Social
Approaches
to Sport

Social
Approaches
to Sport

Edited by
Robert M. Pankin

Rutherford ● *Madison* ● *Teaneck*
Fairleigh Dickinson University Press
London and Toronto: Associated University Presses

Associated University Presses, Inc.
4 Cornwall Drive
East Brunswick, N. J. 08816

Associated University Presses Ltd
27 Chancery Lane
London WC2A 1NS, England

Associated University Presses
Toronto, Ontario, Canada M5E 1A7

Library of Congress Cataloging in Publication Data
Main entry under title:

Social approaches to sport.

   Includes bibliographies and index.
   1. Sports—Social aspects—Addresses, essays,
lectures. 2. Sports—Social aspects—United States—
Addresses, essays, lectures. I. Pankin, Robert M.,
1935–
GV706.5.S64   306'.4   81-65466
ISBN 0-8386-3015-4   AACR2

Printed in the United States of America

For Mark

Contents

Foreword

This book is an intriguing and provocative contribution to the sociology of sport. To use the felicitous phrase of Marcel Mauss and Georges Gurvitch, the various authors have a multidimensional view of sport as, a "total social phenomenon." The unifying theme is social organization, a concept I perceive as very broad in its reach and appreciation by these scholars.

These essays were all written expressly for this publication and do precisely what the editor, Robert Pankin, intends: raise questions. The great merit of this collective effort is to prod the reader to think about issues related to social factors in sport as they exist in modern, postindustrial society. What are the social influences of the wider society, namely social organization, on play, games, and sports and vice versa?

This book underlines a central fact of modern social life. Sport is a part of bureaucratic organization that creeps into the petty pace of daily life. Huizinga's *Homo Ludens* (1959) had the great merit of pointing up the significance of play for the making of culture at a time when the play element was drying up under the withering influence of rational organization. Industrial organization infiltrated religion, law, warfare, and work. Predicting and controlling the future through eliminating risk, uncertainty, and danger are the central goals of bureaucracy. The "new industrial state" described by John K. Galbraith (1978), is new because of economic planning. The corporate giants, numbering perhaps 500, and more likely 200, through complex, organized research-and-development projects plan the future as tightly as they can. Included in their planning is managed consumption. The corporate investment in capital and time for a research-and-development project makes it imperative that consumers will want what is produced. Otherwise the corporation will suffer enormous losses. Numbered among those areas of human life controlled by corporate planning are sports and entertainment.

9

Sports occupy an important place in postindustrial economic society. They are part of crucial changes occurring in the allocation and use of time. Technological innovation has reduced the work force's total time on the job. Automated procedures and machines can do much of the work that formerly was done by human subjects. There is less work for everyone, and most workers can anticipate long periods of unemployment and underemployment in the future. Such a prospect requires a redefinition of what we mean by full-time work, unemployment, and leisure. A result is that people have and will have greater blocks of freed time from work to use in leisure. And sports are a part of it.

U.S. News and World Report (1979) reported that in 1978 an estimated 180 billion dollars had been spent on recreation, travel, theater, sports, and other leisure activities. That represents $1 out of every $8 of consumers' personal spending for the year. "Sales of sporting goods and equipment hit an all time high in 1978. At least 255 million spectators attended major sporting events during the year" (41). Swimming, tennis, basketball, and soccer attracted increasing numbers of fans. In 1965 leisure spending was $58.3 billion. Consumption, therefore, had tripled in thirteen years. Of course, this does not account for inflation, and the new reality of a recession is another factor to consider. The evidence indicates however, that much leisure spending is inelastic, meaning that people now consider leisure as essential to their well-being as food, clothing, and shelter. Leisure and sports have become a basic need.

Sports represent an escape from the routine, especially that of work and, increasingly, of unemployment. There is much in overorganized, bureaucratic work that is dull, boring, mindless, and uncreative. As David MacCannell states:

> Affirmation of the basic social values is departing the world of work and seeking refuge in the realm of leisure. "Creativity" is almost exclusively in the province of cultural, not industrial, production, and "intimacy" and "spontaeity" are preserved in social relations away from work. (1976:6)

MacCannell goes on to suggest that the modern worker is in a partial and limited relationship to the rest of society because of his being restricted to a single position among millions in the division of labor (one of the sources of boredom). Since MacCannell is interested in tourism, he sees that activity as a way in which this individual worker may grasp hold of the division of labor as a total social phenomenon containing both virtue and vice. "Sightseeing is a kind of collective striving for a transcendence of the modern totality, a way of attempting to overcome the discontinuity of modernity, of incorporating its fragments into unified experience" (MacCannell 1976:13).

I would argue that the same could be said of sports. The act of participating in sports either as a player or as a spectator is a collective striving to grasp life as a totality, to make sense out of the fragmented, alienating nature of the differentiation and specialization that are the attributes of modernity—an organic solidarity. The organic solidarity has made necessary the type of organizational society that must deal with the vital question of power and its distribution. This brings us to the central theme of this collection of essays. To my way of thinking the editor and his collaborators have isolated the single most important issue in modern society: how is power organized? Who has it and who doesn't? Highly suggestive is Robert Pankin's idea that social organization creates "masking," which is an individual actor's way of handling the power arrangement in a particular social setting and his or her place in the system.

Sports function to allow modern people to put on different masks than the one they most often have to wear in everyday life. Leisure—of which sports are a part—is creating other measures of status, prestige, and power. Life-style, with its combination of work and leisure variables, is replacing occupation as the single most important indicator of prestige. Yet this is not the issue this book confronts. The authors are dealing with how the existing stratification arrangements differentiate among people of varying backgrounds according to age, gender, race, and income. These classic social forces influence decisively how power is distributed. These social facts operate within the modern industrial oganization that is the prototype for all relationships. It would certainly be interesting to approach this issue from the other direction: namely, that sports represent a way of lifting masks or substituting other ones than those assigned by bureaucratically organized society. I think of the New Games Foundation, which is an outcome of a spontaneously organized event a few years back—an event that brought together persons who wanted to create their own games on the simple basis of playing hard, playing fair, and nobody getting hurt.

Another image which comes to mind is a nudist group. A few years ago a graduate student of mine studied several colonies in

Florida. He found that nudists consider their colonies essentially as leisure settings. They liked the nudist experience because ridding themselves of clothing was like taking off masks they were forced to wear in straight society.

Likewise, new spectators at baseball games include more females and members of varied socioeconomic levels. Wild Bill Hagy of the Baltimore Orioles has become a new symbol for fans. A delightful play element is being reintroduced in spectating at sports events like Oriole games that seems to illustrate the increasingly important role of leisure as the generator of creative, novel ideas, of playfulness and expressiveness. Huizinga's observation (1959) that play and games were becoming too serious may have to be reexamined as leisure becomes more influential.

All this is by way of commenting on the highly seminal notion of social organization and attendant "masking." It certainly raises questions, which is once again the specific aim of this book. Some other questions that I think will interest readers are the following:

1. Is the work-leisure dichotomy a false one? Some would argue that leisure is an extension of the division of labor and that it arose because of the differentiation in social times and consequent roles.

2. Can leisure be usefully distinguished from games and play? Games and play are leisure, but leisure is certainly more than soccer or blind man's buff. Leisure incorporates sculpting, writing poetry, and contemplation, which are far different from play.

3. Can play be the product of culture if it is biologically evolved? The old but still relevant question of nature versus nurture enters here. Is play genetic or cultural or both? If both, is one the senior partner?

4. Why do black athletes dominate certain sports such as professional basketball? Can the genetic or biological be totally rejected? The subcultural-information-pool explanation is the most adequate one, sociologically speaking, but I can already hear the disclaimers.

5. Is there transferability to other social situations of the observation that males act as a positive reference group for both genders in sports participation? It would seem to work well in analyzing the armed services, the operating room, and corporation board rooms.

6. Will the greater emphasis on leisure have an impact on the way older persons see themselves and their likelihood of continuing to participate in strenuous physical activities? The positive

evaluation of leisure in retirement could have a salutary influence on the way old persons judge their physical capabilities. If the wider society is more involved in leisure pursuits and if less negative stereotyping of aging persons' doing strenuous physical activities occurs, then the expectations and self-images of older persons could significantly change.

7. Golf, in one respect, is a game played by persons who occupy positions of importance (power) in the social organization of society. Is the democratization of leisure, i.e., *mass* leisure, affecting prestige sports such as golf, or do these sports remain games of the rich, the prestigious, and the powerful? How does golf reflect organizational society?

8. Is soccer more in tune with the fluid, electronic age than baseball? This is the contention of Louis Kutcher (1978) as a result of his research on the recent growth in the popularity of soccer in the United States.

9. Finally, are certain kinds of sports more in harmony with a certain theoretical paradigm than others? Do sports, like other aspects of culture, reflect the type of society out of which comes a particular theoretical orientation to social reality?

This collective volume on the sociology of sport goes far in expanding the dialogue about the place of sports in modern society. It fills an important void in the literature. We have here professional sociologists, anthropologists, and a psychologist training their sights on important issues which sports reveal for any society.

Phillip Bosserman
Vice President of the Research
Committee on the Sociology of Leisure,
International Sociological Association
Professor of Sociology and Anthropology,
Salisbury State College

Works Cited

Galbraith, John K., *The New Industrial State*, 3rd Edition. Boston: Houghton Mifflin, 1978.

Huizinga, Johan. *Homo Ludens*. Boston: Beacon, 1959.

Kutcher, Louis. "Soccer in America: A Study of Culture Diffusion." Unpublished manuscript, 1979.

"Leisure: Where No Recession Is in Sight."*U.S. News and World Report*, January 15, 1979, pp. 41–44.
MacCannell, David. *The Tourist*. New York: Schocken Books, 1976.

Preface

The originating ideas for this book were generated in the middle to late 1960s. During bull sessions among graduate students at Ohio State University sport was occasionally discussed. Admittedly, in that turbulent time, this was not our major preoccupation, but at one time or another the conversation touched on why there wasn't a better developed sociology of sports. I don't recall any solutions' being advanced then, but we did agree that some day, sometime, someone ought to do more in the area.

Apparently, other people were thinking along the same lines. Just a year or two later sociology of sport books began to be published, and the *International Review of Sport Sociology* began to attract some attention. Nineteen sixty-eight was a landmark year, for that was the time of the black protest and attempted boycott at the Olympic Games in Mexico City organized by Harry Edwards, who was to become a prominent sport sociologist.

Two similar incidents helped crystallize this project in my mind. In Columbus, Ohio, on a sunny spring afternoon, several graduate students and Lee Warshay (who was on the OSU faculty) decided that baseball took precedence over sociology for the day. We went out to the park and spent a pleasant afternoon watching the minor league teams at work. We particularly enjoyed the baseball because Columbus had, at that time, several players who were later to be elevated to the professional Pittsburgh Pirates' championship teams. More importantly, between pitches there was a lively discussion of the game, possible strategies, and various sociological topics: who was the audience for baseball, where the players came from, and the difference between baseball and other sports from a sociological point of view. I remember thinking at that time, "Why doesn't someone put this all on paper?"

Several years later, during a professional meeting, three or four of us decided that instead of listening to the papers being presented

15

we would listen to bats on balls. The earlier game incident repeated itself. The discussion revolved not only around the game and its strategy, but also around its sociological aspects. I wondered again why someone wasn't writing this down. Finally, two years later, and only after completing some research on auto racing, I decided to take matters into my own hands and organize this anthology.

The basic and controlling idea of the anthology was to collect original work (material not previously published) primarily by people who have not been involved in the sociology of sports. This goal was accomplished. I had hoped that these writers would bring fresh views to the sociology of sports and perhaps make a contribution to the social scientific understanding of the pehnomenon. I hope that the completed product has come close to these expectations. Each chapter of this book answers a few questions and raises many more that should keep researchers in the area busy for several years if they follow all of the leads.

The contrast between the first and second chapters of this book suggests another of its parameters. The book is deliberately eclectic from a theoretical point of view. I have not tried to impose my view or anyone else's, on the authors. In the first chapter I tried to raise questions from a macro-social and organizational-structural point of view. The theoretical goal was to fit sports as practiced in the West into a societal whole.

In chapter 2 Laughlin and McManus turn to what they call a "within" perspective. Using a promising anthropological approach called Biogenetic Structuralism, they examine the genetic potentialities involved in play and games. Sport as a concept is, not so incidentally, attacked as an ethnocentric or even humanocentric view. They argue, and I agree with them, that we cannot agree on a definition of what sports are, therefore we must not be bound by a semantic category. Laughlin, McManus, and myself come together theoretically in the attempt to find the basic structural components of the human activity that is designated as sport.

The second part of the book deals with sports during the human life cycle. Kay Johnsen develops the idea that male and female value patterns are developed via contact with sports and games, which have often been overlooked in studies of socialization patterns.

James LeFlore continues the socialization argument by developing a theory of subcultural information pooling to explain why blacks participate in some sports and not in others. I asked LeFlore to write this type of chapter because of his unusual interest in skiing. The original question I asked that motivated his inquiry was, "Why is it that blacks are not generally found on the ski slopes?"

The participation of older people (generally, senior citizens) in sports is the topic addressed by Robert Harootyan in the next chapter. Given our image of vigorous physical activity that is engaged in only by youth, it seems anomalous to even suggest that older people participate in sports. While Harootyan, in his research, does not find a high amount of active participation by older people in sports, he still advocates it. The data marshaled indicate that, not only is it healthier for older people to participate in sports, but they would feel better about their own life-styles if they did participate.

The third part of the book is more specific. In chapter 9, Stanley Eitzen and Norman Yetman update their years of research on discrimination in major professional sports such as baseball, football, and basketball. They examine the organizational structure of these sports, which allows discrimination to continue even though black people have become the prominent stars.

James Davidson is an excellent amateur golfer, and it was his interest in this sport that led me to ask him to write a chapter on it. Golf has traditionally been considered an upper-class sport, although it is becoming more popular with the masses. The class basis of golf is what Davison examines. This chapter follows a classical sociological approach in applying the principles of stratification to a new area. In doing so Davidson has raised many questions about both stratification and golf that should interest researchers.

Finally, Leon Warshay, who was one of the original instigators of this book, produced a chapter on baseball (he was chosen as one of a panel of fans by the *Detroit Free Press* during the summer of 1979). Warshay examines baseball from the perspective of the sociological theorist. He tries to find the best theoretical position to use for analysis. Not surprisingly, he concludes that there is no one sociological-theoretical school that will completely explain the social behavior involved in baseball. In coming to this conclusion and bringing together the evidence, Warshay produces a succinct analysis of what used to be the American pastime.

Acknowledgments

Throughout this book, the many who helped the individual authors prepare their chapters have been given well-deserved credit. The preparation of an anthology is often a lonely task, but one always finds others to help with the various duties involved. Two people in particular who have been invaluable in the preparation of this book are Mark Pankin, who saw to a lot of the organization of detail while I was in Asia, and Eileen Kramer, who helped me with a different view of the literary, social, and editorial process. Reece McGee read an earlier version of the book and made some valuable suggestions that have improved the final product. When the times looked worst during this project, Kathryn Hayes provided the encouragement and support that helped me to continue. Linda Mautner did an excellent job on the graphics. Finally, I would like to thank Alice LaBonte and her staff at Central Michigan University for their clerical efforts, and Bev Risler for her outstanding competence in preparing the final manuscript.

Social
Approaches
to Sport

Part I
Approaches

1
An Approach to Sports

ROBERT M. PANKIN

Introduction

The practitioners of sociology and the other social sciences are increasingly focusing their attention on sports. This book is designed to bring some fresh views to the topic. In order to do this, informed speculation is necessary and provocative questions must be raised. The outcome may not only move toward adding to the general body of social theory but may also provide insights to help improve the quality of life. This process begins with speculation that leads to explanation, which in turn leads to questions provoking further speculation. This chapter is a tentative beginning to that process, which is continued throughout the rest of this book. The thrust of the book, therefore, is toward explaining one area of social life, in hopes that the reader will be left with more questions than answers about sport as a social process.

More specifically, this chapter first speculates about some of the reasons that sports have become a popular area of study in sociology. The issue of definition is raised and problems that are associated with defining leisure, sports, and games are examined. In the course of that examination we look at the well-worn work-leisure dichotomy, which has probably served beyond its usefulness. But the notion of work centers attention on organizational theory. A version of this is suggested for the analysis of sports. Organizations provide a kind of mask in society and that mask is interrelated with the mask provided by sports. The masking occurs on several levels, and questions are raised connected with each of them.

25

Sociologists and Sports

Much of the well-known literature in the sociology of sports and leisure spends considerable time distinguishing among leisure, sports, and games (see for example Loy and Kenyon, 1969; Edwards, 1973; McIntosh, 1968). That material will not be repeated in this chapter. While such classifications may help direct the attention of scholars and help focus their research, it seems that the classifications have more significance in relation to academic politics than in terms of what nonacademic people actually do. Studies of leisure have long been respectable within the social-scientific enterprise. Research about games and their socializing function have been pioneered by anthropologists, but games as such do not play a prominent part in the social-scientific literature.[1]

Sports, on the other hand, have not really been a respectable area for social-scientific study until recently. But now the area has become at least semirespectable and many sociological works focus on sports with their related issues. Unfortunately, the quest for respectability may result in a sterilized view of actual life experiences. A major theoretical problem, in this author's view, is to bring sociological life to the study of sports.

Why have sports now become respectable as an area of study? A possible answer is that during the 1960s there was a large increase in the number of practicing professional social scientists, including many sociologists. In order to advance their careers, sociologists may have been seeking out unexplored areas for study and publication. In other words, the surplus of labor opened up a new area and may have made the study of sports respectable.

Well-publicized, organized sports have burgeoned in the United States and in other countries. Table tennis made world headlines as the first opening of surface diplomatic contact between the People's Republic of China and the United States. But in the United States, sports, which was always a business, has now become a big business. Millions of dollars are spent on television contracts for college and professional football, which has altered the character of those sports which are fortunate enough (or unfortunate enough depending on one's point of view) to receive lucrative contracts. There seems to be nothing else that has the mass viewer appeal of sports. Sports occur live and spontaneously, thereby generating a sense of excitement.

The public, then, accepts sports as part of everyday life and as conversational material. More importantly, millions of dollars are exchanged in sports. It is not only television with its connected advertising, but also equipment manufacturers and other sports-related businesses that have a large stake in the popularization of sports. Ski resorts, bowling alleys, and golf courses are commonplace. A swimming pool seems to be a must for an upper-middle-class family and one has to be provided in the neighborhood for the children of the ghetto. The point is obvious: the conjunction of the surplus of social scientists with the increasing leisure time available to the general population and the large amount of money involved makes the study of sports respectable.

The Definitional Issue

In the view of this author, the category *sport* is impossible to define precisely enough to allow systematic study. If one proposes so narrow a definition that this might be possible then too much is excluded. On the other hand, if the definition is too broad it includes too much and becomes meaningless. One is caught in an inescapable bind when no intermediate definition proves satisfactory. Yet one must face the fact that people, in general, see the linguistic designation *sport* as a real category that represents human activity. It appears that the way out of this dilemma is to recognize that people relate to each other in terms of the category, and then to focus attention on the nature of those social relationships. This point of view is elaborated on in the following material.

To return to the definitional issue, then, one may begin to define *sport* rather simply as contests that involve at least some attempt to dominate another party. That party may be another person, or as in the cases of golf or bowling, for example, it may be a standard of perfection. This is only to say that in sports the aim or goal of the participants is to win.

Sports may be classified in the general category of leisure. Leisure activities range along a spectrum from doing almost nothing (e.g., sleeping) to being very physically and mentally involved. Usually, when we speak of leisure activity, we speak of a substitution of some preferred activity that provides diversion from what people perceive as "normal" social relations. It should be recognized, however, that leisure does not necessarily mean noninvolvement or relaxation. The pressures during leisure time can be just as great as the pressures during work. In discussions of leisure activity a different network of social relationships is either present or implied. At leisure, one deviates from work roles legitimately (see Theodorson and Theodorson, 1969: 229-30). An extreme example of this is getting drunk, which is forgivable during leisure time but gets you fired at work. One's usual social role can be relaxed and many kinds of "deviant behavior" can be excused by saying, "I didn't know what I was doing; I was drunk."

The work-leisure dichotomy must be confronted in discussions focused on Western industrial societies. Such societies have work as a basic value and leisure is often somewhat suspect. Defining leisure as a different pattern of social relations tends to escape the dichotomy by adding categories beyond work or nonwork. The dichotomy, however, still creeps into the discussion.

The problem when studying sports is to focus on the different types of social relations outside of the work place. But it is the relations at the work place that are really dominant, and it is those relations that govern leisure activity. This is easily seen when we refer to "deviation from work roles." It is the work role that is used as the standard of behavior. An unwritten, and in some cases written, clause in work contracts has to do with "conduct" that is "unbecoming." Such rules are particularly prevalent for athletes. Athletes are fined, suspended, and not permitted to play in certain leagues "for the good of the game" (Wolf, 1972). The commissioner of baseball has wide latitude "for the best interests of baseball." Ron LeFlore, an ex-convict who played with the Detroit Tigers and then the Montreal Expos, not only is a star but must be a "model citizen." His work role must dominate his life. In Western society, particularly the United States, people who reject work roles are called bums or hippies (or if rich, playboys or jet setters).

It is this domination of work roles that leads to the almost inescapable conclusion that power structures developed in the work place diffuse to the larger social mileau and will dominate leisure activity. Organizations, therefore, which are formed to engage in so-called nonwork activity will very quickly be modeled after work organizations. As these organizations grow beyond a few volunteers they will provide work for people and become work organizations themselves. When these become large scale sports "clubs" they employ professional athletes and those athletes become workers.

The utility of the work-leisure dichotomy is definitely questionable when one considers the case of the professional athlete.

The games she or he plays while "at work" are the leisure of others. Can it now be said that the work of ordinary people can be the leisure of professional athletes? It would seem ludicrous to point out that the professional athlete might find leisure on the assembly line. It is possible that this kind of consideration will lead us to dispense with the work-leisure dichotomy.

The work-leisure dichotomy adds little or nothing to one's knowledge; in fact, it may add to or create confusion. It is for this reason that the focus should now be placed on social relations. As soon as this is done, attention is focused on the inescapable fact that the dominant relations of what is called the work place are the same that are found associated with sports.

The emphasis here is on social relationships—the "stuff" of social life. If one is to investigate any aspect of social life, including sports, the emphasis must be placed on the social relationships involved. The particular interest here is in how these relationships pattern themselves or become regular. When these patterned relationships emerge, what is recognized is not a static social structure, but one that is constantly changing. And regularity is to be found in the nature and types of that social change. Sports provide an excellent opportunity to look at patterns of change both within the contest situation and the situations that develop outside of the contest; the organizational relationships of sports.

Given this set of assumptions, a definition of sports provided by Harry Edwards seems to fit the assumptions made here and allows us to deal with the linguistic category. Sports are activities having formally recorded histories and traditions that stress physical exertion through competition that occurs within limits set by explicit and formal rules. These rules govern role and position relationships both within and outside the contest. The roles are played by actors who represent or are a part of formally organized associations and they have the goal of achieving some valued item or items through defeating an opposition (Edwards, 1973:57–58).

A more specific category is the notion of the game. A game is always a single or generalized event that can be particularized; it is applicable to sports and occurs in leisure time (except for professional athletes). While social life can be completely conceived of as a game, very few aspects of social life are defined as games except, occasionally, by cynics. The present discussion applies when one speaks of sports games as situations that are socially defined as games.

Tension in game situations tends to be legitimated. The

legitimating factor is the set of rules that govern the game context and establish performance criteria. Participants have a set of roles whether they are players or spectators.

Domination and Subordination

Any examination of sports shows that domination is a desired state of affairs. Subordination is not desirable; the emphasis is always on winning. Children are socialized to win at games but at the same time to get along with other children. The social ethic teaches that nice guys finish first, in spite of Leo Durocher.[2] The emphasis, however, is on finishing first. Poor winners are excused more often than poor losers.

The socialization pattern is continued when the child becomes a fan. It is his or her team that wins or loses, and losing is depressing. The same child may become an athlete participating in organized sports. Athletic training teaches domination. If the child grows up to be a professional athlete, domination continues to be emphasized. But the more one participates in organized sports, the more one has to be subordinate. One is subordinate to a coach, or to management, and is owned and governed by clauses in contracts. This presents a paradox that is present in all sports. An athlete who is trained to dominate must become subordinate for a considerable portion of his or her life. Outside of the game situation, the athlete often must do what he or she is told by sponsors, coaches, or other management officials. Even while the game is played, the athlete must execute as she or he is told.

This last statement is exemplified by a famous baseball legend. A very good slugger was sent up to the plate with a runner on first base and his team trailing by one run. He was ordered to bunt. The first pitch was a ball, and the batter squared to bunt but did not offer. The second pitch was thrown right down the middle. The batter looked, took a full swing, and hit a home run that eventually won the game. Two days later the player was traded. Why? Because he disobeyed orders. Obeying orders or being subordinate was more important than winning the game. Perhaps if the slugger had apologized to the coach for hitting the home run, he might have saved his position on the team.

Any theory, then, that attempts to explain and raise questions about publicly played sports must be a power theory. While other aspects of social relationships certainly come into play when dealing with sports, the aspects of domination and subordination seem to color all other activities.

Organizational Power Theory

For publicly played sports,[3] theories of organizational power are most appropriate. A theory of organizational power must begin by noting that only a few people within any organization control the behavior of all the members of the organization. This includes the play of the star quarterback and the relationship of the seldom-used substitute to the coach. The behavior of organizational members must involve the administrative capacities of the organization and the creation of a public image, as well as decisions regarding who plays, who doesn't, who gets traded, and who is asked to retire.

Who controls sports organizations? This question appears simpler to answer than it really is. The major factor adding complexity to the question is the public visibility of such organizations. Charles O. Finley owned several sports organizations and might be the prototype, today, of the "owner controlling model." But even Finley may not have had complete control because the commissioners of the leagues in which he had teams from time to time have invalidated his decisions.

At the other extreme are the loosely knit organizations of golfers and tennis players—e.g., the Professional Golf Association (PGA). And sports organizations must now count the unions among themselves.[4] In the amateur realm, control seems to lie with national and international associations, colleges and universities, and organizations of organizations such as the National Collegiate Athletic Association (NCAA) or the International Olympic Committee (IOC).

All of this suggests that the question of actual control must be submitted to an empirical test. But it is the question of the means of control that is a major concern here. It is this author's contention that sports organizations (and thus the people connected with them) are controlled in the same way other complex organizations are controlled; through bureaucratic means, modified by the demands of public visibility.

The analysis of ownership and control of sports organizations is crucial for understanding the role sports play in the life of modern capitalist societies. Any analysis will reveal that sports teams are usually owned and controlled by those who have been successful in the outside world of business. The question that one must ask is, How will successful people in business run sports organizations?

The apparent answer to this question is that such organizations are amenable to control by utilizing business principles. Even on an amateur level, one finds thinly veiled or open discussions of a market for sports activity. Given the market concept, it is not surprising that the successful business manager, managing a sports organization, would opt to use the latest management techniques, which would include the principles of marketing and the development of standards of efficiency. Hence, it may be observed that athletes are being judged by various levels of proficiency that are reminiscent, in certain respects of time and motion studies.

One even finds the latest techniques of human relations management being introduced into sports organizations. Athletes are now allowed to participate in some decisions that affect their sports lives, although not often the major ones. One must still be in major league baseball for a considerable number of years before being allowed to participate in the major decision about being traded. At the other extreme are the styles of haircuts, although coaches, managers, and owners still to some extent attempt to control the hair style and mode of dress of the individual athlete. The point, however, is that athletes are managed as employees in any business.

The other aspect of management is the presentation of the team to the public. The "marketing" of the team has effects on the societal level as well as on the team itself.

Sports are interrelated with the social structure of society and the ideas and beliefs that support that structure. The successful athlete playing his or her role as the clean-living member of the community has been prominent for years. Some shock has been expressed when the truth of the private lives of athletes comes out. But even this is in line with the amoebalike effect of the structure of modern society. With the turn toward naturalness, athletes can be a little more human—to the point decreed by their conservative mentors.

Another way in which sport fits into modern society is the use of sports figures for celebrating "normal" political activity. The ceremonies of a quasi-religious and political nature that occur before games and during intermissions support patriotic development and the interest of the national body.

Since competition is a major feature of modern industrial society, (at least on a lip-service basis), sport is a nice fit. Sport provides a legitimation for competition and for notions of winning and losing.

In an interesting way sport supports the alienation of industrial society. Tension builds during the game situation and helps relieve frustrations encountered in the everyday work world. At the end of the activity, one's team has either won or lost. A definite decision has been reached and tension is then released. In contrast, no such definite decisions are reached in the work world except when one is hired or fired. Most employees simply go on working and living with the tensions of the work situation. Tension is an expression of the alienation felt toward work. Sports then transfer alienation from work toward a favorite team and tension is relieved when the team plays. If the team is not doing well, you feel badly about the team, but not about work. If the team is doing well, on the other hand, you feel fine and forget about the hardships of work in modern society.

In addition to supporting alienation one gets used to seeing athletes treated as nonhuman and traded as any other piece of merchandise (or benched, the sports equivalent of being laid off), then why not everybody else?

The Mask of Sports

Sports, then are a kind of multileveled mask that begins with surface masking, as at the start of a baseball game when the catcher puts on his face mask. The catcher's equipment is not the only mask in sports. The face guard on a football helmet comes to mind as well as the scarves and goggles that cover the faces of race drivers.

It is not only the face but the body that is covered in many sports. Football and auto racing are extremes, but hockey, skiing, and fencing are all in the same category. The players are hidden and features are masked with height, approximate weight, and sometimes hair color only being observable.[5] At the other extreme are sports such as swimming and diving, track, basketball, golf, handball, squash, gymnastics, billiards, boxing, tennis, bowling, table tennis, rowing, and weight lifting. In all of these sports the participants are quite visible and their physical identity is readily apparent. There is a middle category, however, of baseball, rugby, lacrosse, horse racing, and soccer. In these sports the participants are partially identifiable, although some body masking does occur.

There is a commonality that runs through this classification. The sports where the most masking takes place seem to be the most dangerous. They are the ones where body contact could produce injury. On the other hand, most of the sports where the participants are unmasked are not considered dangerous. The group of sports in the middle, of course, are less dangerous than the first group but more dangerous than the second. The relationship, obviously, is not perfect (at least boxing and basketball, which have a majority of black players, are exceptions), but the association seems strong enough to look for reasons behind it. The question suggested is, Why do we hide the identity of those who participate in some sports?

Publicly visible sports organizations are governed by norms of presentation. Looking at these norms gives initial answers to the above question. The first answer is obvious: protection is the reason for the body masking in most sports where it occurs. Body masking covers vulnerable parts. Players are partially protected by their equipment. In sports where there is little masking, such as basketball and boxing, the athlete is presumably protected by rules (not very well when we see boxers die from their injuries).

While the necessity of protecting athletes when they engage in dangerous sports is unquestionable, it seems that more than the athletes are being shielded. The fan is also being guarded. But this requires explanation. How is the fan protected by an athlete's padding? A "fan is . . . an individual who has both a high personal investment in and a high personal committment to a given sport" (Loy and Kenyon, 1969:70). When the participants are masked it means that the identification of the fan with the player is no longer person to person; it is with a number and an image. This serves to impersonalize the personal commitment. An example from this author's experience may illustrate the point. I conducted research at an auto racing track and always felt quite tense while watching the races. The reason for my tension was fear—the fear of seeing someone seriously hurt or injured—but I never recognized how different my feelings may have been until I returned to the track as a fan. It seemed that I felt more tension than the people around me were feeling, and I began to wonder why. Then it occurred to me. I was personally acquainted with many of the people driving those cars; most of the other fans were not. The cars and the people were simply names, numbers, and colors to them.

One of the conclusions of that earlier research was that fans at auto racing tracks do not necessarily come to see people killed or injured (Pankin et al., 1974). The problem that arises is, How can people be induced to come and watch not only auto racing but other sports where it at least appears likely that someone can be seriously hurt or killed? A partial answer to this question lies in the phenomenon of masking. Participants are masked; therefore, they are not quite human in the minds of the fans. In fact, the athlete as superhuman is a common image in our society. In some sports, for example, cockfighting, which involve only animals, death is the expected outcome for one participant. Masking, then, limits personal identification and convinces the fan that nobody they know is going to be hurt. The reason the spectator may be persuaded is related to some inability to identify the distorted figures as human beings.

When one becomes aware of the athlete off the field, it is usually through a television image. It is often difficult to reconcile the television personality with the on-field figure, and for most masked athletes a clip of their exploits is shown to help identify the person. (There are exceptions—Joe Namath and Reggie Jackson being the most notable.)

The media and the publicity machines of professional sports go to great pains to build the athletic image. The mild-mannered, clean-living, nonaggressive type seems the norm. One is led to believe that aggression remains on the field and that there is little carryover. It warrants headlines when this pattern is seriously violated.

All of this is possible because the identity and personality of the participant are hidden from the spectator. In the one instance, it is hidden by face covering, padding, and rules. Where no physical masking is present, personality is hidden by rules. It becomes possible to create an artificial identity. One can only imagine what dangerous spots would be like if masking did not take place. For example, touch football, a game that is exciting and has little contact and no masking, is a prototype.

Automobile racing is another good example of the relation of masking to the way a sport is played. As safety equipment in automobiles has improved, so have speeds. The rate of death and injury seems, however, to remain constant. Deaths in automobile racing, while considered normal, must be held within tolerable limits. The 1973 Indianapolis 500-mile race had a death rate that was not tolerable. This produced rule changes that slowed cars down (or at least didn't let them increase speeds further).

Sportsmanship and Masking

Learning good sportsmanship is one of the most ballyhooed of the character-building aspects of sports in our society. But one notices it most when so-called bad sportsmanship is exhibited. The ejection of a basketball player for fighting in a televised basketball game is a good example. The ejection comes when a punch is thrown, but often observers, including the television commentators, note the roughness of the game before the ejection. For example, they comment frequently on the use of elbows. What is noteworthy is that ejection does not usually come until the violence, defined as bad sportsmanship, becomes overt. Similar instances of covert and violent rule breaking are "normal" in football where holding among linemen can be seen on almost every instant replay, and in hockey where subtle spearing with the stick is common. A small fraction of the covert instances are penalized, but all open fighters are punished. There is more outrage when fighting occurs in unmasked sports (boxing excluded) than in the masked variety. In the latter, fighting is almost considered "part of the game."

Sportsmanship apparently does not teach positive obedience to all of the rules. Rather, one might conclude from observing that the lesson is: "Don't get caught!" It is only overt and manifest action outside the rules that is punished as unsportsmanlike conduct.

Sportsmanship, like sports themselves, may be conceived of as preparation for life activity. On the one hand, one learns to violate rules subtly and not to get caught; on the other hand, through sportsmanship one learns to be a good loser. It is only those who find themselves in the top few positions who end up winning consistently. Exhibiting good sportsmanship gives everyone a chance to be a winner. After a loss, one can always be complimented on a display of good sportsmanship. It is an out; a way of saving face. To reinforce the point: most people are not winners most of the time. People, however, do not see themselves as losers. This is because losing is mediated by notions about sportsmanship. People in our society, by being "good sports," can consider themselves winners. They continue to play under these circumstances even though chances for reaching the top are never quite as good as the fifty/fifty that happens in the competitive situation in sports. Sportsmanship then, is a mask for losing.

Competition

Competition is another aspect of the masking process. Sports mask life activity in this case. Most people "root" for a team when they observe sports events. This identification allows people to believe that there is at least a fifty/fifty chance of their winning in their own life situations. These are better odds than almost everyone gets when they confront their daily lives. In most cases, one ends up in a tie or loses; but in any case one does not have a fifty/fifty chance to win.

Competition is one of the fundamental principles of our society. People, ideally, act in their own best interests, competing against the next fellow for advantage in the general marketplace of life. One can refuse to compete and play instead for security. In this situation, a person seems to be assigned to a permanent-loser category that may be redefined via sportsmanship.

This author's argument, however, is that competition in sports and competition in nonsports activities are quite different, not in form but in content. In form, both types of competition are alike. At any given moment a competitive process reduces to a one-on-one situation and one player takes on all comers, one by one, either winning or losing. But the basic similarity ends at this point.

In sports, one presumably competes for the fun of it and even professionals claim to be having fun. The definition of the sports situation is activity for fun and most people get very upset when business rears its ugly head in the sports world. Business aspects are usually kept behind the scenes. For years it has been the owners of teams who engaged in this business, not the players. Now the players have unionized and the owners attempt to apply the image of unsportsmanlike conduct to the players while negotiations are occurring. Both groups tend to shy away from the image of sports as work. The point is that work and sports are considered opposites.

Work is not fun, and it is continuous; sports are fun, and they are discrete. In sports the game always ends and the next game begins with all things equal except in rare cases where there is a series, such as the Canadian football playoffs or the World Series. But even those exceptions have a definite end. In the world of work the company goes on and continues to compete even when one retires. In the world of work what one does is permanent.

How many times has one felt like "telling off" the boss when quitting but forgone the pleasure for fear of reprisals? In sports, however even major transgressions such as gambling (the bête noir of professional sports) can be forgiven. Consider the case of basketball players who were caught in fixing scandals but who have come back to play professional basketball. Or consider the well-known cases of Paul Hornung and Alex Karras, who were suspended for a year and then returned to play professional football with more lucrative contracts. This level of transgression in the world of work would probably have caused the participants to be blackballed.

There are two points to be made about competition. First, the competitive process in sports is different in content but not in form from the competitive process in society. Sports have been maligned on the grounds that they teach competition, and competition is seen in some quarters as a social evil. If the form-content distinction is recognized, the outright condemnation of sports activity as contributing to general social decadence does not necessarily follow. Sports are fun for participants and observers. There is a special quality in competing, enjoying it, and knowing that the competition comes to an end and can be more or less forgotten. Signficantly, it is those people who make a business of sports competition who cannot forget very easily. Managers, general managers, coaches, promoters, and other administrators who formalize the process have translated sports into the world of work for themselves. Players know that if they wish, they can and eventually will retire, but they may worry about being increasingly tied to the world of business by extra deals with the owner. This may be the corruption of sports. Secondly, sports acts as a superstructural cover or mask for what is going on in the rest of society. The anesthetizing feature has been discussed elsewhere (Hoch, 1972), but what is not readily recognizable is that what has happened is that the form of competition for fun is used as an ideological support for those who compete as part of their working lives. A good example of the use of this ideological cover is an ex-president's well-known interest in sports and the consequent usage of sports cliches in running the government.[6]

An easy translation of the competitive process in sports into the competitive process in work creates major difficulties both in the sports world and in the work world. In both worlds, it appears that participants' awards are based on production. To all intents and purposes that production even looks tangible. But in the sports world only statistics are produced. People are paid in terms of how they compare on various statistical measures (e.g., batting averages) with other people. The time spent on the job appears to be irrelevant. In the world of work, however, people are paid more in terms of time spent on the job than in terms of their productive capacity (largely determined by some organizational and/or technical factor). In the work world people are encouraged to compete in order to get ahead by pleasing a boss. It is often problematic, however, whether increased output will, in fact, please the boss. There are academic cases, for example, where people publish *and* perish.

In the sports world one competes in terms of a set of standards, and this differentiates the competition from the world of work. More importantly, as has been pointed out, in sports the game always ends, but in work the game always continues. If the boss is dissatisfied with an employee's performance, the employee is fired. If the boss of a sports team is dissatisfied with a player's performance, personality, or other characteristics, the player is traded. There is a qualitative difference between the two. Since the difference is not recognized, sports appear to be in the same realm as work, and one can presumably be motivated to work via the use of a sports ideology. (For more detail on the nature of sports ideology in this country, see Edwards, 1973:69.)

Summary

Social science, and sociology in particular, is a part of the mask of sports. Insofar as sociologists of sports support the status quo with their work, they are supporting the organizational power structures that are the primary masking agents. Names could be mentioned and studies cited at this point, but it is not this author's purpose to engage in polemic. The purpose has been to raise questions about the role sports (and those who study sports) play in Western industrial society.

Definitional biases lead into an abyss of petty distinctions. Should one really care if they are analyzing a game or sports or leisure? What difference does it make (James, 1955:42)? When focusing on social relationships one can forget about these distinctions and instead take an in-depth look at social life.

Any in-depth look at the social life revolving around sports reveals the complex interrelationship between types of organizational power and the mask that sports provides. Organizations present sporting events in such a way that the players' protection actually protects the fan. Part of the human quality of danger can sometimes be overlooked because the players are considered by the fan to be more than human, sometimes superhuman or even nonhuman. At times one can watch someone get hurt without doing anything to help. (This is an interesting parallel to the cases of street violence where people don't want to get involved!)

Successful organizations produce winners. Making a large profit is defined as a win for a corporation. The winning team will usually draw more fans and make more profit. At the same time, the fans see themselves as winners. They may lose in most of their other social relationships, but in sports they win by proxy. Alienation from work is made tolerable, as sports provides the mask for this as well.

One of the great paradoxes of Western industrial society is that, in general, people expect to win and even think of themselves as winners. The reality of it can be brutal, however. More often than not, people either lose or draw. While doing that, however, some see themselves as winners because they are "good sports." They accept their fate a bit more easily because they learn to think highly of themselves. They can define themselves as winners even when they lose and insist that others look at them in the same light.

Sports may produce some effects that reduce the potential for decent social existence, but they have the potential to contribute positively to the quality of our lives. The form of sports may be the same as that of business, and the drift of sports activity may be toward more of what we experience in other aspects of social life, but the content is different. Sports activities are discrete in the most important ways. This means that the power associated with sports organizations need not be permanent; there is an escape. While escaping into sports only a few are completely captured (those who make it a permanent career).

Sports provides an example for a way of life that need not be a way of domination. This of course raises the interesting possibility of constructing a different kind of social life.

I would like to thank Charles D. Laughlin and Leon Warshay for their critical help in revising this chapter.

Notes

1. This is with the possible exception of mathematically based game theory, which was extracted from notions of rational game playing.

2. Durocher, who managed several contending baseball teams, was quoted as saying, "Nice guys finish last."

3. By this I mean sports that typically draw large audiences as opposed to pick-up games. Sports that draw massive attention, however, even influence pick-up games and how they are played.

4. An interesting comparative study might be done between unionism and professionalism in sports as compared, for example, with academic life.

5. More players now use helmets in hockey; they are required in college, but not professionally.

6. A television news story on President Nixon touring a tornado disaster area in Ohio showed him talking about Hank Aaron's 715th home run and using it to tell people they too would "make it."

Works Cited

Edwards, Harry. *Sociology of Sport*. Homewood, Ill.: Dorsey Press, 1973.

Hoch, Paul. *Rip Off the Big Game*. Garden City, N. Y.: Anchor Books, 1972.

James, William. *Pragmatism*. 1907. Reprint. Cleveland: World Publishing Company, 1955.

Loy, John W., and Kenyon, Gerald S., eds. *Sports, Culture, and Society*. New York: Macmillan Company, 1969.

McIntosh, P. C. *Sport in Society*. London: C. A. Watts & Company, 1968.

Pankin, Robert M.; Cassella, Catherine, and Cassella, Frank. "Supermodified, Super Show: a Study of the Sociocultural Matrix of Supermodified Automobile Racing." *Journal of Popular Culture*, September 1974, pp. 162–67.

Theodorson, George A., and Theodorson, Achilles G. *A Modern Dictionary of Sociology*. New York: Thomas Y. Crowell Company, 1969.

Wolf, David. *Foul! The Connie Hawkins Story*. New York: Holt Rinehart Company, 1972.

2
The Biopsychological
Determinants of Play
and Games

CHARLES D. LAUGHLIN, Jr., and JOHN McMANUS

Introduction

There has been a current surge of interst in the biological and ethological aspects of play (see Loizos, 1966, 1967; Bekoff, 1974; Hinde, 1970; Stevens, 1977; Bruner et al., 1976; Schwartzman, 1978; Sutton-Smith, 1976) and in the sociological aspects and functional correlates of games (see Loy and Kenyon, 1969; Sage, 1974; Lüschen, 1970; Stone, 1972; Stevens, 1976). It is the purpose of this chapter to provide as far as is presently possible the evolutionary biological neuropsychological, ontogenetic, and ethological determinants of play and gaming in *Homo sapiens* and other species of social animals. This task is approached through *biogenetic structuralism*,[1] which argues that play is a fundamental attribute of the ontogenesis of all higher social animals, and that gaming is an evolutionary refinement of play.

The contention of this chapter, supported by the following synthesis, is that phenomena such as play and games *cannot*, in principle, be explained apart from their biological matrix. This allows one to operationalize phenomena, so as to avoid both *ethnocentrism* (aided by the cross-cultural comparative perspective not evident in the work of some sociologists of sports: e.g., Sage, 1974; Ball, 1973; Levine, 1974) and *anthropocentrism*.[2]

The concept of "sport" is quite evidently rife with both ethnocentric and anthropocentric connotations. From a structural perspective, "sport" cannot exist apart from the culturally specific cognitive categories of a society. Put another way, "sport" is the term given to certain culturally compartmentalized games whose outcomes are determined primarily by physical skill. It is felt that for social scientists to place such a category of behavior at the center of theoretical concern is to proceed with blinders. Caillois (1955), for example, not only defines "sport" as an "institutionalized game requiring physical prowess," but also requires that the physical skill involved be "highly developed." It is felt here that any attempt to explain a phenomenon that is so narrowly defined is doomed to failure.

Definitions of sociocultural phenomena become exceedingly problematical when they involve variables both "within" and "without" the organism (Teilhard de Chardin, 1959), and even more problematical when the definition of a phenomenon is couched solely in "without" terms. Preoccupation with behavior is understandable, but scientifically regrettable, as it leads to operationalization delimited by the immediately observable. This leads to a characteristic paradox: everybody knows the phenomenon when he or she sees it, but nobody can define it noncontroversially.

This definitional hassle has resulted in the ascription of a myriad of functions to play—e.g., the development of communication skills (Mason, 1965), set formation learning (Barnett, 1970), experience broadening (Leyhausen in Bekoff, 1972), social interaction development, dominance order and social solidarity (Poirier and Smith, 1974), adult behavior practice (Loizos, 1966), and socialization of aggression (Ruppenthal et al., 1974). Other functions assigned to games are enculturation (Sage, 1974), conflict resolution (Roberts et al., 1959), pattern maintenance, integration, adaptation and goal attainment á la Parsons (Lüschen, 1970), socialization of adults, warfare skills (Lüschen, 1970), and rites of passage (Frederickson, 1960). In point of fact, games have been given virtually all of the functions that have been given to ritual, even to the distinction between rites of intensification and rites of passage (as defined by Chapple and Coon, 1942; van Gennep, 1960; see Schwartzman, 1978).

But enough said in introduction; this study will proceed to a detailed biological exposition of play and games and return to these other questions in due course.

The Biology of Play

The definitional controversy surrounding "play" has at times reached such extremes that some authorities have suggested we dispose of "play" as a useful analytic category (Berlyne, 1969; Beach, 1945). The problem of identifying the boundaries of play may possibly be attributed to the tendency of social and ethological scientists to orient themselves toward the "without" rather than the "within" of the organism. Their definitions are commonly couched in behavioral terms, rather than in terms of the internal structure that may be generating, modulating, mediating, or facilitating that behavior. The result of this analytical bias is nowhere more evident than in the definition of play as activity without practical end (Huizinga, 1938). This must refer to no *obvious* practical end *external* to the organism, whereas it is perfectly possible (it could be argued probable) that play is activity with a practical *internal* end. Since the growth in the predominance of play in the behavioral repertoire of the developing organism increases on the way up the phylogenetic scale (Norbeck, 1974), it is at least inferable that play is linked to other internal evolutionary developments. It is no accident that play is virtually universal among social mammals and birds.

Cognized and Operational Environments

The position taken here is that the evolution of play is intimately bound up with the evolution of the brain's cognizing function. The cognizing function for any higher animal, including *Homo sapiens*, is the construction of an internal model of the external world affecting the organism. The internal model may be called the *cognized environment* (E_c) and the external world the *operational environment* (E_o). The relation between the cognized environment and the operational environment is *not* that found in a simple pictorial representation, but rather of adaptive *isomorphism*.[3] That is, the E_c is so structured that it directs the production of behavior that proves adaptive for the organism within the E_o. During the organism's development, the E_c is constructed by the organism in interaction with the E_o (Piaget, 1929, 1952, 1971; Wolff, 1963; Bruner in Bruner, et al., 1976: 28–34). The construction of an E_c is based initially upon a complex feedback and feedforward arrangement that is termed the empirical modification cycle (EMC) (Laughlin and d'Aquili, 1974). This occurs between inherent neurophysiological models (*neurognostic models*) of the E_o, and the E_o itself (Laughlin and McManus, 1975). These neurognostic models are generalized, malleable structures ("schemes" in Piaget's terms) for processing sensory information and mediating behavior. In virtually all cases, neurognostic models undergo development in ontogenesis in order to bring them into optimal adaptive isomorphism with the E_o. An example would be the development of the infant's initial grasping response or gross motor pattern into a complex and flexible motoric repertoire that over time, becomes increasingly flexible and differentially applicable to a wide variety of objects and situations. Eventually, it becomes subsumed as a subsystem of complex cognitive-motor operations.

Neurognostic models are constructed from actual neural tissues and take the form of pathways through fields of neural connections that increase in sensitivity and stability with frequency of activation (Eccles, 1973). The particular form (i.e., the complexity of interconnections, size of neural components, proportion of support cells, etc.) taken by a neurognostic model is dependent upon both the genetic endowment of the organism and the richness of the organism's environment. Optimal development of neurognostic models (i.e., greatest potential complexity and efficiency of organization) requires the presence of an optimally enriched environment; i.e., just complex or novel enough, but not too complex (Diamond et al., 1964, 1966; Rosenzweig et al., 1962, 1972). This interaction is not passive for the organism, but requires activity on the part of the organism for optimal development of neurognostic models. That is, no matter how enriched the environment, the organism must be able to operate actively upon that environment to promote the most complex development of neural structures.[4] For higher social species, the E_o must be reasonably enriched in two essential aspects relative to optimal development of the E_c: the physical (optimal novelty of physical objects and relations in the environment over time) and the social (the presence of and interaction with conspecifics; Rosenzweig et al., 1972).

As Piaget has repeatedly demonstrated, conceptual development is an interactive process having necessary attributes of both being and becoming. The organism must simultaneously balance the requirements that it be adapted to its current E_o and that it develop into an increasingly complex, "mature" organism. We are compelled to emphasize that the relations obtaining between the E_c and the E_o of an organism are exceedingly complex and operative at a number of levels of systemic organization (see also Hinde, 1970:425–33) all of which must be encompassed in an explanation of cognitive functions, including play (Rubinstein and Laughlin, 1977).

Play and the Cognized Environment

Play may be defined as a subprocess of the EMC by means of which an organism intentionally complexifies its E_o for the purpose of optimizing development of its E_c.[5] In more detail, play consists of a subset of intrinsically motivated, behavioral components of the EMC. Play specifically functions neuro-developmentally to optimize the development of the organism's E_c. The E_o is complexified either by increasing the sensory information about the E_o as previously modeled, or by increasing the spatio-temporal range of the E_o. The former mode seems to predominate in the more mature play of organisms; the latter seems to predominate in early play, particularly in solitary play.

Complexification of the E_c means the organism's knowledge of or exposure to the E_o, the consequence of which is the elaboration of the E_c. The E_c can be complexified, as it exposes itself to a wide range of effects for example, by physical movement of the organism in a spatial context. Alternatively, the more mature organism can come to know its environment more broadly or deeply, thus similarly expanding the effective E_c.

The definition of *play* used here requires some amplification and clarification before proceeding to a discussion of games. It seems evident from a variety of inferences that play is intrinsically motivated ("autoregulated" in Piagetian terms) behavior. A number of scholars have noted the "voluntary" quality of play, and that play is not susceptible to conditioning (Huizinga, 1938; Caillois, 1955; Loizos, 1966). Several authorities have gone so far as to attribute a discrete drive or "mood" motivating play behavior (White, 1959; Morris, 1964; Sade, 1973). While aware of the difficulties in attributing drive to recurrent behaviors (see Bekoff, 1972; Loizos, 1966), the authors are also aware of the data on a number of species indicating the extreme reluctance of young animals to stop playing (e.g., chimpanzee; see van Lawick-Goodall, 1971: 157) and are inclined to the position that the "drive" underlying play behavior is a specific instance of the general motivation discussed elsewhere as the *cognitive imperative* (d'Aquili, 1972; Laughlin and d'Aquili, 1974). *Cognitive im-*

perative refers to an intrinsic motivation present in all vertebrates that compels the organism to complete the EMC so that novelty in the operational environment may be reduced through cognition (modeled within the E_c) and maintained at an adaptive level (see Piaget, 1971 for a similar notion). By using the notion of the cognitive imperative, therefore, no more is attributed to brain than to lungs when their function in oxygenation is noted, or to the intestines when their role in alimentation is indicated.

It must be made clear that play is not simply a necessary condition for the manifestation of a motor pattern, the construction of an E_c, or even for the occurrence of sociality in adult interaction. Play, as has been stated previously, is a *subset* of behaviors comprising the behavioral phase of the EMC. But it is a crucial subset. Play is characteristic of the EMC in organisms phylogenetically complex enough (i.e., all mammals, and a few of the more intelligent birds; Wilson, 1975) to construct an E_c capable of feeding forward beyond the bounds of the immediate spatio-temporal press; that is, they are progressively less "stimulus-bound" (see Piaget, 1971; Pribram, 1971). Higher organisms are capable, within the genetic limits characteristic of any given species, of a more or less flexible E_c (see Poirier and Smith, 1974). The more complex and predominant the play on the part of a species the more complex will be its E_c (Welker, 1956a; Sutton-Smith, 1967; and Wilson, 1975: 164). Furthermore, the data seem to indicate that play is requisite for the enhancement of complex motor patterns in relation to the environment (van Lawick-Goodall, 1971; Menzel et al., 1963, 1970).

An organism, however, will not intrinsically seek to complexify an operational environment that is already perceived as superoptimal. This does *not* mean that the organism will not develop an E_c. The EMC still functions and will continue to function in order to bring the organism's E_c into more adaptive alignment with the stressful elements in the E_0. In terms of later E_c functioning, the play-derived organism's decision process remains more concrete in its alternative responses and choices. Perceptual-conceptual evaluations are more restricted in this case than that of the play-enriched organism.

How Play "Works"

Play, as a particular activity of the EMC, is important to the construction of an E_c among the higher animals. The infant's first autonomous actions, however, follow fairly quickly after the initial period of maternally structured play (Menzel, 1968) with the beginning of solitary play—a set of repetitive sensorimotor actions upon objects in the infant's immediate environment (Harlow, 1963; Bekoff, 1972; Norikoshi, 1974). This early period of involvement between organism and environment is necessary to the successful construction of an adaptive E_c (Piaget, 1952; Menzel, 1968; Laughlin and d'Aquili, 1974).

Sufficient play activity during an early period is requisite, for example, to optimal acquisition of curiosity and refined motor skills in later life (Welker, 1956a; Sutton-Smith, 1967; Menzel et al., 1970) and adaptation to novel environments (Menzel et al., 1963; Berkson et al., 1963; Menzel, 1964, 1966). Curiosity in an organism would appear to be the manifestation of the cognitive imperative in relation to novelty in an otherwise well-cognized E_o. It is known that a number of higher vertebrates are more interested in novel objects than familiar ones; e.g., primates (Menzel, 1963, 1966), ungulates (Thorpe, 1966; Darling, 1964), and dolphins (Tavolga, 1966). Play objects or "toys" are of intense interest to captive dolphins, who will complete tasks with such objects as the sole reward (Pepper and Beach, 1972).

Involvement with novelty is an interactional process requiring not only the presence of novelty in the E_o but intrinsic motivation on the part of the developing organism to act upon that novelty. Menzel et al. (1972) have shown that restricted rearing of chimpanzees may result in a sufficient fear reaction so that approaching novel objects is inhibited. Yet it is argued that cognization of novelty requires intrinsically generated "disadaptation" on the part of the organism (Wolff, 1963: 486). In a very real sense the organism itself may create novelty by acting upon attributes of the E_o (see, for example, Breland and Breland, 1961). The adaptation process modifies the neurognostic models comprising the E_c so that behaviors directed by the models are adaptively synchronized with the E_o.

Play[6] is the principal mechanism that generates novelty by intrinsic action. By inference, if the organism exists in a developmentally suboptimal E_o and is for one reason or another deprived of the opportunity to play (i.e., inhibited from intrinsically generating the requisite novelty), then potential development of the organism's E_c will be severely impaired (Hebb, 1949; Harlow and Harlow, 1962, 1966; Harlow, 1969).

Play behavior affects the quantum of novelty in the E_o, and thus the complexity of the E_c. It involves the free concatenation of motor patterns, all of which are found in other action contexts (Miller, 1973; Loizos, 1966; Welker, 1961). Play provides the experimental combination and recombination of a variety of motor patterns, thus increasing the probability of discovering the most adaptive variations. It is not the mere practice of motor patterns that makes play adaptive; it is the coordinated refinement of motor patterns that is crucial.

Lest this view be taken as too simplistic, it should be noted that an increase in experience and skill (i.e., coordination of motor patterns) enters a feedback relationship with novelty encountered in the E_o. When an organism has a broad range of experience and a complex behavioral repertoire available it will be found in the presence of a greater range and complexity of sensory stimuli. This is another way of stating Uexküll's (1909) contention that objects in the E_o operate as transducers, transforming action on the part of the organism into sensory stimulation that the organism assimilates.

In play, the organism may intrinsically impede the direct efficacy of coordinated motor patterns. In this way change and complexity are added to the range of stimulation available in the E_o. Miller (1973) noted this in human game playing and called the phenomenon *galumphing* (see also Piaget, 1951). It is also clear that galumphing is a universal and significant attribute of vertebrate play. Donald Stone Sade,[7] for example, has noted that young rhesus monkeys on Cayo Santiago will occasionally place a coconut fragment over their eyes and run about bipedally, bumping into whatever is in their paths. Free concatenation of motor patterns, experimentation with coordination, and intrinsic manipulation of the stimulus conditions in experience are all casually operative in the acquisition of neoteny, the maximal range of means to ends (Miller, 1973). Patterns developed in other contexts may be incorporated into play, further refined in coordination with other motor patterns and reciprocally assimilated to each other. Also, patterns developed in play may become operative in nonplay contexts (see Köhler, 1927: 69 for examples among chimpanzees).

Play is adaptive because it is a "within" function that optimizes information about the E_o and thus optimizes cognitive structural development (see Sutton-Smith, 1967: 365 for a consonant position). Taken in toto, play is intrinsic modulation to enrich the operational environment.

Social Play

Social scientists are often the victims of their own categories. This is quite apparent in the commonly made distinction between "physical" or "solitary" play on the one hand and "social" play on the other. An individual organism's conspecifics compromise a significant set of elements and relations in the organism's E_o. Thus adaptation to the E_o requires cognization of those elements and relations. In particular, social play functions to optimize E_c development in relation to the cognizing individual's conspecifics. Social play derives its distinction as "social," not because it is fundamentally different as a process from other play, but rather because of the intended object. Social play (especially in early years) functions neurobiologically to establish or modify channels of neurophysiological entrainment[8] requisite for optimal interorganismic coordination within and between social groups. The details of play (i.e., what motor patterns appear in social play, when the play occurs, and with what objects are not as important here as the central fact that organisms during social play are "taking each other's rhythm" (Count, 1958, 1973; Poirier and Smith, 1974; Chapple, 1970; Chapple and Coon, 1942; d'Aquili et al.,1979). Whereas "physical" play involves free concatenation of motor patterns and galumphing in relation to inanimate or non-socially relevant animate elements in the E_o, "social" play involves the same manipulation of free variation in interaction with conspecifics.

A fundamental, universal neurognostic structure underlies social play in mammals and it is demonstrated by a number of universal features. Probably the most important indicator is the inevitable symbolic marking of social play bouts as "play." All primates, for instance, seem to initiate social play by exhibiting distinctive facial gestures and postures that communicate to potential play partners, "I want to play" (Chevalier-Skolnikoff, 1973; Bateson, 1955, 1956; Loizos, 1967; Sade, 1973; van Lawick-Goodall, 1968). The same feature has been noted as well for many other mammalian species (Loizos, 1966; Bekoff, 1974).

Another indicator of the universal structure of play is the ease with which interspecific play may occur with little misunderstanding of intent (Thorpe, 1966; Norbeck, 1974; van Lawick-Goodall, 1968, 1971). The apparent universality of sexual differentiation in patterns of social play, evident in macaques, baboon, chimpanzees, and human beings (Poirier and Smith, 1974, Owens,

1975; Ruppenthal et al., 1974; Roberts and Sutton-Smith, 1962), as well as an apparently distinctive difference between patterns of play exhibited by arboreal and terrestial species (Poirier and Smith, 1974; Redican and Mitchell, 1974), are additional indicators of the biological structure of social play.

Social play becomes a much more complex affair than solitary play. This is seen as other organisms not only exhibit greater variation per se but also often make that variation contingent upon the behavior of the other interacting organism. Interaction between two organisms is much more flexible and more multideterminant than interaction with the physical world. The organism can have more effect, in some cases, on another animal than it can have on certain aspects of the physical environment. Similarly, since two biological systems have their own direction in an interaction, in addition to factors specific to that interaction, the organisms' prediction of the results of behavior are somewhat different than prediction vis-à-vis the inanimate world. This interaction has important consequences for individual development and motivation (Piaget, 1971; Langer, 1969; Seligman, 1975).

Social play is more than a necessary condition for social interaction (Baldwin and Baldwin, 1973). Other forms of social interaction involving the developing organism also result in adaptive neural entrainment and social coordination. Social play, however, provides a potent arena for the optimization of these functions and may be expected among all social mammals (at least) during periods of peak neural development when internal and external stress are absent. A long series of ingenious experiments (Harlow, 1963, 1969; Harlow and Harlow, 1962; Harlow et al., 1971) have demonstrated the importance of social interaction in the development of rhesus monkeys. Even in animals deprived of other significant forms of social involvement social play is so potent a factor in social development that only a few minutes a day will result in near-normal development (Harlow, 1969; see also Fox and Clark, 1971). A minimal amount of social play appears to be a necessary condition for certain types of complex social skills (Harlow, 1969; Bekoff, 1974).

Social play is behaviorally characterized by repetitive motor patterns, more or less synchronously coordinated, on the part of two or more individuals of either the same or different species. According to Piagetian theory, not only are conceptual operations in human beings constructed from earlier sensorimotor interaction with the physical world, but a conceptualized social organization is constructed from early motoric interaction with conspecifics in the environment (Piaget, 1932; Kohlberg, 1969). It is not the simple refinement of specific motor patterns that appears to be the crucial result of social play, but rather the *interorganismic coordination* of these motor patterns. For example, the motor patterns basic to aggressive interaction among primates appear at or near birth in virtually complete form (Hinde, 1974: 283; Sade, 1975, personal communication). Repeated involvement in aggressive social play would appear to modulate the skillful and appropriate use of these patterns. Commonly, aggressive play has a cumulative and incremental effect upon the interaction complexity between peers and others, frequently leading to the emergence of dominance relations between the animals. Another way to view this process is that social play provides a principal nexus for the blending of inherent proclivities of temperament (Fox, 1973, 1974, 1975) and action into incrementally more flexible and competent social responses.

Social organization and patterns of social interaction are somewhat fluid among social mammals. The social cognized environments of (even adult) group members must be minimally open to modification in order to assure isomorphism with a changing E_o. For this reason, adults in virtually all mammalian species participate in social play to some extent, although generally with far less frequency than infants and juveniles (Loizos, 1966). Adult social play continues to facilitate optimal fit between E_c and E_o, or as Miller (1973) has said, it maintains a maximal range of means to ends. Etkin (1967) has suggested that through social play animals maintain "familiarity" with each other. The presence of social play as a significant factor in the behavior of developing organisms will probably result in more complex and flexible social relations in, and between generations within the same society (Wilson, 1975: 167). This factor, as Count (1973) and Sade (1974) have pointed out, has important implications for fitting social form to ecological niche in a progressively changing E_o.

The Biology of Games

Anthropology has exhibited an interest in the cross-cultural aspects of games, that dates to the work of Edward B. Tyler (1879, 1896). Yet there continues to be disagreement and confusion regarding a clear definition of "game" (Stone, 1972; Sage, 1974;

Schwartzman, 1978). The problem of defining the nature of games will remain intractable so long as the "within" of the phenomenon is systematically ignored.

Play plus Ritual Equals Game

F. S. Frederickson notes that "the most cursory acquaintance with sports in the cultures of man will reveal their importance as ritual" (1960: 433). *Games are ritualized play.*[9] More properly, the game is a nexus between two biologically structured processes, play and ritual. The "within" of play has been described above; now the "within" of ritual will be briefly discussed. Ritual is a complex form of behavioral communication involving a number of conspecifics that: (1) has a predictable pattern or form; (2) recurs with some regularity; (3) operates to synchronize affective, perceptual, conceptual, and motor subsystems of the participants' nervous system; and (4) decreases social distance between participants such that (5) corporate action is facilitated on the part of participants, within or outside the context of the ritual (d'Aquili and Laughlin, 1975; d'Aquili et al., 1979).

Ritual is the locus of adjustment and readjustment of cognized relations between animals (generally conspecifics). Cognized adjustment involves neurobiological changes over a wide area of the nervous system, including autonomic, limbic, cerebellar, and cortical subsystems. Barbara Lex (1979) has, for example, discussed the crucial role of ritual in "tuning," or adjusting, sympathetic-parasympathetic reactivity to external stimuli. Of equal importance is ritual's part in standardizing cognitive and perceptual functions of the central nervous system—stabilizing both the level of conceptual functioning (see below) and the appropriate identification of stimuli within the context of each participant's cognized environment. Finally, ritual is a major stage for enactment of perceived coping behavior. It would appear to be a characteristic of the cognitive imperative that the organism perceive its own behavior and the behavior of those with whom it is acting in concert as operating effectively upon the E_o (Weiss, 1972; Laughlin and d'Aquili in d'Aquili et al., 1979; Seligman, 1975).

A game, then, is the coalescence of ritual and play. To *game*[10] is to participate in a ritual, involving play behavior. It is interesting in this regard that Fox (1973) reports play bouts among adult wolves acting as "tension-reducers" where food is scarce and when the alpha-male has just eaten his fill. Haber (in Fox, 1973) reports that play will also occur after failure on the part of a wolf hunting party to kill a moose. In these cases, the play bout operates as ritual to tune autonomic junctions and establish equanimity for the commonweal.

Human games have long been conceived as "models" or "rituals." Lüschen (1970) has offered a number of case examples. Roberts et al. (1959, 1963), have called games of strategy "models of social integration" and games of change "models of the supernatural." Most sociological analyses, however, have stressed correlational contingencies and social functions at the level of surface structure (e.g., the different social functions of wrestling in Frederickson, 1960). The concern here is the deep structural question: variations in the details of gaming aside, *why* do games in all societies, in some sense mirror or model social relations and action? It is quite certain that gaming does model social action, not only in *Homo sapiens* but among other species. This is nowhere more apparent than in ritualized mammalian aggressive play (e.g., among immature and adult male elephants; Douglas-Hamilton and Douglas-Hamilton, 1975) that is often highly socially structured and in which dominance relations emerge, are established, reinforced, and adjusted through time.

Just as play provides a "context" (Piaget, 1951) or "frame" (Bateson, 1956) within which action may optimize the congruence between E_c and E_o, a game (being an amalgamation of play and ritual) provides a more socially complex and standardized frame within which participants, and spectators as participants, may optimize the development of social coordination with the E_c and E_o. Play also optimizes perceived mastery over obstacles either impinging upon participants' E_c's from the operational environment, or imposed upon the E_c via galumphing (i.e., intrinsically generated obstacles). Typically, obstacles imposed by galumphing are at least minimally isomorphic with obstacles encountered in other nonplay contexts. For this reason, games may be called *rituals of mastery*.[11] As with play proper, skills and social coordinations developed in gaming have ramifications for effective social action that transcend the game frame.

Mammalian Games

The amalgamation of play and ritual is not a phenomenon unique to human beings. Gaming, as it has been defined here, is a process to be found among a wide variety of higher social animals.

The point in phylogenesis at which this amalgamation occurred is not certain. Neither play nor ritual are necessary conditions for a societal adaptation. Rather, play and ritual seem to emerge phylogenetically among creatures who are sufficiently complex to exploit both the solidarity of corporate response and flexibility of response from population to population in relation to different environments, and from generation to generation in response to environmental change. It is our considered opinion that play and ritual are both attributes of an evolving nervous system. They developed at the same time and at the same pace as distinct and independent structural elaborations with discrete selective advantages. It seems likely that during some period just prior to the phylogenetic stage represented by the highest stages of play and ritual there resulted a more complex form of play behavior—the game.

Wolfgang Köhler describes such gaming among young chimpanzees:

Two chimpanzees would wrestle and tumble about playing near some post; soon their movements would become more regular and tend to describe a circle round the post as centre. One after another, the rest of the group approach, join the two, and finally they march in an orderly fashion and in single file round and round the post. The character of their movements changes; they no longer walk, they trot, and as a rule with special emphasis on one foot, while the other steps lightly; thus a rough approximate rhythm develops, and they tend to "keep time" with one another. They wag their heads in time to the steps of their "dance" and appear full of eager enjoyment of their primitive game. (1927: 314–315)

This "ring around the post" game illustrates a number of interesting facets of the gaming process, including (1) game spontaneous initiation, (2) complex social coordination, (3) rhythmic motor activity (Gellhorn and Loofbourrow, 1963; Gellhorn and Kiely, 1972, 1973; see especially Lex, 1979) as a possible driving mechanism of autonomic functions, and (4) repetitive, non-random patterns of motor sequencing, appearing almost "rule structured." Complex gaming is also apparent among dolphins (Caldwell and Caldwell, 1972).

In considering the evolution of play and games, and especially in considering the relationship between games evidenced by species like the dolphin, chimpanzee, or wolf, it is necessary to distinguish those attributes of games characteristic of *Homo sapiens* alone;

i.e., highly symbolic game elements, conceptualization of games qua games, and the institutionalization of games. These features are evolutionary elaborations facilitated by the more highly developed conceptual and symbolic capacity of the human brain. To what extent species such as some dolphins or the chimpanzee are capable of conceptualizing a game (i.e., aware that "this strip of behavior is a game and must be conceptually distinguished from other sorts of behavior") and, further, symbolizing a game or the elements within a game (i.e., able to incorporate a behavior that communicates "this is x game" or "this element x stands for y") remains uncertain. We stand greatly in need of the sort of information about the "within" of gaming and the evolution of gaming that answers to these questions should bring. It has been demonstrated elsewhere (Laughlin and McManus, 1979) that there is at least the possibility of chimpanzee capacity for both conceptualized and symbolized ritual behavior per se.

Human Games

It has been argued above that play and gaming are activities of the developing cognitive function of brain. Within a game the differentiation, symbolic nature, and the level or levels of organization of elements will be constrained by (be a function of) the optimal cognitive capacity of brain. We may speak of a ceiling to optimal complexity of brain, both in relation to the individual and his or her ontogenesis, and in relation to the species or population in terms of its evolution. It may be stated axiomatically, therefore, that optimal cognitive functioning is a necessary, but not a sufficient condition, for optimal differentiation and organization of gaming behavior. Following this line of reasoning, everything else being equal, a greater complexity of gaming behavior among chimpanzees than among macaques may be expected. Such a judgment, in fact, has been made by Bernstein (1962) and DeVore (1963).

The emergence of play behavior in ontogenesis appears to be graded in stages, both for the developing human[12] and for the developing nonhuman primate.[13] In all cases solitary play involving the physical aspects of the environment seems to emerge before play involving complex social interaction. In human beings, of course, the greatest range of complexity in ontogenesis from infancy to adulthood, the greatest variety of play and games, and the greatest elaboration of primordial play-game patterns with symbolic material is found—the latter to such an extent that the elements of play and games may be wholly symbolic (e.g., as in "word games," "blind" chess, etc.). Indeed, the importance of play and games has reached such importance in *Homo sapiens* that Huizinga (1938) was moved to call the species *Homo ludens.*

In the individual case, the optimal level of cognitive functioning reached at any point in his or her ontogenesis will be a function of the interaction between his or her nervous system and the environment (Piaget, 1971). As has been seen already, if the individual is deprived of an optimally enriched social or physical environment, then her or his cognitive development will probably be inhibited (Piaget, 1951; Feldman et al., 1974; Harlow, 1966; Harlow et al., 1971; Bruner et al., 1966; McManus, 1979). This will have an inevitable effect upon the nature, direction, and organization of play and gaming, not to mention other forms of individual coping behavior.

Games and Cognitive Development

From what has been discussed before, it makes sense now to say that the surface form of a game depends upon both the environment and the participants' cognitive structural development. Lüschen (1974: 57) has noted, in the cases of the Mandan Indians and the Australian aborigines, that the complexity of games and the size of game repertoires do not necessarily depend on the complexity of the techno-economic system. The interactional model that is being proposed is depicted here in Figure 1. Game participation in developing persons is an EMC activity. It is a phenomenon intimately bound up in a feedback relationship intervening between complex developmental variables and efficient variables in the E_o. Gaming is both determined by, and is facilitated by, conceptual development. Just how gaming operates at the interface between E_c and E_o in the developing human is the central issue addressed in the remainder of this chapter.

A Biogenetic-Structural Theory of Games

From a biogenetic-structural perspective it is possible to devise a theory of human games and game preference that allows one (1) to treat the "within" of gaming as well as the "without"; (2) to treat the phylogenetic and ontogenetic aspects of gaming simultaneously; (3) to predict to many cross-cultural correlations adduced by

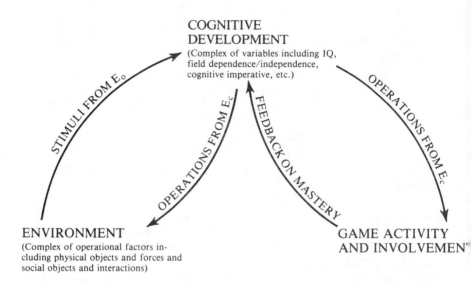

Figure 1. Cognitive development and involvement in games.

other scholars in support of their theories; and (4) to make predic-
tions about further cross-cultural relationships between game
preference and environmental factors facilitatory or inhibitory for
conceptual development.

The "Conflict-Enculturation" Theory of Games

In the interests of theoretical continuity, the authors wish to
utilize some facets of the work completed by other scholars. John
Roberts, Brian Sutton-Smith, and their associates seem to provide
the most comprehensive and anthropologically tenable approach
to understanding the function and evolution of games. In a
lengthy series of studies (Berry and Roberts, 1972; Roberts et al.,
1959, 1963; Roberts and Sutton-Smith, 1962, 1966; Sutton-Smith,
1966, 1967, 1978; Sutton-Smith and Roberts, 1964, 1967, 1970;
Sutton-Smith et al., 1963) these scholars have explored the
worldwide incidence of human games. They define games "as
recreational activities characterized by organized play, competition, two or more sides, criteria for determining the winner, and

agreed-upon rules'' (Roberts and Sutton-Smith, 1962). Three types of games are defined: *physical skill*, where winning is determined primarily by the exercise of motor skills; *strategy*, where winning is primarily determined by competency in rational decision-making; and *chance*, where winning is determined solely by guessing or some mechanism for randomizing outcomes (e.g., a die). Games of physical skill and strategy are not pure types. Games of physical skill may involve only strategy or chance, or both strategy and chance; games of strategy may involve an additional chance element, but may not involve physical skill. Games of chance must involve only chance outcomes (Roberts and Sutton-Smith, 1962).

In an attempt to explain the distribution of game types cross-culturally, Roberts and Sutton-Smith used a neo-Freudian model. Children seek games that model the internal conflict characteristic of their culture. Thus, physical-skill games are associated with high achievement training and cultural complexity; games of chance with high social responsibility and punishment for individual initiative, as well as with uncertainty and belief in benevolent supernatural beings, and games of strategy with obedience and discipline (Sutton-Smith et al., 1963). They also argued for an evolutionary sequence in the emergence of games from a period of no games, followed by the origins of games in the order of physical skill, chance, and strategy (Berry and Roberts, 1972; Roberts and Sutton-Smith, 1966).

A lengthy critique of the work of Roberts and Sutton-Smith is not necessary here, especially since the authors find more to praise in their efforts than to deprecate. It will be far more useful to incorporate their findings and insights into the authors' model wherever possible. A critique of those aspects in which there is disagreement will be left to a later time. Where a difference of opinion or construction exists between the authors and Roberts and Sutton-Smith, exception will be taken for clarification.

The Evolution of Cognition and Games

As stated previously, games are rituals of mastery. They are formed by the intersection of play and ritual in phylogenesis and ontogenesis. Games may or may not incorporate the element of competition between participants (in contradistinction to the Roberts/Sutton-Smith definition). Furthermore, although a game may involve physical skill, that skill may be solely *verbal expression* (e.g., dirty dozens, Wolf-Buzz-Bark-Oink, charades).

It is probable that games, *as the authors have defined them*, have been part of the hominid behavioral repertoire since at least the time of *Ramapithecus* (roughly 12–14 million years ago). The structural matrix that has evolved in relation to game behavior is found in the complexity of the cognitive function of the hominid brain (see Laughlin and d'Aquili, 1974). Increase in cognitive function complexity resulted in a brain capable of increased perceptual differentiation of alternatives, cognization of alternatives within the E_c, and increased capacity to operate upon cognized alternatives without the necessity of trial-and-error motor activity (Piaget, 1971).

Gaming, as an EMC activity, will reflect the complexity of the cognitive operations underlying behavior. This will not be a simple one-to-one correspondence, however. One may participate in a game at a level of complexity equal to or below that of the optimal capacity of one's cognitive system, but one may not effectively participate in a game at a higher level of complexity than one's cognitive capacity. It seems highly unlikely that a chimpanzee can play chess within the rule structure usual for human play. Yet this does not mean that the chimpanzee cannot and does not play games.

One may speak of a physical dimension that may or may not be present in a game, and a rational (decision-making, choice-making) dimension that in humans at least, may or may not be present in a game. A particular game may be sufficiently generalized that it may range from totally physical to totally rational, depending upon the level of the operational-conceptual structure of the individual participant. From the vantage point of Piagetian theory, however, one would predict that games of high physical involvement would precede the more rational in phylogenesis (as has been already shown) and in ontogenesis. Since children are most likely to play games in any society, and the first games they are likely to play have a predominant physical component, therefore, it is predictable that games having a high physical component will predominate cross-culturally. This prediction is borne out by cross-cultural data (Roberts and Sutton-Smith, 1966).

The rational dimension of games may be cognized by players as having two loci of choice or decision making: decisions cognized as made internally (inside self), and decisions cognized as made externally (outside self). The internalization of choice may be termed *strategy*, and the externalization of choice/*chance*. The two modes of rationality in relation to institutionalized games in our society are schematized in Figure 2. It should be noted that Figure 2, to some extent, misrepresents the real complexity of the view presented here. The presence of a physical skill is a third dimension. A number of games may have elements of both internalized and externalized rationality; that is they may combine both strategy and chance. Poker is an obvious example, but so is chess when one includes the drawing for black or white.

Figure 2. The dimensions of rationality and locus of choice in games.

How Cognitive Systems Work

A detailed consideration of the underlying cognitive system allows the full appreciation of the "within" dimension of games, game preference, and sociocultural association with games. It has been shown experimentally that the human conceptual system does not operate at the same level of organizational complexity upon all aspects of the E_o (resulting in so-called developmental decalages;

see Inhelder et al., 1974), nor does it operate at peak (optimal) complexity upon the same aspect of the E_o at all times (Schroder, Driver, and Streufert, 1967). It is the latter finding that is the major concern here, for it underscores the importance of comprehending the interactional nature of cognitive functioning and development.

Optimal complexity and efficiency in cognitive system functioning, in relation to the E_o, requires the maintenance of an optimal degree of novelty (uncertainty) in E_o stimuli (Hebb, 1949). The cognitive system, however, is not passive in this process. The system takes part in the admission of E_o stimuli into itself (see Geertz, 1973: 81–82). The human cognitive system functions to maintain an optimal balance between predictability on the one hand and uncertainty on the other (Seligman, 1975). As depicted in Figure 3, where the balance is optimal, the cognitive system will function at peak efficiency and complexity (Harvey et al., 1961; Schroder et al., 1967). If the operational environment produces superoptimal uncertainty, then the cognitive system becomes overloaded; then it will act to minimize uncertainty, in part by reducing the complexity of its own functioning. On the other hand, if uncertainty is suboptimal, the system again functions below optimal complexity. Severe superoptimal or suboptimal levels of uncertainty will often result in aberrant cognitive system activity.[15]

How any particular individual cognizes uncertainty depends upon a complex of cultural and developmental factors. Of principal structural importance, however, is the level of operational complexity of which the individual is capable. In a series of remarkable experiments, Piaget and Inhelder (1975) have shown that a person's conception of "chance" or uncertainty depends on the point reached in development. At the preoperational level (the level prior to true thought) the person is capable of differentiating only between the expected and the unexpected. At this level the E_c is insufficiently complex to model and attribute causal necessity. At the level of concrete operational thought (true thought) a person becomes capable of differentiating between possible and necessary events (Piaget and Inhelder, 1975: 227). The former are events in the E_o, for which no causal models exist in the E_c preceding and anticipating the events. The latter are events for which such causal models exist. For the concrete operational person, then, events in the E_o fall roughly into two classes: the predictable and the unpredictable. Only with the development of formal

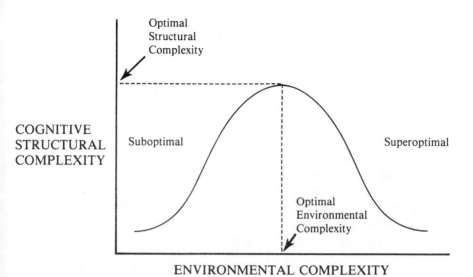

Figure 3. The relationship between optimality of uncertainty and optimality of cognitive-system operation (after Schroder et al., 1967).

thought is the person capable of cognizing events in the E_o *in terms of probabilities of occurrence.* Probability, for Piaget and Inhelder (1975: 230), is the coalescence of "chance" (the unpredictable) with "deductive necessity" (the predictable). The formal operational person is capable of reasoning to degrees of certainty based upon a cognized model of a total distribution of "unpredictable events." That person is capable of making judgments based upon likelihood or unlikelihood, rather than simple certainty or uncertainty that is characteristic of the previous stage.

A point that is critical to the present discussion is that most persons in the majority of societies never fully develop formal operational thought, and some evidence (Dasen, 1972) points to societies in which no one becomes formally operational. The discussion of the conception of "chance" by the concrete operational person will be returned to momentarily. First, however, it is important to complete the dissection of the cognitive system and its function.

The E_c is inevitably only partially isomorphic with the E_o (see note 2). Thus, between the two environments, there lies a "realm" of perceived effects whose causes remain unperceived, and, given the finite constraints of the human nervous system, are possibly unperceivable. This realm of potential mismatch between E_c and E_o has been termed by the authors the *zone of uncertainty*. The presence of a zone of uncertainty for all human societies is manifested in what Paul Tillich (1951) called matters of ultimate concern—that is, of course, precisely the focus of all religion (d'Aquili, Laughlin, and McManus, 1979; Laughlin and Brady, 1978).

Karl Pribram (1971: 211-13) has shed further light on how cognitive systems work. He argues that affect expresses the relationship between the organism's behavioral repertoire and its perceptions. Affect in this sense is a statement about the coping relationship between the E_c and E_o. When incoming information about the E_o is conceived to be more complex than the set of actions available for response, the cognitive system "heats up" to peak performance and the organism feels "interest" and "motivation" (Pribram, 1971: 212). An attempt will be made by the organism to cope and to improve the range of coping actions available. If, however, the coping response is perceived by the organism as failing, then the organism feels "emotion"; i.e., fear, frustration, depression, etc. (see also Seligman, 1975). If, on the other hand, the repertoire of responses is conceived as being greater than that required by the organism's perceptions of the E_o, the organism manifests "a relatively 'flat' motivationless and emotionless state" (Pribram, 1971: 212). In fact, perceptions may be insufficient to obtain an orientation response from the organism and may result in an internal affective state of boredom.

An affective state of "pleasure," "satisfaction," or "fulfillment" may accompany the perceived optimal range of match-mismatch of the behavioral repertory or conceptual operation and expectancy in relation to the E_c. This affective state, so common in human play, has been termed *Functionslust* by Buhler (1930). *Functionslust* may be described as the pleasure taken in the action itself. It is presumably the subjective experience of the intrinsic motivation to play and is the affective component of mastery—the cognitive component of mastery is the increased match between action and operational expectation (see Csikszentmihalyi, 1975, for relevant data). The literature is rife with evidence that *Functionslust* also accompanies the play of non-human species (Bekoff, 1974).

Play, games, and sport allow a restriction of the stimulus domain to a manageable level, permit involvement that transcends self-consciousness, provide situations that allow a feeling of predictability and control commensurate with the players' skills, contain clear mechanisms of feedback concerning performance and result in a level of absorption in which one loses, at least in some cases or moments, an awareness of the self. Furthermore, activity without overt, external reinforcement would seem to provide intrinsic emotional and motivational experience—experience that would appear to be requisite for fulfillment of human life.

From these considerations it may be seen that the organism is moved to reduce uncertainty—the mismatch between E_c and E_o—by a complex cognitive-affective system. It has been argued elsewhere (McManus, 1979) that ritual per se operates as a mechanism for conceived coping in human social action, and is particularly evident and effective in relation to the zone of uncertainty, that "gray area" of chronic potential mismatch between the E_c and the E_o.

A Biogenetic Structural Theory of Games

Figure 4 demonstrates how these various "within" considerations may be placed into a more coherent theory of game function and preference. Games of "pure" strategy (e.g., chess) are those in which mastery derives from matching internalized processes (i.e., differentiated alternatives, available motor or operational skills, decision making) to the rule structure and goals of the game. Games of strategy will be sought and played by actors who think their repertoire of skills and capacities match a range of game requirements; that is, the complexity of the game is neither suboptimal nor superoptimal.

The chance element in games has the effect of regulating uncertainty by either *reducing* or *increasing* perceived unpredictability in the E_o. This operates by externalizing (or "projecting") the locus of choice or environmental complexity. There is a well-known association between games of chance and both religion and environments of conspicious uncertainty. Roberts and Sutton-Smith (1966; Sutton-Smith and Roberts, 1970) have, on the basis of this fact, referred to games of chance as "models of uncertainty". Games of chance predominate in societies confronting great variance in crucial resource availability—resources upon which survival depends—and in societies confronting chronic warfare.

In traditional societies, outcomes in games of chance are rarely

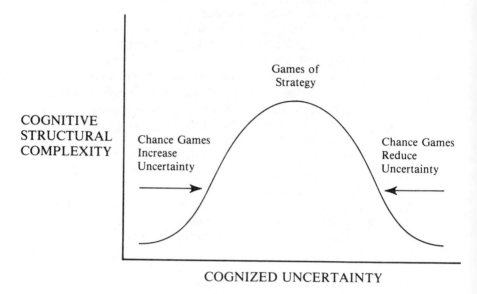

Figure 4. The effect of games of chance and strategy upon cognitive-system activity.

cognized in terms of probability (Roberts et al., 1959). And, in many societies, such games are conceived as being divinatory—the intervention by supernatural entities and the interjection of information and choice by external forces. These cross-cultural facts are understandable if one views them in light of the discussion of cognitive development and uncertainty.

For most members of the majority of societies (and all adult members of some societies), events in the E_o are cognized roughly into two categories: the expected and unexpected (for persons at a stage prior to operational thought), or the predictable and unpredictable (for persons, including most adults, who have reached full operational thought). It is the occurrence of events ("chance" events) in the unpredictable category that cause superoptimal noxity for concrete operational persons. The stressful uncertainty category constitutes precisely the zone of uncertainty, the target of religious cognization and ritual action. Small wonder then that games of chance—rituals of mastery involving the externalization of rationality—should be found among a society's repertoire of coping mechanisms related to uncertainty and stress. It is with a sense of irony that we continue to refer to these games in terms of "chance," considering that their real effect is the removal of chance and the satisfaction of the cognitive imperative.

A point commonly missed by scholars who are interested in games is that chance may also operate to increase uncertainty in the E_o. Games may act as one of a set of such mechanisms in society. Indeed, Peckham (1965) has argued that art also operates to create uncertainty in the environment. Games of chance would in this case operate to "heat up" cognitive system complexity and efficiency, bringing it toward optimal functioning. But chance does not have to be cognized as pure chance in order to have the effect of increasing uncertainty. More often a game of chance must be cognized as a blend of internal and external choice—as both strategy and chance. The duel, an example of ritual aggression and gaming from Western cultural history, was once cognized as an affair of skill, yet, there was considerable chance involved (Bryson in Frederickson, 1960). Chronic gamblers "have a system," carry their "good luck piece," cognize a run of wins as "Lady Luck is with me," or feel that their "mojo's working."

Within the context of a game of chance the stimulus from the E_o is perceived to some extent as being unpredictable, yet the realm of unpredictability is socially and environmentally contained. In most cases the uncertainty does not spill over into non-game contexts. But the effects of entering and participating in a game has corresponding effects upon an actor's outside life. People experience affective states, including perhaps *Functionslust*, while playing and these states remain, effecting their perceptions of the extra-game cognized environment, and especially their place within it. Above all, boredom from suboptimal stimulation has been momentarily banished, neuropsychological arousal obtained, and reinforcement for repetition of the experience registered. It is interesting to note in this regard that Elias and Dunning (1970) describe certain sports that appear as the locus of controlled excitement expression. Although there is not sufficient space to go into it here, these factors go a long way toward explaining the chronic gambling problem. A person may become addicted to gaming as his/her only source of *Functionslust* and escape from grinding boredom.

The element of strategy in games functions to stimulate intrinsic cognitive activity and judgment to peak activity. The "pure" strategy game (that is a game without a significant chance element; e.g., chess or go) is one in which alternatives within the context of rules, evaluation of alternatives, and choice of alternatives resides within the volition of the player. The E_o imposes neither suboptimal nor superoptimal novelty upon the field of play. Many games, of course, combine strategy and chance to varying degrees, depending upon the E_c of the participant. Games such as backgammon or "draw" poker combine externally generated alternatives with intrinsically generated evaluation and choice. For the coach, a football game may be predominantly one of strategy, but in actual play, elements of chance (variables beyond the coach's control such as weather, injury, ground conditions), as well as elements of physical skill (degree of motivation on the part of players to excel over their counterparts on the other team) may provide alternatives external to the coach's internal plan. As a matter of fact, extreme measures may be taken to remove the element of chance from gaming; e.g., synthetic playing fields, field houses, and "domes."

Environment, Socialization, and Game Preference

Given the same E_o, different actors will respond in different ways vis-à-vis optimality of novelty depending: (1) on the potential complexity of organization of their cognized environments, and (2) on social constraints to action. Individuals attaining higher structural development are less vulnerable, if operating at peak complexity, to the pernicious effects of stress. Persons having high cognitive structural complexity are just beginning to operate at their peak when persons of lower structural complexity are showing a decrement due to superoptimal stress (see Schroder et al., 1967 for a summary of relevant research).[16]

High potential structural complexity has been shown to be significantly correlated with measures of high IQ[17] (Sullivan, McCullough, and Stager, 1970; Kohlberg and deVries, 1969). Development of perceptual differentiation and independence from external cues about perceptual material, as well as high cognitive structural complexity may be strongly influenced (inhibited or facilitated) by the nature of the environment and by the nature of socialization procedures (Witkin, 1971; Harvey et al., 1961; Dasen, 1971; Cross, 1965; Kohlberg, 1969).

With everything else being equal, it is predicted here that persons who are highly field independent and highly developed in cognitive structural complexity will prefer a greater proportion of strategy and a smaller proportion of chance in the games they play.

Conversely, persons who are highly field independent and of lower structural complexity will tend to prefer more chance and less strategy in the games they play. Schematized as a Markov process, it might be said that IQ and field independence are necessary but not sufficient conditions for structural complexity, and structural complexity is a necessary but not a sufficient condition for preference for strategy games (see Figure 5).

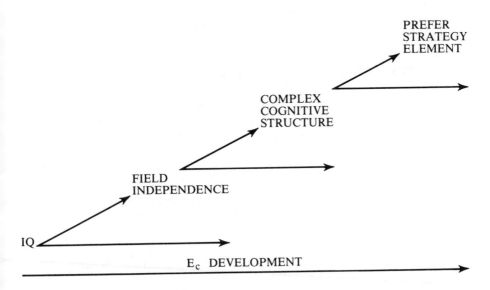

Figure 5. The relationship of IQ, cognitive variables, and game preference.

The Roberts and Sutton-Smith (1964) data indicate a significant correlation between high IQ and preference for strategy games. It is suspected that field independence is a hidden dimension in their measure, but there is no way to be certain at this point. On the other hand, persons who have a low IQ tend to be field dependent and low in cognitive complexity, and should tend to prefer a predominance of physical skill, with or without the accompaniment of the other two elements.

It is easy to see that, assuming the above relationships obtain between cognitive and gaming variables, *any environmental or socialization variables facilitatory to cognitive development should also have a determinant effect upon game preference.* Thus, heterogeneity of physical environment, socialization procedures emphasizing independence of judgment, nonauthoritarian guidance, noninterference by elders in peer-related affairs, lack of corporal punishment, etc., are shown in various studies to be conducive to the development of field independence and structural complexity (Witkin, 1971; Dasen, 1972; Cross, 1965). Conversely, homogeneity of physical environment, and socialization procedures based upon authoritarian principles, corporal punishment, mediation by elders of peer disputes, and emphasis upon independence of judgment generally are shown to be inhibitory to field independence and structural complexity. Thus, one might expect to find games of strategy prevalent (accompanied or unaccompanied by other types of games) in societies fitting the former characteristics, and games of chance and physical skill prevailing among societies fitting the latter characteristics (see Figure 6.) Alternatively, a significant correlation between the presence of high field independence or high structural complexity and the presence of games of strategy may be predicted.

CONDITIONS INFLUENCING
STRUCTURAL DEVELOPMENT

		FACILITORY	INHIBITORY
GAMES OF STRATEGY	PRESENT	EXPECTED HIGH LOADING	
	ABSENT		EXPECTED HIGH LOADING

Figure 6. Conditions Facilitory or Inhibitory to Cognitive Structural Development and the Presence or Absence of Games of Strategy.

Although an attempt has been made to test these hypotheses the results are unfortunately equivocal, due in large measure to the paucity of, and ambiguity in, the cross-cultural data. As they now stand, the associations suggested here must await further research for confirmation or disconfirmation.

Conclusions

In addressing issues surrounding the nature of play, games, and "sport" the concern here is with a complex phenomenon. In this chapter, an attempt has been made to demonstrate that such phenomena can be explained, and that the requisite explanation entails consideration of biological, neuropsychological, ontogenetic, cognitive, and social factors. The inclination here is to think that the social sciences are growing intolerant of simplistic, unidimensional, and discipline-bound theory. This intolerance is in keeping with the fact that as social scientists our task is the explanation of the most complex systems in the known universe. Nothing short of a free exchange of information and insight across disciplinary boundaries will suffice. This chapter has been one small step in that direction.

The study of play and games underscores an important shift occurring in the social, not to mention the biological, sciences. Scientists are beginning to appreciate the fact that to explain a phenomenon in the adult system requires a consideration of the ontogenesis of the phenomenon.[18] The increased concern for ontogenesis, in turn, underscores the importance of close scrutiny of the neurobiological systems underlying the developmental process (Fox, 1971; Laughlin and d'Aquili, 1974); that is, the neurophysiological "within" of the phenomenon. It is predicted here that the shift to a neurophysiologically grounded, ontogenetic perspective, will change the epistemological status of certain phenomena from peripheral concern to central concern. This is quite evident in the enhanced interest in play and games (see Schwartzman, 1978: 325). What was once considered childish behavior, hardly worthy of serious scientific concern, has become what Dolhinow and Bishop (1970) see as a major category of adaptive behavior.

Finally, it should be fairly evident from the above considerations, as well as from material found elsewhere in this volume (see chapter 1), that defining our object of scientific reference as "sport" is to incumber ourselves with myopia. The notion of "sport" is ethnocentric (a product of the E_c) and anthropocentric (incapable of ethological operationalization). Furthermore, "sport" is our cultural category for a set of behaviors that solely constitute the "without" of the phenomenon that should concern us. A suggestion is that we take off our blinders, put on our X-ray glasses and take a good, long, healthy look at the "within" of the phenomenon in which we are so vitally interested.

We wish to acknowledge the invaluable assistance of Phillip Stevens, Jr.; Ivan Brady; Sue Horan; Janie Brady; Patricia Kolarik; Robert Pankin; Anthony Annunziata; Beth, Sarah and Kate Allgeier; and Miriam Barron.

Notes

1. Biogenetic structuralism is a neurobiological theory of human sociocultural phenomena that was initially presented in Laughlin and d'Aquili (1974). It has subsequently been expanded and applied to several substantive issues in the social and behavioral sciences (see also d'Aquili, Laughlin, and McManus, 1979; and Laughlin and Brady, 1978.)

2. Aided by the ethological approaches to games; e.g., Norbeck (1974) and Frederickson (1960) explicitly eschew any theoretical link between the play of human beings and that of other species.

3. A more detailed discussion of this section, including the concepts of "adaptive isomorphism" and "cognized and operational environments" is to be found in d'Aquili et al., (1979) and in Laughlin and Brady (1978). The latter distinction we borrowed from Rappaport (1968), although it is of much greater vintage, dating at least to the writings of Uexküll (1909).

4. Failure to understand the intrinsic origins of conceptual activity has led to needless misunderstanding of the structuralist position (Sutton-Smith, 1966; Piaget, 1966). The organism is not a passive recipient of a poorly copied image of reality. Rather, the organism actively constructs a model of reality based upon neurognostic prototypes and feedback from the E_o in response to activity upon the E_o by the organism (Piaget, 1952).

5. Play, as we conceive it, includes certain features attributed to "exploration" by some ethologists (Wilson, 1975: 165; Welker, 1961). We are willing to accept the dichotomization of "play" and "exploration," but only under certain complex structural conditions too lengthy to go into in the present chapter.

6. Piaget (1951, 1966) gives a more restricted meaning to the concept of "play." We would subsume his "play" and "imitation" under our concept of play.

7. Personal communication (1974).

8. The term "entrainment" refers to the process by which neural subsystems become linked together in a causal sequence.

9. There is some dissonance between the ethological notion of "ritualization" and the anthropological notion of "ritual." We have discussed this issue elsewhere (d'Aquili et al., 1979).

10. Our language lets us down at this point, for the words "to game" and "gaming" denote gambling or stakes play. We mean to denote merely the act of participating in a game.

11. For similar reasons, although from a different theoretical context, Sutton-Smith and Roberts (1970) call games "models of power."

12. Piaget (1951) explicated three stages in the development of human play.

13. Harlow (1963) defined five stages of play development in the macaque, while Poirier (1970) found at least four stages among nilgiri langurs.

14. By chance we do not mean to imply probability. Few of the world's societies cognize chance as strategy based upon probability, but rather as interjection of choice by some external, usually supernatural, rational entity (see Roberts and Sutton-Smith, 1966).

15. Piaget (1952, 1971; Piaget and Inhelder, 1969) has demonstrated through many experiments that rational operations are constructed by the organism out of earlier sensorimotor activities. Since the young child is rather stimulus-bound and required to act directly upon his or her world in order to cognitively cope, the older child and adult may run through various alternative activities mentally and select the best alternative before acting, or choosing not to act.

16. See Seligman (1975) and Laughlin and Brady (1978) for the effects of superoptimal stress; see also Zubek (1969) for the effects of severe sensory deprivation.

17. Herman Witkin (Witkin, 1971; Witkin et al., 1973) and his associates have formulated the notion of "cognitive style" that is a composite concept covering a number of cognitive functions cemented into an integrated whole. The cognitive style of an individual combines the "self-consistent modes of cognitive functioning" that develop via the interaction between his or her cognitive potentiality and his or her cognitive and social environment (Witkin, 1971). Some of the aspects of development subsumed by the concept are differentiation of defense structure, development of autonomous analytical structure, and the development of perceptual differentiation. The latter factor (perceptual differentiation or "field dependence/independence") is the one most widely researched and is a measure of the degree to which a person makes judgments about differentiated perceptual material grounded in cues internal to the person rather than given in the external perceptual field. Cognitive style may be influenced by environmental and socialization factors (Witkin, 1971).

18. See Bekoff (1972) for a similar conclusion.

Works Cited

d'Aquili, E. G. *The Biopsychological Determinants of Culture*. Reading, Mass.: Addison-Wesley, 1972.

d'Aquili, E. G., and Laughlin, C. D. "The Biopsychological Determinants of Religious Ritual." *Zygon* 10 (1975): 32–58.

d'Aquili, E. G.; Laughlin, C. D., and McManus, J. *The Spectrum of Ritual*. New York: Columbia University Press, 1979.

Baldwin, J. D., and Baldwin, J. I. "The Ecology and Behavior of Squirrel Monkeys (*Saimiri   oerstedi*) in a Natural Forest in Western Panama." *Folia Primatologica* 18 (1972): 161–84.

———. "The Role of Play in Social Organization: Comparative Observations on Squirrel Monkeys (*Saimiri*)." *Primates* 14 (1973): 369–81.

———. "Exploration and Social Play in Squirrel Monkeys *Saimiri*)." *American Zoologist* 14 (1974): 303–15.

Ball, D. W. "Ascription and Position: A Comparative Analysis of 'Stacking' in Professional Football." *The Canadian Review of Sociology and Anthropology* 10 (1973): 97–113.

Barber, R. *The Knight and Chivalry*. Totowa, N.J.: Rowman and Littlefield, 1974.

Barnett, S. A. *Instinct and Intelligence*. London: Pelican, 1970.

Barry, H., and Roberts, J. M. "Infant Socialization and Games of Chance." *Ethnology* 11 (1972): 296–308.

Bateson, G. "A Theory of Play and Fantasy." *Psychiatric Research Report* 2 (1955): 39–51.

———. The Message "This Is Play." In *Group Processes*, edited by J. B. Schaffner, pp. 164–68. New York: Macy Foundation, 1956.

Beach, F. A. "Concepts of Play in Animals." *American Naturalist* 79 (1945): 523–41.

Bekoff, M. "The Development of Social Interaction, Play and Metacommunication in Mammals: An Ethological Perspective." *Quarterly Review of Biology* 47 (1972): 412–33.

———. "Social Play in Mammals." *American Zoologist* 14 (1974): 265–436.

———. "Social Play in Coyotes, Wolves, and Dogs." *Bioscience* 24 (1974): 225–30.

Berkson, G.; Mason, W. A., and Saxon, S. V. "Situation and Stimulus Effects on Stereotyped Behaviors of Chimpanzees." *Journal of Comparative and Physiological Psychology* 56 (1963): 786–92.

Berlyne, D. E. "Laughter, Humor and Play." In *Handbook of Social Psychology*. Vol. 3, edited by G. Lindzey and E. Aronson, pp. 795–852. New York: Addison-Wesley, 1969.

Breland, K., and Breland, M. "The Misbehavior of Organisms." *American Psychologist* 61 (1961): 681–84.

Bruner, J. S.,; Jolly, A., and Sylva, K. *Play—Its Role in Development and Evolution*. New York: Penguin Books, 1976.

Bruner, J. S.; Olver, R. R., and Greenfield, P. M. *Studies in Cognitive Growth*. New York: Harcourt Brace, 1966.

Caillois, R. "The Structure and Classification of Games." *Diogenes* 12 (1955): 62–75.

Caldwell, D.K., and Caldwell, M.C. *The World of the Bottlenosed Dolphin*. Philadelphia: J. B. Lippincott, 1972.

Chapple, E. C. *Culture and Biological Man*. New York: Holt, Rinehart and Winston, 1970.

Chapple, E. D., and Coon, C. S. *Principles of Anthropology*. New York: Henry Holt, 1942.

Chevalier-Skolnikoff, S. "The Primate Play Face: A Possible Key to the Determinants and Evolution of Play." Paper given at annual meeting, American Anthropological Association, New Orleans, 1973.

———. "The Ontogeny of Primate Intellectual Development and its Implications for Communicative Potential." Paper presented at the conference on Origins and Evolution of Language and Speech, New York Academy of Sciences, New York City, 1975.

Count, E. W. "The Biological Basis of Human Sociality." *American Anthropologist* 60 (1958): 1049–85.

———. *Being and Becoming Human*. New York: Van Nostrand Reinhold, 1973.

Cove, J. "Survival or Extinction: Reflections on the Problem of Famine in Tsimshian and Kaguru Mythology." In *Extinction and Survival in Human Populations*, edited by C. D. Laughlin and I. Brady, pp. 231–44. New York: Columbia University Press, 1977.

Cross, H. J. "The Relation of Parental Training Conditions to Conceptual Level in Adolescent Boys." *Journal of Personality* 34 (1966): 343–65.

Csikszentmihalyi, M. *Beyond Boredom and Anxiety*. San Francisco: Jossey-Bass, 1975.

Darling, F. F. *A Herd of Red Deer*. Garden City, New York: Doubleday, 1964.

Dasen, P. R. "Cognitive Development in Aborigines of Central Australia: Concrete Operations and Perceptual Activities." Unpublished Doctoral Dissertation, Australian National University, 1970.

———. "Cross-Cultural Piagetian Research: A Summary." *Journal of Cross-Cultural Psychology* 3 (1972): 23–39.

DeLemos, M. M. "The Development of Conservation in Aboriginal Children." *International Journal of Psychology* 4 (1969): 255-69.

DeVore, I. "Mother-Infant Relations in Free-Ranging Baboons." In *Maternal Behavior in Mammals*, edited by H. L. Reinhold. New York: Wiley, 1963.

Diamond, M. C., et al. "The Effects of an Enriched Environment on the Histology of the Rat Cerebral Cortex." *Journal of Comparative Neurology* 123 (1964): 111-19.

———. "Increases in Cortical Depth and Glia Numbers in Rats Subjected to Enriched Environment." *Journal of Comparative Neurology* 128 (1966): 117-26.

Dolhinow, P. J., and Bishop, N. "The Development of Motor Skills and Social Relationships among Primates through Play." *Minnesota Symposium on Child Psychology* 4 (1970):141-98.

Douglas-Hamilton, I., and Douglas-Hamilton, O. *Among the Elephants.* New York: The Viking Press, 1975.

Eccles, J. C. *The Understanding of the Brain.* New York: McGraw-Hill, 1973.

Elias, N., and Dunning, E. "The Quest for Excitement in Unexciting Societies." In *The Cross-Cultural Analysis of Sports and Games*, edited by G. Lüschen, pp. 31-50. Champaign, Ill.: Stipes Publishing Co., 1970.

Etkin, W. *Social Behavior from Fish to Man.* Chicago: University of Chicago Press, 1967.

Fagen, R. M. "Selective and Evolutionary Aspects of Animal Play." *American Naturalist* 108 (1974): 850-58.

Feldman, C. F., et al. *The Development of Adaptive Intelligence.* San Francisco: Jossey-Bass, 1974.

Fichtelius, K. E., and Sjohander, S. *Smarter Than Man? Intelligence in Whales, Dolphins and Man.* New York: Random House, 1972.

Fox, M. W. *Integrative Development of Brain and Behavior in the Dog.* Chicago: University of Chicago Press, 1971.

———. "Social Dynamics of Three Captive Wolf Packs." *Behavior* 47 (1973): 290-301.

———. *Concepts in Ethology: Animal and Human Behavior.* Minneapolis: University of Minnesota Press, 1974.

Fox, M. W., ed. *Evolution of Social Behavior in Canids. The Wild Canids.* New York: Van Nostrand and Reinhold, 1975.

Fox, M. W., and Clark, A. "The Development and Temporal Sequencing of Agonistic Behavior in the Coyote (*Canis latrans*)." *Z. Tierpsychol* 28 (1971): 262-78.

Frederickson, F. S. "Sports and the Cultures of Man." In *Science and Medicine of Exercise and Sports*, edited by W. R. Johnson, pp. 429-36. New York: Harper and Row, 1960.

Geertz, C. *The Interpretation of Cultures.* New York: Basic Books, 1973.

Gellhorn, E., and Kiely, W. F. "Mystical States of Consciousness: Neurophysiological and Clinical Aspects." *Journal of Nervous and Mental Disease* 154 (1972): 399-405.

———. "Autonomic Nervous System in Psychiatric Disorder." In *Biological Psychiatry*, edited by J. Mendels, pp. 235-62. New York: John Wiley, 1973.

Gellhorn, E., and Loofbourrow, G. M. *Emotions and Emotional Disorders: A Neurophysiological Study.* New York: Harper and Row, 1963.

Harlow, H. F. "Basic Social Capacity of Primates." In *Primate Social Behavior*, edited by C. H. Southwick, pp. 153-60. Princeton: Van Nostrand, 1963.

———. "Age-mate or Peer Affectional Systems." *Advanced Studies of Behavior* 2 (1969): 333-38.

Harlow, H. F., and Harlow, M. K. "Social Deprivation in Monkeys." *Scientific American* 207 (1962): 137-46.

Harlow, H. F.; Harlow, M., and Suomi, S. "From Thought to Therapy: Lessons from a Primate Laboratory." *American Scientist* 59 (1971): 538-50.

Harlow, M. K., and Harlow, H. F. "Affection in Primates." *Discovery* 27 (1966): 11–17.
Harvey, O. J.; Hunt, D., and Schroder, S. *Conceptual Systems and Personality Organization*. New York: Wiley, 1961.
Hebb, D. O. *The Organization of Behavior*, New York: Wiley, 1949.
Hinde, R. A. *Animal Behavior*. 2d ed. New York: McGraw-Hill, 1970.
———. *Biological Bases of Human Social Behavior*. New York: McGraw-Hill, 1974.
Hubel, D. H., and Wiesel, T. N. "Receptive Fields, Binocular Interaction and Functional Architecture in the Cat's Visual Cortex." *Journal of Physiology* 160 (1962): 106–54.
Huizinga, J. *Homo Ludens*. Boston: Beacon Press, 1938.
Inhelder, B.; Sinclair, H.; and Bovet, M. *Learning and the Development of Cognition*. Cambridge: Harvard University Press, 1974.
Jewell, P. A., and Loizos, C. *Play, Exploration and Territory in Mammals*. New York: Academic Press, 1966.
Kelly, M. R. "Some Aspects of Conservation of Quantity and Length in Papua and New Guinea in Relation to Language, Sex and Years at School." Territory of Papua and New Guinea *Journal of Education*, 1970, pp. 55–60.
King, G. "The Biological Limits of Human Sociality." Presented at annual meeting American Anthropological Association, San Francisco, Calif., 1975.
Kohlberg, L. "Stage and Sequence: The Cognitive Developmental Approach to Socialization." In *Handbook of Socialization Theory and Research*, edited by D. Goslin, pp. 347–480. Chicago: Rand McNally, 1969.
Köhler, W. *The Mentality of Apes*. 2d ed. London: Routledge and Kegan Paul, 1927.
Kummer, H. "Tripartite Relations in Hamadryas Baboons." In *Social Communication among Primates*, edited by S. A. Altmann, pp. 63–71. Chicago: University of Chicago Press, 1967.
Laughlin, C. D. "Deprivation and Reciprocity." *Man* 9 (1974): 380–96.
Laughlin, C. D., and d'Aquili, E. G. *Biogenetic Structuralism*. New York: Columbia University Press, 1974.
———. "Ritual and Stress." In *The Spectrum of Ritual*, edited by E. G. d'Aquili; C.D. Laughlin; and J. McManus, pp. 280–317. New York: Columbia University Press, 1979.
Laughlin, C. D., and Brady, I. A. *Extinction and Survival in Human Populations*. New York: Columbia University Press, 1978.
Laughlin, C. D., and McManus, J. "The Nature of Neurognosis." Paper presented at annual meeting American Anthropological Association, San Francisco, California, 1975.
———. "Mammalian Ritual." In *The Spectrum of Ritual*, edited by E. G. d'Aquili, C. D. Laughlin, and J. McManus, pp. 80–116. New York: Columbia University Press, 1979.
Levine, N. "Why Do Countries Win Olympic Medals?" *Sociology and Social Research* 58 (1974): 353–60.
Lex, B. "The Neurobiology of Ritual Trance." In *The Spectrum of Ritual*, edited by E. G. d'Aquili et al., pp. 117–51. New York: Columbia University Press, 1979.
Loizos, C. "Play in Mammals." In *Play, Exploration and Territory in Mammals*, edited by P. A. Jewell and C. Loizos, pp. 1–10. New York: Academic Press, 1966.
———. "Play Behavior in Higher Primates: A Review." In *Primate Ethology*, edited by D. Morris, pp. 176–218. Chicago: Aldine, 1967.
Loy, J. "Behavioral Responses of Free-Ranging Rhesus Monkeys to Food Shortage." *American Journal of Physical Anthropology* 33 (1970): 263–72.
Loy, J. W., and Kenyon, G. S. *Sport, Culture and Society*. New York: Macmillan, 1969.
Lüschen, G. *The Cross-Cultural Analysis of Sport and Games*. Champaign, Illinois: Stipes Publishing Company, 1970.
———. "The Interdependence of Sport and Culture." In *Sport and American Society*, edited by G. H. Sage, pp. 46–60. Reading, Mass.: Addison-Wesley, 1974.

Mason, W. A. "The Social Development of Monkeys and Apes." In *Primate Behavior*, edited by I. DeVore, pp. 514–43. New York: Holt, Rinehart and Winston, 1965.

McBride, A. F., and Hebb, D. O. "Behavior of the Captive Bottle-Nose Dolphin." *Journal of Comparative and Physiological Psychology* 41 (1948): 111–23.

McManus, J. "Psychopathology as Errors in Cognitive Adaptation." Annual meeting of American Anthropological Association, San Francisco, California, 1975.

———. "Ritual and Social Cognition." In *The Spectrum of Ritual*, edited by E. G. d'Aquili, C. D. Laughlin, and J. McManus, pp. 216–48. New York: Columbia University Press, 1979.

Menzel, E. W. "The Effects of Cumulative Experience on Responses to Novel Objects in Young Isolation-Reared Chimpanzees." *Behavior* 21 (1963): 1–12.

———. "Patterns of Responsiveness in Chimpanzee Reared through Infancy under Conditions of Environmental Restriction." *Psychol. Forsch.* 27 (1964): 337–65.

———. "Responsiveness to Objects in Free-Ranging Japanese Monkeys." *Behavior* 26 (1966): 130–50.

———. "Primate Naturalistic Research and Problems of Early Experience." *Developmental Psychobiology* 1 (1968): 175–84.

Menzel, E. W.; Davenport, R. K., and Rogers, C. M. "Effects of Environmental Restriction upon the Chimpanzee's Responsiveness in Novel Situations." *Journal of Comparative and Physiological Psychology* 56 (1963): 329–34.

———. "The Development of Tool Using in Wild-Born and Restriction-Reared Chimpanzees." *Folia Primatologica* 12 (1970): 273–83.

———. "Protocultural Aspects of Chimpanzee's Responsiveness to Novel Objects." *Folia Primatologica* 17 (1972): 161–70.

Miller, S. "Ends, Means and Galumphing: Some Leitmotifs of Play." *American Anthropologist* 75 (1973): 87–98.

Morris, D. "The Response of Animals to a Restricted Environment." *Symposium of the Zoological Society* 13 (1964): 99–118.

Murdock, G. P. "The Common Denominator of Cultures." In *The Sciences of Man in the World Crisis*, edited by R. Linton, pp. 123–42. New York: Columbia University Press, 1945.

———. *Ethnographic Atlas*. Pittsburgh: University of Pittsburgh Press, 1967.

Norbeck, E. "The Development of Peer-Mate Relationships in Japanese Macaque Infants." *Primates* 15 (1974): 39–46.

Owens, N. W. "Social Play Behavior in Free-Living Baboons, *Papio anubis*." *Animal Behavior* 23 (1975): 387–408.

Peckham, M. *Man's Rage for Chaos*. Philadelphia: Clifton Books, 1965.

Pepper, R. L., and Beach, P. A. "Preliminary Investigation of Tactile Reinforcement in the Dolphin." *Cetology* 7 (1972): 1–8.

Piaget, J. *The Child's Conception of the World*. London: Routledge and Kegan Paul, 1929.

———. *The Moral Judgment of the Child*. London: Routledge and Kegan Paul, 1932.

———. *Play, Dreams and Imitation in Childhood*. London: Heinemann, 1951.

———. *The Origins of Intelligence in Children*. New York: International Universities Press, 1952.

———. "Response to Brian Sutton-Smith." *Psychological Review* 73 (1966): 111–12.

———. *Biology and Knowledge*. Chicago: University of Chicago Press, 1971.

Piaget, J., and Inhelder, B. *The Psychology of the Child*. New York: Basic Books, 1969.

———. *The Origin of the Idea of Chance in Children*. New York: Norton, 1975.

Poirier, F. "Nilgiri Langur Ecology and Social Behavior." In *Primate Behavior*, edited by L. A. Rosenblum, pp. 215–24. New York: Academic Press, 1970.

Poirier, F. E., and Smith, E. O. "Socializing Functions of Primate Play." *American Zoologist* 14 (1974): 275–87.

Pribram, K. H. *Languages of the Brain*. Englewood Cliffs, N.J.: Prentice-Hall, 1971.

Price-Williams, D. R. "Abstract and Concrete Modes of Classification in Primitive Society." *British Journal of Educational Psychology* 32 (1962): 50–61.

Prince, J. R. *Science Concepts in a Pacific Culture*. Sydney: Angus and Robertson, 1969.

Rappaport, R. A. *Pigs for the Ancestors*. New Haven: Yale University Press, 1968.

Redican, W. K., and Mitchell, G. "Play between Adult Male and Infant Rhesus Monkeys." *American Zoologist* 14 (1974): 295–302.

Roberts, J. M.; Arth, M. J., and Bush, R. R. "Games in Culture." *American Anthropologist* 61 (1959): 597–605.

Roberts, J. M., and Sutton-Smith, B. "Child Training and Game Involvement." *Ethnology* 1 (1962): 166–85.

———. "Cross-Cultural Correlates of Games of Chance." *Behavioral Science Notes* 3 (1966): 131–44.

Roberts, J. M.; Sutton-Smith, B.; and Kendon, A. "Strategy in Games and Folk Tales." *Journal of Social Psychology* 61 (1963): 185–99.

Rosenzweig, M. R., et al. "Effects of Environmental Complexity and Training on Brain Chemistry and Anatomy: A Replication and Extension." *Journal of Comparative and Physiological Psychology* 55 (1962): 429–37.

———. "Brain Changes in Response to Experience." *Scientific American* (March 1972), pp. 22–29.

Rubinstein, R., and Laughlin, C. D. "Bridging Levels of Systemic Organization." *Current Anthropology* 18 (1977): 459–81.

Ruppenthal, G. C., et al. "Development of Peer Interactions of Monkeys Reared in a Nuclear-Family Environment." *Child Development* 45 (1974): 670–82.

Sade, D. S. "An Ethogram for Rhesus Monkeys: I. Antithetical Contrasts in Posture and Movement." *American Journal of Physical Anthropology* 38 (1973): 537–42.

———. "The Vertebrate Ego." Paper presented before the annual meeting of the American Anthropological Association, Mexico City, 1974.

Sage, G. H. *Sport and American Society*. Reading, Mass.: Addison-Wesley, 1974.

Schroder, H. M.; Driver, M.; and Streufert, S. *Human Information Processing*. New York: Holt, Rinehart and Winston, 1967.

Schwartzman, H. B. *Transformations: The Anthropology of Children's Play*. New York: Plenum Press, 1978.

Seligman, M. *Helplessness*. San Francisco: W. H. Freeman, 1975.

Stevens, P. "Laying the Groundwork for an Anthropology of Play." *Newsletter of the Association for the Anthropological Study of Play* 3 (1976).

———. *Studies in the Anthropology of Play*. Cornwall, N.Y.: Leisure Press, 1977.

Stone, G. P. *Games, Sport and Power*. New Brunswick, N.J.: Transaction, 1972.

Sullivan, E. V.; McCullough, G.; and Stager, M. "A Developmental Study of the Relation between Conceptual, Ego and Moral Development." *Child Development* 41 (1970): 399–412.

Sutton-Smith, B. "Piaget on Play: A Critique." *Psychological Review* 73 (1966): 104–10.

———. "The Role of Play in Cognitive Development." *Young Children* 22 (1967): 361–70.

Sutton-Smith, B., and Roberts, J. M. "Rubrics of Competitive Behavior." *Journal of Genetic Psychology* 105 (1964): 13–37.

———. "Studies of an Elementary Game of Strategy." *Genetic Psychology Monographs* 74 (1967): 3–42.

———. "The Cross-Cultural and Psychological Study of Games." In *The Cross-Cultural*

Analysis of Sport and Games, edited by G. Lüschen, pp. 100-108. Champaign, Ill.: Stipes Publishing Co., 1970.

————. *The Dialectics of Play*. Schorndoff, West Germany: Verlag Hoffman, 1978.

Sutton-Smith, B.; Roberts, J. M.; and Kozelka, R. M. "Game Involvement in Adults." *Journal of Social Psychology* 60 (1963): 15-30.

Symons, D. "Aggressive Play and Communication in Rhesus Monkeys (*Macaca Mulatta*)." *American Zoologist* 14 (1974): 317-22.

Travolga, M. C. "Behavior of the Bottlenose Dolphin (*Tursiops truncatus*): Social Interactions in a Captive Colony." In *Whales, Dolphins, and Porpoises*, edited by K. S. Norris, pp. 718-300. Berkeley: University of California Press, 1966.

Teilhard de Chardin, P. *The Phenomenon of Man*. New York: Harper and Row, 1959.

Thorpe, W. H. "Ritualization in Ontogeny: I. Animal Play." *Philosophical Transactions of the Royal Society of London*, series B., vol. 251: 311-19, 1966.

Tillich, P. *Systematic Theology*. Chicago: University of Chicago Press, 1951.

Tylor, E. B. "On the Game of Patolli in Ancient Mexico and Its Probably Asiatic Origin." *Journal of the Royal Anthropological Institute* 8 (1879): 116-29.

————. "On American Lot-Games as Evidence of Asiatic Intercourse before the Time of Columbus." *Internationales Archiv für Ethnographie* 9 (1896): 55-67.

Uexküll, J. V. *Umwelt und Innewelt der Tiere*. Berlin: Julius Springer, 1909.

Van Gennep, A. *The Rites of Passage*. Chicago: The University of Chicago Press, 1960.

Van Lawick-Goodall, J. "The Behavior of Free-Living Chimpanzees in the Gombe Stream Reserve." *Animal Behavior Monographs* 1 (1968): 161-311.

————. *In the Shadow of Man*. Boston: Houghton Mifflin, 1971.

Waddell, V. "Some Cultural Considerations on the Development of the Concept of Conservation." Unpublished paper presented to a Genetic Epistemology seminar, Australian National University, October 1968.

Weiss, J. M. "Psychological Factors in Stress and Disease." *Scientific American* (1972): 104-13.

Welker, W. I. "Effects of Age and Experience on Play and Exploration of Young Chimpanzees." *Journal of Comparative and Physiological Psychology* 49 (1956a): 223-26.

————. "Variability of Play and Exploratory Behavior in Chimpanzees." *Journal of Comparative and Physiological Psychology* 49 (1956b): 181-85.

————. "An Analysis of Exploratory and Play Behavior in Animals." In *Functions of Varied Experience*, edited by D. W. Fishe and S. R. Maddi, pp. 93-111. Homewood, Ill.: Dorsey Press, 1961: 93-111.

White, R. "Motivation Reconsidered: The Concept of Competence." *Psychological Review* 66 (1959): 297-333.

Wilson, E. O. *Sociobiology: The New Synthesis*. Cambridge, Mass.: Harvard University Press, 1975.

Witkin, H. A. "Social Influences in the Development of Cognitive Style." In *Handbook of Socialization Theory and Research*, edited by Goslin, pp. 687-706. Chicago: Rand McNally, 1971.

Witkin, H. A.; Price-Williams, D.; Bertini, M.; Christiansen, B.; Oltman, P. K.; Ramirez, M.; and van Meel, J. "Social Conformity and Psychological Differentiation." Research Bulletin, Educational Testing Service, Princeton, N.J., 1973.

Wolff, P. H. "Developmental and Motivational Concepts in Piaget's Sensorimotor Theory of Intelligence." *Journal of the American Academy of Child Psychiatry* 2 (1963): 225-43.

Zubek, J. P. *Sensory Deprivation: Fifteen Years of Research*. New York: Appleton-Century-Crofts, 1969.

3
Summary

On the surface these first two chapters seem to present very different approaches. Chapter 1 proceeds macro-sociologically while chapter 2 explores some of the same issues from a biogenetic-structural point of view. But in spite of these differences there are similarities worth discussing.

While Laughlin and McManus deal with a micro or biological approach their point of view is, in another sense, macro. It is macro because they deal with evolution and how within that evolutionary process the human species has managed to organize itself. Social organization is the crucial point of similarity between the two chapters.

Chapter 1 argues that the well-worn work-leisure dichotomy has little further usefulness in explicating the nature of human social organization. Different sets of social relationships may very well occur at work, and during what we call leisure time, but close examination will show these social relationships to be more similar than different. Laughlin and McManus indicate that there is a biological interaction between play, which we usually consider as leisure, and modeling the world. The organism, through play behavior, learns how to cope with the world in a nonthreatening environment. The very nature of play behavior allows us to produce models of the world that carry over into other forms of social relationships. From another angle this raises the question that occurs in chapter 1: Why do games model social relationships?

Laughlin and McManus argue that play, initially, makes the environment more complex than it had been for the organism. This is not true, however, if the environment is already perceived as superoptimal. In that case the organism will play in that environment as it is, without complexifying it any further. During both of these processes play optimizes information about the environment. In other words, play is another way of learning social relationships. As one wins and loses they learn domination and subordination. In other words, one learns to deal with the environment as an organization of power in a nonthreatening way.

Social play becomes social when the objects of its inception are other organisms. For a human being social play may help to teach us to treat another as a play object. Athletes in society are more than just play objects and are made that way partly through the process of masking discussed in chapter 1. In Western society one learns to relate to people in play as things to be moved out of the way, beaten or defeated. At the same time that one learns this behavior, it is also learned that the objects do not move at will; rather, one must respond to other objects (human beings) and from time to time be gotten out of the way, beaten, or defeated. It is through this biosocial process that one learns to engage in "proper" relationships outside of play behavior.

Chapter 1 argues that play and games, particularly those designated as sport, provide a mask, or, a superstructural cover for much that remains hidden in Western society. This could be due to the institutionalization of a fundamental biological process called galumphing. Laughlin and McManus argue that play and games put up false obstacles that can be overcome. Overcoming these false obstacles helps develop social coordination. The institutionalization of overcoming false obstacles is another way of talking about superstructural cover. Play and games are institutionalized in the West and perhaps in other societies as false obstacles that we see ourselves overcoming. These obstacles, however, are found outside of normal day to day social relationships. And they are overcome via a very real social fantasy life in games.

Finally, it is worth pointing out another basic similarity between the two chapters. Laughlin and McManus argue that sport is an ethnocentric or anthropocentric category that cannot be properly defined outside of a specific culture. Chapter 1 explicitly agrees. Sport may be used as a semantic category but it does not enable one to engage in any fruitful social analysis.

The two remaining parts of this book deal with these and other issues. Sport as a socializing agent that leads to social differentiation at different points in the life cycle is examined in part II. Part III provides an analysis of some specific sports and highlights differentiation factors within them. The following chapters in the book serve to illustrate many of the points that have already been raised, partially answer some of the questions that have previously been brought up, and go on to raise some additional questions.

PART II
Life Cycle

4
Introduction to Part II

It is a sociological truism that socialization processes produce similarities among some people, but these same processes that produce similarity often produce differentiation. This part of the book treats the interrelationships of socialization processes with sports focusing on how they produce social differentiation. Since the socialization process continues throughout the lifetimes of human beings, the authors of these chapters concentrated on three different phases of the life cycle; childhood, youth and young adulthood, and old age.

Although these three chapters were written independently, and from somewhat different perspectives in terms of their focus, there is a remarkable degree of similarity among them. They all treat minority groups but draw attention to them by discussing the "out-groups" for those minorities. Males are an out-group for females, whites are an out-group for blacks, and younger people are an out-group for older people. As females, blacks, and older people develop patterns of behavior and values throughout their life cycles, they compare themselves with those out-groups that are generally seen positively by most people. Although members of the minority groups may in fact reject some of the values of the majority, they have little choice but to accept most of the ways of life and values of that majority group. But even when what the majority group has to offer is rejected, minorities must somehow cope with majorities.

All three of these minority groups are generally seen as lacking some abilities. Girls are generally seen as weak and emotional, blacks lack intelligence and have been "culturally deprived," and the old are seen as weak and infirm. All of these prove to be myths when we compare large groups of minority group members with their respective out-groups. This means that based on physical or mental ability, there is no reason to socialize people to play various sports or to accept particular positions within sports. But sports are defined and controlled by white males. The white male definition of the situation leads to perceived differences among all groups in the society, which in turn leads to a socialization process that produces differentiation. For example, Johnson points out that perceived differences among young boys and girls are based on what adults think and not on the abilities of children. The same may be said about the perceived differences between blacks and whites. These are based on white definitions of the situation and have been shown time and again to have no factual basis. Harootyan's data, additionally, indicates that older people are not as disabled as is commonly believed and could (if they themselves did not accept the dominant definition of the situation) participate more fully in all sorts of physical activity, including team sports.

These perceived differences and definitions of the situation lead to differential criteria for participation in various sports. Boys are channeled toward team sports while girls are directed toward individual sports. White males as a group end up in diversified sports, both team and individual, short and long duration, violent and nonviolent; while blacks participate primarily in either team sports, sports of short duration (track and field), or a combination of violent and short duration sports (boxing). Young people participate in diversified sports while the old do not participate except for the few that do on the individual level. These social definitions of the situation allow us to downgrade the individual accomplishments of girls, blacks do not end up in the central positions that are involved in the outcome of games (see chapter 9), and the old don't even count.

According to James LeFlore this results from a system of learning. An information pool is available for each group and the group draws on that pool of information in making decisions about what sports or physical activity to engage in. That information is partially derived through an interaction of dominant or controlling groups with the dominated or controlled groups. Part of that knowledge is a definition of winning and how to go about it. Girls win when they become women by becoming attached to males. Blacks win when they become dependent on whites who control outcome. Old people simply lose.

Kay Johnsen, in her chapter, goes beyond standard analyses to look for unintended consequences of gender differences socialization. She examines the role of sports in maintaining these differences. Her analysis is unique, for she looks at the socialization process as it affects young boys, from the point of view of the negative out-group of those young boys and girls. Insofar as sports teaches positive and negative values she finds that a gender reference to women is a negative expression for boys.

Because the participation of girls in sports is passive, boys learn from this that men are the in-group and women the out-group in terms of what most people value. "Males become a positive reference group for both genders." This process begins very early as girls are socialized to participate in individual sports while boys get into team sports. This is based not on the physical attributes of the individual but rather on gender roles that in turn are based on perceived differences between adult males and females, not on the real differences between young boys and girls. As boys grow older they do develop some increased physical superiority (not all boys do, but most *believe* that they are superior). In this process boys learn relative to other boys, but girls are still around for comparison. If girls do achieve individually it is easy to downgrade them. Even the sensational golfer Nancy Lopez had to get married before she achieved real social respectability.

In looking at the socialization differences that result from sports, Johnsen was in part answering the question, Why do we find girls in some sports and not in others? LeFlore explicitly addresses this question. Why are blacks found in certain sports and not in others? Why are they found in certain positions in the sports they are in and not in others? He rejects the older genetic and socioeconomic-environmental explanations for this phenomenon and proposes an extension of systems theory in terms of information pooling. He sees information pooled in the subculture—seen as a subsystem—and adds the insight of Max Weber that people behave rationally in each other's presence. Black athletes engage in intentional behavior based on the information in their subcultural information pool.

The crucial considerations from the surrounding social system are the types of sports that are visible and played, the social class origins of these sports, as well as the social class of the participants. Subcultural considerations include class and racial differences, social mobility opportunities via sports, and factors from the general culture such as known discriminatory patterns. All of this information is used by subculture members to define their general situation. And this subtly channels athletes toward certain sports or positions. The information available from the surrounding culture is then incorporated into the athletic subculture. This includes "knowledge" about good or bad, opportunities in various sports, and whether those chances are enhanced by playing various positions. In particular, information may relate to a sport's environment and whether that environment is or is not hostile to blacks.

Robert Harootyan adds another dimension to the question of who participates. He begins with the observation that when people get older they suddenly stop participating in sports, which has aggravating effects on people that show up particularly under stress. He takes the position, therefore, that one must value sports and physical activity for older people. He further points out that theories like functionalism and functional conflict theory (as opposed to the different conflict theories of either Gumplowicz or Marx) lead to the position that old people ought to adjust to an unfavorable status in society. Harootyan explicitly rejects this.

Harootyan indicates that the patterns of socialization related to older people are based on negative values toward old age. He points out that available roles decrease but that role specificity decreases also. Roles of older people are broader. Contrary to the view of younger people, older people do not see their increased freedom and leisure time as positive. They value their role changes, however, and their ability to control their lives more fully than they have before. The general public, on the other hand, has generally negative perceptions of older people that have the effect of keeping them out of physical activity. Older people are seen as having a lot of leisure time but not much ability, personal resources, or individual worth. As a result, younger people do not include older people in physical activity such as sports. Harootyan points to serious disjunction between beliefs and reality. He discovers that the experience of older people does not follow the stereotype. They are much more active than one would expect.

Although older people are more active than one would expect, they are not as active as they could be. This phenomenon occurs because they internalize stereotypes about themselves. They accept their negative status and in certain respects this becomes a self-fulfilling prophecy. The similarity between the situation of older people, women, and blacks is striking.

Harootyan also reports some original research on older people. The bulk of their physical activity is found in walking, gardening, and conditioning exercises. When these three physical activities are eliminated the decrease in activity among older people is a drastic 84.3 percent. It seems that people give up sports actively simply because of a general definition of the situation—a response to the generalized other. Yet, at the same time, there is evidence to indicate that to stay active is to stay healthy. The most active older people are those who have been to college, and those who have had blue-collar jobs. More research on this issue is required. Harootyan concludes by pointing out that the Senior Olympics are a way to encourage old people to participate in sports.

There are several points of interest in these chapters that are useful for theory development along the lines suggested in chapters 1 and 2. These points will be discussed further in the final chapter.

5
The Development and Maintenance of Gender Differentiation through Sports[1]

KATHRYN P. JOHNSEN

The identification of social-structural variables that aid in the maintenance of gender-differentiation patterns within our society has attracted considerable attention in recent years. This author's interests in this topic have been concentrated on the processes by which values associated with masculinity and femininity are transmitted and are embedded in the behavior patterns and self-concepts of boys and girls as they grow to maturity (Christensen and Johnsen, 1971: chapters 5, 6, 7).

Much attention has been focused on those social systems, especially the family and educational systems, which have the intended (or at least the expected) consequences of maintaining the pattern of gender differentiation (Lynn, 1969; Grams and Waetjen, 1975). The resulting differences and similarities between males and females in childhood, adolescence, and adulthood have been exhaustively studied, discussed, and evaluated (for recent summaries see Maccoby and Jacklin, 1974; Yorburg, 1974). Numerous theories have been introduced concerning the source of these differences including the effects of hormone differences during fetal development and adolescence (Money and Ehrhardt, 1969), anatomical differences (Erikson, 1964), socialization influences (Maccoby, 1966; Lynn, 1969), and structural constraints in the society (Halter, 1970). Other theories have been presented that attempt to account for the supposed universality of certain of these differences (Kohlberg, 1966; Goldberg, 1973).

Less attention has been devoted to those patterned activities that perhaps unintentionally contribute to the development of gender-associated attributes, either by differentially structuring the activities in which boys and girls participate or by promoting different attitudes toward similar or related activities (for a discussion of manifest and latent functions see Merton, 1957: 61–66). Recent pressures for increasing the support given organized team sports for females and for including girls on little league baseball teams draw attention to the world of sport as one set of such patterned activities that has largely been overlooked in the socialization literature. The contribution of the "game" that involves rules, coordinated activities, and group goals to the development of self and the potential for social organization is, of course, basic to the developmental theories of Piaget (1932) and Mead (1934). But the application of these ideas to differences in the socialization patterns of boys and girls has received practically no attention (recent exceptions are Grams and Waetjen, 1975: 103–6, and Lever, 1976).

The sports literature contains discussions of sports as reflections of the dominant values in a society (Boyle, 1963; Edwards, 1973; Snyder and Spreitzer, 1974). Helanko (1963) specifically uses the Piaget framework to examine the changing nature of play, games, and sports as these relate to the male's socialization process. However, the contribution of organized sports to the maintenance and transmission of gender differentiation patterns appears to have been overlooked.

A personal experience ended my rather academic reflections on the relationship between sports and value transmissions and turned me toward an active analysis of the process. My young son was a new member of his high school football team and I was vitally aware of some of the values he was expressing. I heard him speak about how he was learning to get his fingers through the face mask of another player, keeping his arm in the way so that the referee wouldn't see him. He was learning where and how to hit so hard that it hurt the other player rather than just take him out of the play. When I asked if this was really in the spirit of the game, he said: "Sure, our coach says hit them as hard as you can so you scare them so bad they'll stay out of your way. Do anything you can—just so the ref doesn't see you do it."

I was also aware of some other developments: his growing appreciation of the contributions of some of his teammates, even though their plays were not noticed by the crowd; his growing pleasure in participation, and his lessened need to make "the big play," although that too was enjoyed when it happened. I noted an occasional complimentary remark about an opposing player or team when there had been a particularly good play. After a loss, the comment, "They really outclassed us," might be followed by, "Of course they have a bigger school," but the appreciation of their competence was still evident.

What seemed to be developing in him was an intrinsic motivation toward competence that was overriding the extrinsic motivation of crowd or social approval. There was also an ability to appreciate competence in others regardless of who they were or what team they played on, and to appreciate the range of the contribution of the other boys, whether spectacular, the same as his, or not. I was impressed by the development of these values through his participation in school sports.

But I heard something else that alerted me to the possible importance of school athletic programs for the maintenance of value systems that ostensibly have little to do with the intended functions of team sports. After a big win one night, we were congratulating our son and his response was: "Oh, that was nothing. The other team was a bunch of women." More and more I heard comments such as: "Did you see him mess up tonight? What a woman!" "We'd have a better team if we didn't have so many women in our school"—meaning not females, but males who failed to measure up to the expectations for masculine behavior.

His growing appreciation of the so-called masculine characteristics of competence, aggressiveness, toughness, independence, and objectivity, as well as the tendency to relegate those males who did not exhibit these traits to membership in the opposite gender category, appeared to be a classic example of in-group/out-group behavior utilized in analyzing relationships between other categories of people (Sumner, 1906; Merton, 1957). The control mechanisms used by team members to idealize and maintain "masculine" behavior seemed very similar to those in the larger society in which the negative stereotype of the female provides the script for behavior to be avoided by the "real" male (Johnsen, 1969).

The tendency of females to accept the negative stereotype that is applied to them not only is in keeping with in-group/out-group behavior but further suggests the lack of a comparable in-group formation among females. Defined by both themselves and males as an out-group, women along with men assign in-group virtues to males and out-group vices to themselves (Merton, 1957: 425). Males become a positive reference group for both genders. The acceptance and appreciation of a female by the male in-group, then, becomes dependent upon the degree to which she exhibits the characteristics attributed to the out-group and "stays in her place" relative to in-group members.

The fit between the values that were being expressed by our son and those supported in the larger society concerning differences between the genders seemed to support the notion of the maintenance of gender patterns through sports. But when does it start? By the high school years many of the male-female differences are already apparent—especially those concerning athletic competitions, the in-group orientation of males, and the more individual friend orientation of females (Lynn, 1969). Obviously, training for masculine-feminine behavior begins well before children enter school or are old enough for team sports. Infants are treated differently, depending upon whether they are boys or girls, are given different toys and portrayed differently in children's books (Money and Ehrhardt, 1969; Weitzman et al., 1972). But they play together and do not seem to develop much antagonism for each other just because they represent different genders until they reach the age of approximately six or seven.

Several things come together at this stage of development. First, by this age, if not before, children know for certain that they will remain male or female (Money and Ehrhardt, 1969; Kohlberg, 1966). All the other categories by which they are labeled will change, or can be changed, with the exception of race, ethnic origin, and gender.

Second, little boys especially have become aware of some of the demands of developing masculinity. They have very likely developed some anxieties about how to be "good" children and "real" boys at the same time. Much of the training for boy behavior involves negative appraisal of the same behavior that is either accepted or rewarded when it comes from little girls. Boys' training for masculinity is much more restrictive in these early years than is girls' training for feminity, and much of it is in terms of not being like little girls. The label "sissy" carries a much more negative connotation than "tomboy" does for girls (Lynn, 1966).

Third, it is at about this age that children are entering the period when, if left alone, they begin to form loosely knit play groups based upon the proximity of others. Through experience in these groups, they begin to learn the rudiments of social organization. They begin to learn to develop group norms and be guided by them, to find their relative status among their peers in terms of valued abilities and contributions to the play group. These groups are likely to be neighborhood play groups, and the play games are likely to be those in which they make and change their own rules (Helanko, 1963).

Fourth, their motor skills have progressed far enough so that now children can begin to play known games in the culture; cognitive skills have developed to the point where they can understand externally applied rules of the game. These competencies create the readiness for participation in more closely knit groups, gangs, or teams within which they begin to learn to substitute group goals for egocentric ones, to develop loyalty to the group, to cooperate with others, and to compete with other groups (Piaget, 1932). These are important parts of the socialization process, but tend to involve boys more than girls This gender difference in participation in team or group games tends to be supported cross-culturally as well as in our own society (Robinson, 1970). This is partially the result of the prevalence of adult males in professional team sports and the tendency of organized sports to reflect the "masculine" values of risk taking, thrill, speed, combat, and potential danger (Kenyon, 1970). As children imitate same-sex role-models as they appear in high school sports, community sports programs, or on television, boys are likely to see their heroes participating on teams, while girls most often find their gender represented as cheerleaders, ice skaters, gymnasts, swimmers, or tennis players—all individual athletic pursuits, even though their individual points may contribute to a group score. Thus, little boys seek out other boys to form a team requiring complex rules, organization of varying abilities and cooperation, while little girls practice baton twirling, cheerleading, cartwheels, and tumbling—activities that they may do in unison but without the tight social organization and cooperation required by team sports (see Lever, 1976, 1978). This difference in activity is still apparent even though support for girls' team sports is increasing.

Fifth, it is quite likely that by the age of seven or eight the main distinguishing factor for children between adult males and females is still seen in terms of dress, physical size, physical strength, and physical competencies. Young children have not yet learned that physical differences between adult males and females carry with them connotations of power, intelligence, courage, competence, and the myriad things differentiating the adult stereotypes of masculinity and femininity. As these things come together at about age seven or eight—the recognition of the constancy of gender, the anxiety of little boys about appropriate boy behavior, readiness for group formation, readiness for team sports, and the use of physical size and strength as the main distinguishing factors between adult males and females—the expanding social experiences are structured as we segregate the genders in gym classes for certain kinds of activities, differentiate between boy and girl push ups, differentially encourage athletic competencies, organize intramural teams, little league baseball, football, and so on.

Reflecting our norms of fairness, we control the competition: seven- and eight-year-olds play seven- and eight-year-olds; seventh-graders play seventh-graders; reserve teams play reserve teams—and boys play boys! In other words, the only criterion for team placement that is not based realistically on age, size, and experience to equalize the competition is the characteristic of gender. Girls are ruled out categorically—not because of age, size or physical capabilities, but because they are not boys. Of course, the same norms of fairness provide the rationale for keeping the competition strictly sex-segregated. Little girls are seen to be weaker, more likely to be hurt, and so must be protected from the "unfair" competition with the supposedly stronger, more rugged boys in these contests of physical strength, courage, and risk taking. In other words, the sports, defined in masculine terms, take on an apparent intrinsic characteristic of their own that appears to make girls, stereotypically appraised, unable to compete except with other girls.

Little girls play, run, jump, skip rope, and develop athletic skills—in fact, during the early years they tend to excel in certain motor abilities and physical activities requiring coordination. But when individual motor activities begin to be used in team sports, girls begin to be viewed as too weak, vulnerable, and too easily hurt to play on the teams reserved for boys. Little girls are kept off the boys' teams and away from competition with them because of real and imagined differences between *adult* males and females, not because of physical differences between *prepuberty* boys and girls. The within-gender variation among prepuberty children in size, strength, and agility is undoubtedly greater than the between-gender variation. But as they grow the ensuing encouragement of physical competence among boys and the discouragement or lack of support for the development of the same competencies in little girls widens the gap between the genders.

For the boys, the beginning of team sports offers them a way of being "real" boys at the same time that they win approval. The little boy who hits his first two-bagger hears the cheers even if he is wetting his pants as he waits excitedly on second, or is crying a little as he skins his knee sliding into a tag at third. Participation in the game probably does offer some release for his anxiety about developing boy characteristics at the same time it builds more anxiety as he is pressed to excel and to win. The structure of the team enhances the development of those things that participation in any group helps teach. Competition with other groups helps develop strong loyalties, elevation of group goals over personal ones, appreciation of the varying contributions of others, and the hard recognition that one does not always win.

Boys learn among their peers that some people are better in some things and others excel in other things; that some lose more than others in many things. They slowly learn their own relative status among their peers and learn to protect their self-esteem whether they win or lose. They know that if the other team is bigger or faster they probably can't win. The seven-year-olds do not really expect to beat the twelve-year-olds—although they can dream about it. Boys learn many important things as they participate in sports; but they learn them *relative to other boys*.

The little girls, though, do not go away. They stay right there, available for comparison purposes. As physical competence becomes more and more important in distinguishing the "real" boy from the "sissy," and as girls fail to develop physical competencies, the "real" boy becomes more and more unlike girls.[2]

The in-group feeling among boys, developed through team formation and competition, heightens the importance of these abilities, as does the cheering of the crowd. At the same time, the anxieties created by the need to find status within the male group makes girls a natural target for the out-group phenomenon. Boys have already learned to use girls as a negative referent. Now, the increasing importance of physical competence for in-group status and the widening of the gap between the sexes in this same competence add some reality to the element of superiority that the males begin assigning to their own sex. Once established in this visible area of behavior, superiority more easily can be generalized to other areas of behavior and competencies, since these are attached to the physical superiority of males in the cultural stereotypes.

Boys are, of course, forced to observe areas in which girls tend to excel them, such as spelling, reading, and neatness in writing. These are individual pursuits, and few stand up to cheer such accomplishments. Lacking the visible, immediate group acclaim that excellence in sports brings, the girls' less visible, individual accomplishments become easier to downgrade.

Gradually, even the male who lacks physical competencies can establish some feelings of self-worth merely because he is male—a member of the in-group. Thus, we find evidence that as boys grow up, they develop an ever-stronger identification with their own sex, develop a higher opinion of themselves and males in general, while they increasingly develop a lower opinion of females. Girls tend to do just the opposite as far as identification with their own sex is concerned. As they grow, their identification with their own sex weakens; they seem to accept the in-group definition of male-female differences. They develop poorer opinions of themselves and other females and more positive opinions of males (Christensen and Johnsen, 1971: 125–27).

One may wonder why females do not develop the same in-group feelings among themselves and relegate males to a negatively defined out-group; why they accept the male's definition of them as being inferior. Girls have the same tendencies toward group formation, but their groups are structured differently, and their games do not seem to demand the role behavior of organized sports. Even when girls' teams are organized, they receive neither the same support for developing competencies nor the same acclaim for winning that would push them toward developing in-group loyalties. For girls lack of strong support for competitive teams is likely to prolong a play attitude toward sports, if they continue to participate, rather than the competitive attitude associated with males. This is not intended to suggest that a competitive attitude is better or worse than a play attitude; only that the masculine-feminine values in society support competitiveness for males and not for females and that, in the early years, this is reinforced by the differential treatment of the genders in the organization of team sports.

Group loyalties formed by girls are likely to develop toward their class in school or the school itself, which, of course, includes both males and females. As the school is primarily represented in competition by all-male teams, girls also learn to value these now masculine attributes that bring acclaim to the whole class or school. They root for the home team the same as boys do. They become cheerleaders and support the team. They form booster-blocks and cheer the team to victory. Even though there is increasing competition among all-girl teams, without the opportunity for developing and testing their own competencies in competition with boys, they are led to accept the conclusion that the boys have already come to—males are superior. This is reinforced by the different rules by which many girls' sports are played and the relative lack of attention given their games by fans and the local press. As they continue to grow, girls discover that the quickest and safest route to receiving some of the rewards of male in-group competition is to be selected out of the female group as the special girl of a winning male, who will allot her a portion of his status. She wins, not so much by developed competencies, but by having by nature or by chance those characteristics that a particular male is attracted to. The competencies that may aid in the continuation of this favored position, once she is selected for it, are likely to be personality attributes that may or may not fit the desires of the male, or that may fit for awhile until he seeks some other kind of support for his changing concept of self. In other words, when the judge of her interpersonal competencies becomes one particular male, who may not be sure of what he likes himself during these adolescent years, or a series of them with differing criteria for judging, she has no reliable standard for judging her own relative status among other girls—her status must continually be reestablished, forming no firm basis for stable social organization among females.

From this analysis of the contribution of gender segregation in team sports to the development and perpetuation of values concerning masculinity and femininity some most interesting consequences arise. In review, the key elements are (1) the importance of physical competence in the early years of a child's life for accentuating the difference between the sexes; (2) the encouragement among boys of an in-group/out-group formation oriented around gender, and its lack among girls; (3) the acceptance of negative out-group status by females; (4) the development of competitive attitudes in males and the continuance of play attitudes in females toward sports extending to many other activities for both sexes; and (5) the inevitable one-to-one pairings of males and females in dating and marriage.

A man learns to compete, to win, to lose, to find his status in many competencies among other males. He learns not to expect to win over every other male in everything regardless of age, size, or skills. It does not hurt his feeling of self-worth if, at age fifty-five, he loses to an equally skilled twenty-nine-year-old male tennis player. Without loss of face a man can say that another man is more intelligent, thinks more logically, or is a better golfer. He has ample opportunity while growing up to find his relative status among males—to cope with success and defeat. But males have little or no practice in finding status among females or coping with defeat by a female in a one-to-one relationship.

One would expect that the more strongly a man is identified with the male in-group, the more he bears the burden of upholding the prestige of his in-group when he does compete with a female in the one-to-one pairing. He must win over her or if defeated, feel disgrace regardless of the differences between them in age, size, skill, or experience. This need to win, started perhaps by the importance of physical competence, does not stop with physical superiority but extends to many other areas. In marriage, if both spouses work, he suffers if his wife makes more money, has a more prestigious position, or wins more recognition. In a work situation, he is likely to be uncomfortable working for a female boss, or even interacting with a woman in an equal, cooperative situation that lacks the sexual element.

In all likelihood, woman's probable play attitude toward games makes it less important for her to win. Besides, she has learned that to lose to a particular male is to win in the long run. If a woman sets out to defeat a man and does, she runs the risk of winning not only *his* disapproval but the disapproval of other females as well. One rule of the game that she learns well is that the bigger, the stronger, and the more intelligent she makes men feel, the more she actually stands to win. She learns to gain power by appearing not to have it.

Influenced by these attitudes, individual men and women pair off in ways that accentuate and make more visible the average male-female differences. Some females are larger and more muscular than some males although, on the average, men are larger and more muscular than women. Some females are more intelligent, however measured, than some males. Some females are more physically competent than some males, although on the average males are more physically competent than females. But in individual pairings one is more likely to find that, where there are differences between them, the male is generally taller, stronger, more muscular, more intelligent, and so on than the one particular female he is paired with. The selection process downplays the individual variation within each sex and accentuates the average differences in the individual pairs, especially in the more visible physical characteristics. This sets up a view of gender differences that reinforces the stereotype of little girls' being too fragile to play team sports with the boys.

Conclusion

This chapter has been an analysis of the way in which the segregation of the genders at an early age in team sports accentuates and helps to transmit the whole value system concerning masculinity and femininity.

Obviously team sports are not the only nor even the most important vehicle for transmitting these values. But to the extent that they do play a part, changes in the present organization of team sports should be carefully evaluated so that they reinforce the values concerning masculinity and femininity that we want to develop in boys and girls. There are a number of alternatives.

If the gender differences in competitiveness, aggressiveness, and the other "masculine" characteristics continue to be valued in *males only*, then no change is needed. Team sports for females should not be encouraged. Either competition in one-to-one relationships should be controlled even more closely or the development of physical competencies in individual females reduced. This would help assure that the outcome in one-to-one competition would be more predictable. If, on the other hand, it is desired to encourage these same "masculine" traits in *females only*, while developing supportive characteristics in males, the present pattern should be reversed. All-female teams would then represent the class or school and be cheered on by male cheerleaders and booster-blocks.

A third alternative may be more in keeping with recent changes that are associated with the entrance of more females into occupational competition with males. This would be a pattern supporting the encouragement of competitiveness, aggressiveness, competence, and in-group formation in both genders, with potential rivalry between them. In this case, the early segregation of the genders in team sports should continue. They should be given equal support and training, and should compete against each other.

However, if our value system supports the downplay of physical aggression, toughness, and thrill-seeking, while encouraging individual competencies in both genders, then all competitive team sports should be removed from the school years and a play attitude toward sports encouraged for boys and girls alike. Perhaps the nature of games should be reconsidered, patterned less after the professional sports of football, ice hockey, and others that emphasize physical toughness, and concentrate on individual athletic competencies such as track and gymnastics in which prepuberty boys and girls can compete equally.

There is also a fifth alternative that would encourage the appreciation of the varying contributions of individuals regardless of gender and their cooperation with each other in reaching shared goals. These are the values important in family life and in the work situation where inter-gender interaction as cooperative "team" members is increasing. To encourage these values putting prepuberty boys and girls on the *same* teams should be considered where group loyalties, cooperation, and rivalries could develop in terms of interests, skills, and shared goals rather than on the arbitrary basis of gender. Of course, new games may have to be devised, organized less around developing the traditional "masculine" characteristics of strength, force, and physical toughness, and more in terms of developing equally valued, complementary activities and physical fitness for both genders as they compete, win, and lose together. It may be difficult to conceive of such games if sports do reflect the dominant value system of society and that value system continues to include the traditional values associated with masculinity and femininity.

The third alternative discussed above appears to be the one toward which North American society is moving. If so, then it becomes imperative that the effects of participation in competitive team sports on girls be studied in order to discover the contribution of these activities to personality development. From the theoretical perspective of this analysis, the timing of the child's introduction into the "team" experience appears crucial, although empirical support for this claim is lacking.

The fourth alternative, which downplays the development of physical aggression, toughness, and thrill-seeking for both genders, appears to have some support in the larger society. The recent attacks on the television networks for the amount of violence in their programming indicates concern about this source for the increased tolerance for violent and aggressive behavior in adults and children alike. Perhaps the approved and applauded "violence" in professional sports,—introduced to children in early competitive team sports and based on the adult model—has been overlooked as a source of both tolerance for and participation in violent behavior.

If research supports the conclusion of this analysis that early sports participation is an important contributor to the transmission and maintenance of important value systems, then careful attention must be directed to the values that *are* reflected in the "games children play" with the active encouragement of their parents and teachers.

Notes

1. This is a revised and expanded version of a paper published in the Proceedings of the National Conference on the Development of Human Values through Sports, held at Springfield College, Springfield, Massachusetts, October 1973. Published by AAHPER, 1974.
2. This tendency in our society has been associated with the need among boys to reject feminine behavior as they seek a masculine self-image; masculinity among small boys being described as "ungirllike" behavior rather than as positive "boylike" behavior (Lynn, 1969). This encourages a rejection of girls as well as the behavior associated with them.

Works Cited

Boyle, Robert H. *Sport: Mirror of American Life*. Boston: Little, Brown, 1963.
Christensen, Harold T., and Johnsen, Kathryn P. *Marriage and the Family*. New York: Ronald Press, 1971 (chapter 7).
Edwards, Harry. *Sociology of Sport*. Homewood, Ill.: Dorsey Press, 1973.
Erikson, Erik. "Inner and Outer Space: Reflections on Womanhood." *Daedalus*, Spring 1964, pp. 582–606.
Goldberg, Steven. *The Inevitability of Patriarchy*. New York: William Morrow and Company, 1973.
Grams, Jean D., and Waetzen, Walter B. *Sex, Does It Make a Difference?* Scituate, Mass.: Duxbury Press, 1975.
Helanko, R. "Sports and Socialization," in *Personality and Social Systems,* edited by Neil J. Smeltzer and William T. Smeltzer, pp. 238–54. New York: John Wiley and Sons, 1963.
Johnsen, Kathryn P. "Progress Report on a Study of the Factors Associated with the Male's Tendency to Negatively Stereotype the Female." *Sociological Focus,* Spring 1969, pp. 21–35.
Kenyon, Gerald S. "Attitude toward Sport and Physical Activity among Adolescents from Four English Speaking Countries." In *The Cross-Cultural Analysis of Sports and Games*, edited by Günther Lüschen, Champaign, Ill.: Stipes Publishing Company, 1970.
Kohlberg, Lawrence. "A Cognitive Developmental Analysis of Children's Sex Role Concepts and Attitudes." In Maccoby, Eleanor E. *The Development of Sex Differences*. Stanford, Calif.: Stanford University Press, 1966.
Lever, Janet. "Sex Differences in the Games Children Play." *Social Problems*, April 1976, pp. 478–87.

———. "Sex Differences in the Complexity of Children's Play and Games." *American Sociological Review*, August 1978, pp. 471–83.

Lynn, David. *Parental and Sex Role Identification*. Berkeley, Calif.: McCutchan Publishing Corporation, 1969.

Maccoby, Eleanor, E., ed. *The Development of Sex Differences*. Stanford, Calif.: Stanford University Press, 1966.

Maccoby, Eleanor, E., and Jacklin, Carol N. *The Psychology of Sex Differences*. Stanford, Calif.: Stanford University Press, 1974.

Mead, George Herbert. *Mind, Self and Society*. Chicago: Chicago University Press, 1934.

Merton, Robert K. *Social Theory and Social Structure*. Glencoe, Ill.: The Free Press, 1957.

Money, John, and Ehrhardt, Anke. *Man-Woman*; *Boy-Girl*. Baltimore: Johns Hopkins Press, 1969.

Piaget, Jean. *The Moral Development of the Child*. London: Routledge and Keagan Paul, 1932.

Robinson, John P. "Daily Participation in Sports Across Twelve Countries," in *The Cross-Cultural Analysis of Sports and Games*, edited by Günther Lüschen. Champaign, Ill.: Stipes Publishing Company, 1970.

Snyder, Eldon E., and Speitzer, Elmer. "Sociology of Sport: An Overview." *The Sociological Quarterly* 15 (1974): 467–87.

Sumner, William Graham. *Folkways*. Boston: Ginn and Company, 1906.

Weitzman, Leonore J.; Eifler, Deborah; Hokada, Elizabeth; and Ross, Catherine. "Sex-Role Socialization in Picture Books for Pre-School Children." *American Journal of Sociology* 77 (May 1972): pp. 1125–50.

Yorburg, Betty. *Sexual Identity*. New York: John Wiley and Sons, 1974.

6

Athleticism among American Blacks

JAMES LEFLORE

Introduction

Boxing, track and field, football, baseball, and basketball have a disportionately high number of black participants who are outstanding achievers. How have black American athletes become stars in a number of amateur and professional sports? This question has peaked the interest of coaches, sportsmen, and social scientists in recent years.

In his encyclopedic sport data volume, George Gipe (1978) notes that by the late 1970s, approximately fifty percent of the players in professional football were black, while the figure approaches seventy percent for professional basketball. In the 1976 Montreal Olympic Games, black athletes won twenty-two of the thirty-one American medals (Gipe, 1978: 330). This trend has continued almost yearly over the past generation, and black achievements in these sports have been outstanding. In baseball, between 1949 and 1968, the National League awarded fifteen of twenty Most Valuable Player Awards to black players (*All-Sports World Record Book*, 1977: 57). The individual scoring leaders in professional basketball between 1959 and 1978 were blacks (*All-Sports World Record Book*, 1977: 62). The names Wilt Chamberlain, Dave Bing, Elvin Hayes, and Bill Russell in the 1950s and 1960s, and Kareem Abdul-Jabbar and Julius Erving in this decade, are all synonymous with stardom. Except for 1962 the National Football League's leading rushers between 1957 and 1968 were black. With the exception of 1961, the leading ground gainers in the American

Football League during the years 1960 to 1968 were all black. Ever since the merger of twenty-eight teams in the National Football League in 1970, the leading ground gainers in both conferences have been blacks (*NFL's Official Encyclopedia History of Professional Football*, 1978: 261). After Ernie Davis won the coveted Heisman Trophy in 1961, a number of other black players have also received the honor.[1] In boxing, the domination of black fighters continued as the U.S. Olympic team scored impressively in Montreal while Muhammad Ali won the heavyweight championship for a record third time. These athletic successes are even more interesting when they are juxtaposed against the list of organized and professional events where black Americans have made almost no impact, or where their contributions have been negligible: rowing, cycling, skiing, bowling, skating, hockey, swimming, polo, chess, tennis, golf, lacrosse, fencing, and gymnastics. There appear to be two common explanations for the success and participation of black athletes in some sporting events but not in others. The longest standing explanation is biological and the more recent, and somewhat more enlightened, is sociological.

The Genetic Paradigm

The biological explanation suggests that the musculature and physiognomy of blacks makes them more naturally adept and proficient at games such as boxing, baseball, basketball, track, and football than at other sports. The argument maintains that the skeletal and muscular development of blacks is particularly advantageous in those sports where bursts of speed and limb qualities are required. In those events where compactness and toughness of form are required (contact sports) blacks are, again, allegedly gifted.

Genetics, according to this argument, would appear to play a large part in the athleticism of populations, particularly in the area of special abilities and subsequent group participation. Implicit in this approach is the assumption that sports in which this ethnic (racial) group appear not to excel or participate, demand other genetic foundations and other physical attributes. While one would not argue about the association between particular sports and unique individual physical characteristics, there is no body of scientific data to support a claim of correlation between racial characteristics and specific athletic events.

Often such claims are made more in the spirit of ethnic pride than from scientific data. Examples that have been heard frequently are the somewhat flippant response of O. J. Simpson, "We are built a little differently, built for speed—skinny calves, long legs, high asses are all characteristics of Blacks" (Michener, 1976: 164), and the comment of Joe Morgan, "I think Blacks, for psychological reasons, have better speed, quickness, and agility. Baseball, football, and basketball put a premium on those skills" (Michener, 1976: 164). And Calvin Hill, "It boils down to the survival of the fittest. Think of what the African slaves were forced to endure in this country merely to survive. Well, Black athletes are their descendants. They are the offspring of those who are physically tough enough to survive" (Michener, 1976: 164). Even the considered and usually penetrating thoughts of E. B. Hendersen lean in this direction:

> Much is inherited. Negroes were bought and sold for a physique that portended hard and long work experience. A premium price was paid for strength and health. For 350 years they have been the toilers and have survived largely because of these resources. Isn't it possible that Negro athletes should seem superior when they bring these abilities onto the athletic fields and compete with youth, whose more civilized, effete ways of living have lessened their physical abilities (Henderson, 1970: 55)

These views stressing physical superiority of blacks seem to overlook the shorter life span of black Americans and the unsettling higher percentages of many diseases afflicting black youngsters. This view carries sociopolitical implications when people are willing to grant physical "superiority" to blacks while denying mental or intellectual equivalence and potential.

Physical anthropologists and geneticists continually point to the great range of genetic variation among members of so-called racial groups; a variation so great as to make unintelligible the concept of races or racial groupings.[2] In fact, the variation within so-called racial groups is greater than that between them. The speciousness of the biological and racial explanation for athletic abilities becomes more apparent when one realizes that a majority of blacks are not even athletes, do not run with agility and blazing speed, and do not handle spheroids with particular dexterity. The biological explanation also fails to explain the large number of successful athletes in these so-called black advantaged events whose genetic background emanates from other than African breeding populations. What, for example, are the biological-determinist explanations for all of the superb "white" athletes in baseball, football, basketball, and boxing? In the modern Summer Olympics the following data must be explained by biological-determinants: (1) in boxing, more gold medals have been won by athletes from countries outside of Africa (excluding South Africa), the U.S.A., and the Caribbean—98-38 (*All-Sports World Record Book*: 200-201); and (2) even so-called black-advantage sports (i.e., the short distances), gold and silver medals have been taken recently by non-blacks, e.g., V. Borzov, gold in '72 in 100 meters; G. Drut, gold in '76 in 110-meter hurdles; P. Norman, silver in '72 in 200 meters; Y. Tarmak, gold in '72, and J. Wszola, gold in '76 in high jump (*All-Sports Record Book*: 215-18).

In an article in *Sports Illustrated* in early 1971, senior editor Martin Kane attempts to substantiate the biological-determinist posture with bits of research drawn from a number of disciplines. He notes that the data indicate "that the black American, *on the average*, *tends* to have a shorter trunk than his white counterpart. His bones are denser, and therefore heavier, than those of whites. He has more muscle in the upper arms and legs, less in the calves. There is *reason to believe* that his fat distribution is patterned differently in the trunk" (Kane, 1971: 75; italics added). But he attempts to remove Kipchoge Keino, Naftali Temu, and other East African athletes from the category of black athletes because of their "white features" and hence, possible ancient white genetic admixture. Based on this logic, he would then have to remove the overwhelming majority of black American athletes, who certainly share a direct and traceable admixture with Europeans.

Harry Edwards has aptly critiqued these views, viewing Kane's arguments as invalid since "it is clear that black athletes of a variety of shapes and sizes have dominated many sports events over white athletes who themselves embodied a variety of shapes and sizes. There are far too many variables that determine athletic excellence to rely upon observable differences in individuals for explanation" (Edwards, 1973: 50). Moreover, "the real determinant of Black superiority in sports lies in this society which implicitly demands that Black youth strive first and foremost to be the world's greatest athletes. . . . Black culture as does the White culture teaches its members to strive for the most desirable among *achievable* goals. Athletics, then, appear to be the most achievable goals" (Edwards, 1973: 53).

The Socioenvironmental, Economic Paradigm

The more recent sociological explanation examines the impact of economic and environmental deprivation upon urban black youngsters. The socioenvironmental side of the argument indicates that the alleged reason that large numbers of blacks play and, subsequently, are successful in boxing, football, and the like is the availability of certain athletic facilities as they are growing up. The explanation compares urban and rural children. Rural youngsters are seen at a disadvantage with regard to some activities and "choose" sports whose prerequisites for excellence are readily at hand; e.g., large open areas, hills, ice ponds (Levine, 1974: 353–60). These conditions help produce long-distance runners, skiers, ice skaters, and lacrosse players.

The economic side of the environmental-economic paradigm discusses the paucity of means available to acquire the equipment and the facilities of sports other than "street" and urban sports or the costs of learning certain skills (Medoff, 1976: 189–90). The majority of black and impoverished children, therefore, will participate in sporting events in which the initial and continued outlay of funds are comparable with their socioeconomic status. Tennis courts, swimming pools, and downhill ski slopes, hockey arenas, fencing strips, golf courses, and bowling alleys and their related equipment appear to be out of the ecological and economic reach of the mass of black children.

We cannot argue with parts of this paradigm. Individuals living in many urban areas would incur added expenses and a considerable loss of practice time if the only facilities were miles away. They might not be able to afford the expense if the only skating rinks, tennis courts, swimming pools, or other practice facilities were accompanied by entry fees or yearly membership costs. One could suggest any number of problems and economic burdens to individuals and groups participating in most organized athletic activities, but the explanation seems an oversimplification of a much more complicated social situation. Black youngsters increasingly spend money to take karate lessons and buy record albums, clothing, and various necessary and unnecessary devices and equipment. Moreover, the paradigm assumes a homogeneity of impoverished social and economic conditions across an entire ethnic population that obviously is not the case. The heterogeneity in urban and black communities is well documented in the sociological literature (Hetner, 1979; Staples, 1976; Frazier, 1957).

Neither does this theory explain the large number of facilities in most metropolitan areas, such as bowling alleys, ice skating rinks, swimming pools, golf courses, and tennis courts, which do not seem to entice black children's use to the degree that basketball courts, baseball diamonds, football fields, and tracks do.

The Subcultural and Informational Pooling Paradigm

Although the two paradigms discussed above are not altogether false, and genetic, environmental, and economic factors must, in varying degrees, impinge upon a discussion of blacks and athleticism, a more comprehensive answer lies in other directions. The approach or paradigm that seems to provide a broader explanation of the way various decisions are made and the predilections of some athletes is what this author terms *subcultural* and *informational pooling*.

Social systems may be viewed as pools or units of discrete information. These pools of information as units are, simultaneously, the possessors of numerous subunits. The investigation of social systems at one level of abstraction might be *between* social systems (e.g., the comparison of social systems, as in cross-cultural analysis) while at another level of investigation the analysis might remain *within* the particular social system (e.g., the comparison of various components within the social system, such as the various subcultural units constituting the subsystem). The level of analysis undertaken is determined by the scope and nature of the problem. The data being sought are information about the various components of the system and their relationship to it. But at the same time, the system is part of another system and is one of its subunits or components.

An intuitively appealing example might clarify this approach to systems analysis and the key role played by information. If one were to study a tree, one level of analysis might examine the relationship of that particular tree and its surrounding environmental elements—e.g., other trees, soil, pollutants, water. On the other hand, the study of the tree might address itself to the components of the tree itself—the bark, the veinous system, the leaves, and their interrelations. At another juncture of analysis the study might be directed at the level of a leaf where it is both a component of the larger tree system and a system itself with parts consisting of cells, circulatory mechanisms, etc. The crucial point is that in systems analysis the investigation should always focus on one plane of inquiry and extend into the next *higher order* of systemness, and into the next *lower order* of systemness, in order to more fully understand the organized range of relationships.

To be fully understood, the decision making and the predilections of black athletes, should be placed in a context (the next higher order of systemness) and broken down into the various areas of content where personal and specific decisions are made. These personal actions or decisions immediately become integrated with those of the subculture. The social action of a single athlete takes place in concert with other such individuals who share common goals, aspirations, world views, concepts of a particular sport, notions of excellence, and other commonly held *subcultural pools*, or bodies of information.

Max Weber reminds us that the action of individuals, insofar as it is social, must be (1) intentional; (2) oriented toward the actions of others; and (3) goal-directed (Weber, 1947: 88). When a person acts, therefore, it is within some frame of reference that utilizes the full range of information at his or her disposal about his or her social and biological system within a specified social group (system). In this framework, black athletes, then, cannot be seen so simply and automatically using the most readily available athletic facility, attempting the event at which they might be more physically adopt or even participating in the sport that might be the least expensive. The decisions about athletic involvement are goal directed and shared by that person's group (social system). This point shall be returned to shortly, but at this juncture the various types of *information* employed to reach goal directed and intentional decisions will be examined more closely.

Information may be of three different kinds (Deutsch, 1951: 185-223). First, there is information about conditions external to the system or organization. This refers to external, but impinging variables that effect or may interact with internal relations of the system. The second kind of information relates to the past. This may include a wide range of recall and recombination about conditions, events, or acts that may, at this time, but may not at another time, hold significance for social actions within the system. The third kind of information relates to the internal operations and participants in the system itself.

These kinds of information are interrelated with, or utilized by, three kinds of feedback: (1) goal seeking—a feedback of new external data into the system whose operational channels remain unchanged; (2) learning—feedback of new external data for the changing of these operating channels themselves, that is, change in the organization of the system; and (3) consciousness or "self-awareness"—feedback of new internal data via secondary messages; messages about changes in the state of the system parts. These kinds of feedback and information allow for four successively higher orders or purposes: (1) immediate satisfaction seeking; (2) self-preservation, which may require overruling the first; (3) group preservation; and (4) preservation of a process of goal seeking beyond any one group (Deutsch, 1951: 185–223). Of course, these orders of purpose require successively higher order feedback networks. In essence, *information* types coupled with feedback networks allow for various levels of purpose to be attained within the organization. Information, then, obtained or shared by individual actors orients social action to specific or general goals. These "objectives" or goals are manifested as the behavior that, for example, the social researcher observes.

The crucial element for a lucid analysis of social organization or system is the linkages among *information pools*. These "pools" of communication and information constitute the complex adaptive system (not simply an equilibrated or homeostatic one) operating as an ongoing process that is continuously generating, maintaining, or altering meaning and behavior patterns to which we attach various labels such as competition, cooperation, success or conflict. An information pool as a carrier of "meaning" is not an entity that exists some place or flows from one place to another but a relation or "mapping" between structured variety sets contained in goal-oriented adaptive systems and their environments. "Communication" involves a "process of selection" from among such sets.

George Miller sums up the relationship between "information" and "organization":

A well-organized system is predictable—you know almost what it is going to do before it happens. When a well-organized system does something, you learn little that you didn't know already—you acquire little information. A perfectly-organized system is completely predictable and its behavior provides no information at all. The more disorganized and unpredictable a system is, the more information you can get by observing it. Information, organization, and predictability room together in this theoretical house. (1953: 3)

The problem for the social researcher is to discover the substance of the "information pool" so that the level of predictability can be determined; realizing that the fluid nature of complex systems *never* allows for total prediction of behavior.

An Application of the Paradigm

The Surrounding Social System

We may now return to look at the subcultural *pooling of information* that includes decisions concerning athletic participation. The society sets the context, becoming the large systemic frame for sporting activity where events are played, emphasized, deemphasized, or totally rejected. Within the United States a host of events, ranging from baseball, football, and billiards to curling and kite flying are available in organized competition. In this country, however, soccer (internationally famous) is deemphasized and cricket is uncommon while one of our most popular sports, football, is rarely played in other countries. Moreover, some sporting events occur almost solely in the college context or in private clubs—e.g., rugby, rifle and pistol shooting, lacrosse, and yachting.

The overall athletic ventures of a society are an outgrowth of its social, economic, and environmental conditions and its cultural history. The Caribbean is a clear example. In that area of the world cultural and environmental variables preclude participation in the Winter Olympics. Snow-laden hills and ice rinks (natural or man-made) do not exist, and there is a lack of cultural or psychological disposition to experience wintry or frigid environments. While doing field work in Trinidad, this author was often asked about coping with the snow and the ice of upstate New York winters. The conditions of ice, chilling winds, and deep snow are often disparaged and disdained by members of cultures whose traditional environments are tropical.

Cultural history also differentiates between the various islands in terms of games emphasis, since cricket and rugby are played in those areas whose cultural history is Spanish. On the other hand, soccer, with its international reputation, is avidly pursued throughout the Caribbean.

Certain athletic events in the U.S. have grown out of the social activities of the leisure class and retain this label in spite of increasing popular participation (see chapter 10); e.g., polo, tennis, golf, equestrianism, sports car and Grand Prix racing, sailing, fencing, chess, skiing, and squash. Participation in these sports does not entirely depend on spending large sums of money, but, perhaps more, on access to facilities, such as membership in private clubs and the availability of leisure time. The time frame of most sporting events practiced by the elite members of society is greatly extended compared to the time frame of sporting events practiced by the masses of the population. Moreover, the quality of the interaction among participants is more leisured. Compare for example, the tempo, the time frame, the noncombatant and genteel quality of golf, sailing, or cricket to the dynamism, short time frame, and physical competition of boxing, ice hockey, or basketball, yet the most leisured category of people in the U.S. are the unemployed poor. Even in modern times participation, then, in certain activities still connotes elitism, snobbism, and a general aura of social sophistication where the outcome of the event is measured less by the scores but more by congeniality and the demonstration of social grace, followed by the personal mastery of prescribed athletic skills.

Interrelations between the Larger System and the Subsystem

Conditions within the larger social system have informational importance to the subculture—e.g., class and ethnic (racial) differentiation, desired and urged social mobility. Particular elements within the larger cultural setting may be seen as *bits* of information used by the potential black athlete. The information that the black athlete gathers about our culture is well documented in the sociological literature (Marden and Meyer, 1973; Hunter, 1964; Hunt and Walker, 1974). Information about the issues of racism, democracy or the lack of it, poverty, ghettos, slums, various avenues of relative upward social mobility, and segregation, are perceptions most blacks have regarding themselves and their cultural milieu. These are all informational inputs from the larger system.

Members of the black subculture define their social context using a generalized and specific pool of information. Participation in athletic events and use of facilities that foster negative sanctions from the larger social system are generally avoided behaviors. Alternatively, events where blacks are expected to take part gather large number of participants. Football, basketball, and boxing are excellent examples of this phenomenon. Even within these sports, certain positions or roles are deemed more appropriate than others. Quests for leadership positions such as quarterback, coach, or manager have, until recently, received negative reactions and sanctions from the larger social system (except, of course, where the positions were within a homogeneous black population).

The use of athletics as a vehicle for social mobility (participation at the professional level in sports or acquisition of college scholarships) has required the black athlete to be skilled at those positions and in those sports that the larger system tolerates, expects them to be good at, and is willing to reward. John Loy and Joseph McElvogue (1970) discuss the notion of *stacking* where certain positions on teams are "reserved" for blacks and others for whites. In positions where generalship is required, e.g., linebackers, quarterbacks, centers, offensive guards in football, or infielders, catchers, and pitchers in baseball, these were overwhelmingly occupied by white players. Offensive halfbacks, defensive cornerbacks, and wide receivers in football and outfielders in baseball were essentially black positions. In basketball, the playmaker (usually a guard) is a generalship position and hence most often a "white" position. The third-base coaching job is very important in professional baseball and nearly always given to whites when the coaching staff is racially integrated (see chapter 9 for further information on stacking).

Young black players quickly learn the positions at which they have a better chance for success and develop the necessary skills, causing intense intragroup competition at those positions. Even if social conformity is not always as severe as is suggested, the information or data in the world view of the subculture and its individual actors seems to suggest this cognized pattern. The context of the larger social system impinges directly upon the organization and system of black athletes, their behavior, and decision-making regarding sports. Although it might be wearisome for whites to hear, there is no denying that discriminatory and racist attitudes and institutions are commonplace in the American milieu. These are well-documented in almost every American sociology textbook in discussions of social stratification, social classes, racism, ethnicity, social and economic inequity, and political disenfranchisement. The social, political, and economic stratification of classes and ethnic groups of the larger society is real and realized by all of its cultural constituencies.

Although these conditions are external to the system under

scrutiny (black athletes), they impinge in a most direct way. Any black athlete can point to instances of these larger system conditions affecting their lives. These accounts are sometimes poignant and intimate although sometimes indirect. Knowledge of the impingement of these conditions and their implications is ubiquitous.

Spencer Haywood recalls:

> The moment I got to Chicago I saw what it was. A ghetto. Filthy streets. Rat-infested tenements. People living in rat-traps. People living on welfare. People without hope. But it was better than any life I'd known. A black man could get work there, in the big city. He could buy a car on time and keep it as long as he could hide from the re-po man. He could buy a bottle and get a girl and get together with some people and have a party. A black man could act like a man there. He could swell up his chest and curse at whitey and get drunk or get a fix but say screw you to the world. It was better than being beat down in the south, you see. And I wasn't ever goin' back to live in Mississippi. No way, Not ever. I got an education of the streets of Chicago and later in Detroit. By the time I was 16, 17 years old I knew things some people don't live in the ghettoes will ever know. (Libby and Haywood, 1972: 24)

In response to just such impinging, larger system conditions, and racial hostilities, Muhammad Ali reveals a sense of relief after throwing his Olympic Gold Medal into the Ohio River.

> I remember thinking that the middle of the Ohio was probably the deepest part, and I walked over to the center of the bridge. And Ronnie, with that extra sense people have who have known and loved each other for a long time, anticipated my actions. Dropping the bike, he ran toward me, yelling. But I had snapped the ribbon from around my neck. I held the medallion just far enough out so that it wouldn't tangle in the bridge structure, and threw it into the black water of the Ohio. I watched it drag the red, white and blue ribbon down to the bottom behind it. The medal was gone, but the sickness had gone too. I felt calm, relaxed, confident. . . . My holiday as a White Hope was over. I felt a new, secret strength. (Ali and Durham, 1975: 79–80)

The observant coach, Gene Smith, discusses another aspect of input from the larger system in *Foul*.

Players in Harlem run more. They dribble and drive better, and they're tougher. But Brooklyn kids shoot better. That's because when you played halfcourt in Harlem you didn't have to take the other team's rebounds back over the foul line before you could shoot. You just put it back up. That makes for a lot of rebounding and shooting around the boards. In Brooklyn, you had to pass it back first, so there was more outside shooting and more passing. I think that's why kids from Brooklyn did better in college and pro ball. They had the outside shots to overcome the big centers. (Wolf, 1972: 35)

The second kind of information needed to fully understand black athletes at their level of social organization relates to the past. Popular information that is not written down is subject to a wide range of recall and recombination referring to conditions, events, or acts that may, at this time, but may not at another time, hold significance for social actions within the system. Black athletes learn from each other, from past athletes, and in general disseminate information relevant to potential successes or failures. Position stacking is an example of information used in recombination relating to past events that hold significance for subcultural decision making.

Jack Olsen (1968), Harry Edwards (1968), and Eitzen and Yetman (1976), among others, point to information extant among black athletes that holds significance for them as they make decisions regarding choice of sports and positions. Emulation of successful black athletes in their events and their survival life-ways are instructive to young blacks.

In addition, the lack of certain information within the subculture about the nuances and athletic rewards of certain sports preclude participation of black athletes in them. How many members of this subculture are aware of the thrill of a "touch" in fencing or the magic of "checkmating" an opponent in chess or the physical exhilaration of downhill skiing? Information about these joys is socially absent and consequently not learned in the same way that children learn about a slam-dunk or a touchdown. If the necessary impetus growing out of available information is absent, then decisions about athletic participation move in directions where information is available. Emulation of Reggie Jackson, O. J. Simpson, and Dr. "J" have no doubt, prompted thousands of black youngsters to pursue an athletic career or, minimally, to participate in the sports where these heroes are legends. From among the scores of culturally available sports, the Black Hall of Fame covers only football, baseball, basketball, track and field, boxing, tennis, and golf. This list is manifestly selected from the major professionalized sports in the United States and conspicuously excludes hockey, auto racing, horse racing, rodeo, and bowling.

The Subcultural System of the Black Athlete

There is information that relates to an understanding of the internal operations and individual components of the system. These elements include the individual black athletes, who collectively and informationally, compose our principal focus. William Grier and Price Cobbs (1968: 58) discuss the personality development of young black men (that may be typical of black athletes) as they acquire adulthood in our society:

> The family has lived in a ghetto, and all their socialization has been within that framework. But Jimmy is part of a historical legacy that spans more than three hundred years. He lives in a large city but he shares his insight with every Black child in every city in this country. He must devise individual ways to meet group problems. He must find compensations, whether healthy or unhealthy. There must be a tremendous expenditure of psychic energy to cushion the shock of learning that he is denied what other men around him have. When he states his desire to attack a White man, he consciously acknowledges his wish to attack those who keep him powerless [no doubt a component for participation in combatant sports]. . . . Throughout his life, at each critical point of development, the Black boy is told to hold back, to constrict, to subvert and camouflage his normal masculinity. Male assertiveness becomes a forbidden fruit, and if it is attained, it must be savored privately. (1968: 59)

Connie Hawkins' experience of his early peer relations and masculine growth provides a good example:

> For many young men in the slums, the schoolyard is the only place they can feel true pride in what they do, where they can move free of inhibitions (even from coaches) where people applaud their accomplishments, and where they can—by being spectacular—rise, for the moment, above the drabness and

anonymity of their lives. Thus, when a player develops extraordinary "schoolyard" moves and shots, these become more than
simple athletic skills. They are an inseparable part of his personality. The level of his "game" becomes his measure as a
man. So it was—and still is—with Connie. (Wolf, 1973:40)

The desire to mature, with increased status, while not running,
suicidally, into obstacles from the larger system is a perceptual
dilemma for these young men. Christina and Richard Milner point
out:

As the profession is paracticed among those players as studied
and interviewed, pimping is a unique ghetto adaptation to the
universal American desire for material success, without "selling
out" to a "square job" for "chump change" or a way of life
away from the familiar streets.
. . . The position of this subculture with regard to both the
larger Black subculture and the still larger American culture
enables one to learn much about the larger systems which may
not at first be apparent. For the player's world is based on the
elaboration of certain American values and certain ghetto
values at the expense of other strong values of both. Thus, their
preoccupation with manhood and the symbols of upward
mobility (a strong ghetto characteristic) and their absorption
with money and power (a strong American characteristic) are
pursued at the expense of sexual and other behavioral norms
held sacred by the larger groups. Yet the very existence of The
Life is based entirely on failures of the larger cultural entity. At
the juncture between "real" and "ideal" behavior in Black and
White America thrives The Life, the subculture of Black pimps
and their prostitutes. As we explored their world we also glimpsed
these larger cultures in sharp and sometimes unexpected focus.
What began as a study of "prostitution" led us to inquire into
Black ghetto hustling culture, into the nature of man and
woman, and into the larger questions about race, sex, and
money in contemporary America. (Milner and Milner, 1972:
8-9)

Athletics could certainly be added to this list. The key elements of
their participant observations are "adaptation," "acquiring
manhood," and "upward mobility." Each young black male attempts, given particular abilities, skills, and information, or the
lack of same, to maximize future successes.

At the personal level, the decision *not* to pursue certain athletic events also has a great deal to do with the subculture's view of these events. The black who knows of chess or fencing and decides to participate in these sports will have to confront the perceived status of these sports. If that perception is negative within the subculture, either because the activity is deemed unworthy, perhaps unmanly, or because the group judges the sport as snobbish and of an elitist nature, then the individual in his or her decisions must take account of this negativism. Continued pursuit of these activities may affect or alter future in-group relations.

The availability of other members of the subculture for participation in some sports and not others may enter into the decision-making process. If a person has to enter into relations that take place in alien or hostile environments in order to enjoy hockey or tennis, the personal decision may be to conform to traditional and more socially acceptable patterns of athletic participation.

Conclusion

Three types of information from each system level are utilized and interrelated with three kinds of feedback discussed earlier: *goal-seeking*, *learning*, and *self-awareness* (consciousness). Membership and actions by individual participants must be understood within the context of the society, and include the decisions of other actors as well as the individuals who may or may not have certain physical attributes, and who finally possess and integrate information regarding their future lives.

This chapter has shown that the explanation for the disproportionately large number of black athletes in certain sports and their paucity in others seems to be more complicated than biological adaptation or economic deprivation theories can explain. The cultural setting in which ordinary blacks and athletes find themselves, the information available to the individual and the subcultural group, plus the cybernetics of the juxtaposition of the social units are all involved in bringing about social action. The *subcultural and informational pooling* of data gives rise to intentional decisions made by people within a particular social environment. The black athlete configures his or her world based upon available *information*, interprets the feedback data and ultimately makes choices, with the necessary adjustments, which hopefully result in positive social rewards.

Notes

1. Mike Garrett, U.S.C.; O. J. Simpson, U.S.C.; Archie Griffin, (twice) Ohio State; Billy Simms, University of Oklahoma; Charles White, U.S.C.; and George Rogers, North Carolina.
2. A crucial and immediate concern is with the definition of a race as a genetic entity. Miscegenation over the centuries has caused the genetic pool of so-called isolatable races to be more complicated and heterogeneous than the average person might assume. See, for example, Livingstone (1962), Montagu (1962 and 1964), Brace (1964), Gould (1975), Brace and Livingstone (1975), Barzun (1965), Osborne (1968), and Banton and Harwood (1975); or any modern textbook in the field of physical anthropology for analyses spelling out the inexactitudes of popular and unscientific views of race, and the difficulties inherent in correlations between race and specific attributes.

Works Cited

Ali, M., and Durham, R. *The Greatest*. New York: Ballantine Books, 1975.
All-Sports World Record Book. New York: Grosset and Dunlap, 1977.
Banton, M., and Harwood, J. *The Concept of Race*. New York: Praeger, 1975.
Barzun, J. *Race: A Study in Superstition*. New York: Harper, 1965.
Brace, C. L. "On the Race Concept." In Montagu, A. *The Concept of Race*, New York: Glencoe Press, 1964.
Brace, C. L., and Livingstone, F. "On Creeping Jensenism." In A. Montagu, ed. *Race and I.Q.*, London: Oxford, 1975.
Buckley, W. *Sociology and Modern Systems Theory*. Englewood Cliffs: Prentice-Hall, 1967.
Deutsch, K. "Mechanism, Teleology and Mind," *Philosophy and Phenomenological Research* 12 (1951): 185–223.
Dobzhansky, T. *Mankind Evolving*. New Haven: Yale University Press, 1962.
Edwards, H. "Why Negroes Should Boycott Whitey's Olympics," *Saturday Evening Post Magazine*, 9, March 1968, p. 241.
———. *The Revolt of the Black Athlete*. New York: Free Press, 1969.
———. "The Black Athlete: 20th Century Gladiators for White America," *Psychology Today* (November 1973): 43.
Emery, F. E. *Systems Thinking*. New York: Penguin Books, 1969.
Frazier, E. B. *Black Bourgeoisie*. Glencoe: Free Press, 1957.
Gipe, G. *The Great American Sports Book*. Garden City, N.Y.: Doubleday, 1978.
Gould, S. *Racist Arguments and I.Q.*, London: Oxford, 1975.
Grier, W., and Cobb, P. *Black Rage*. New York: Basic Books, 1969.
Hefner, James A. "The Economics of the Black Family From Four Perspectives." In C. V. Willie, ed. *Caste and Class*. Bayside: General Hale Publishers, 1979, p. 80–91.
Henderson, E. *The Negro in Sports*. Washington, D.C.: Associated Publishers, 1949.
———. *The Black Athlete*. Washington, D.C.: United Publishers, 1969.
———. "The Negro as Athlete," *Crises* (February 1970): 51–56.
Hunt, Chester, and Walker, Lewis. *Ethnic Dynamics*. Homeland, Ill.: Dorsey Press, 1974.
Hunter, David. *The Slums*. Glencoe: Free Press, 1964.
Kane, M. "An Assessment of 'Black Is Best'." in *Sports Illustrated* (18 January, 1972).

LeFlore, J., ed. *Community Action for Minority Groups.* Syracuse, N.Y.: Syracuse University Press, 1971.

———. "An Analysis of a Third World Slum: Urbanism in Trinidad," unpublished dissertation, 1973.

Levine, Ned. "Why Do Countries Win Olympic Medals." *Sociology and Social Research* 58 (July 1974): 353–60.

Libby, B., and Haywood, S. *Standing Up for Something: The Spencer Haywood Story.* New York: Tempo Books, 1972.

Livingstone, F. "On the Non-existence of Race." *American Anthropologist* 64 (1962): 282–95.

Loy, J., and Elvogue, J. "Racial Segregation in American Sport." *International Review of Sport Sociology* (1970): pp. 5–24.

Marden, Charles, and Meyer, Gladys. *Minorities in America.* New York: Van Nostrand, 1973.

Michener, J. *Sports in America.* New York: Random House, 1976.

Milner, C., and Milner, R. *Black Players: The Secret World of Black Pimps.* New York: Bantam, 1972.

Montagu, A. "The Concept of Race." *American Anthropologist* 64 (1962): pp. 919–28.

Montagu, A. *Race & I.Q.* London: Oxford University Press, 1975.

Montagu, A. *The Concept of Race.* New York: Glencoe Press, 1964.

National Football League. *NFL's Official Encyclopedia History of Professional Football.* New York: MacMillan, 1978.

Osborne, Richard, ed. *The Biological and Social Meaning of Race.* Englewood Cliffs, N.J.: Prentice-Hall, 1968.

Olsen, J. "The Black Athlete—A Shameful Story." *Sports Illustrated* (29 July, 1968): 15–27.

Rothstein, J. *Communication, Organization and Science.* New York: Falcon Press, 1958.

Staples, Robert. *Black Sociology.* New York: McGraw-Hill, 1976.

Weber, M. *The Theory of Social and Economic Organization.* Glencoe: Free Press, 1947.

Wolf, D. *Foul: The Connie Hawkins Story.* New York: Warner, 1972.

Yiannakis, A.; McIntyre, T.; Melnick, M.; and Hart, D. *Sport Sociology: Contemporary Themes.* Dubuque: Kendall-Hunt, 1976.

7

The Participation of Older People in Sports

ROBERT A. HAROOTYAN

Introduction

Despite the growing international research interest on the aging process, information about physical or sports activity patterns among older people remains negligible. Research during the last two decades, however, has produced a wealth of information regarding the physiological changes that occur with chronological aging. But questions remain concerning how much of the loss in physiological function is directly related to the biology of aging, and how much is due to long-term, socially induced reduction in physical activity.

Some evidence exists that the social factor is more important in age-related declines in physiological function. Kraus and Rabb (1961) coined the term *hypokinetic disease* to describe the problems of physical decline directly related to insufficient activity. Their research was a pioneering effort that showed the negative effects associated with inadequate physical activity, obesity, arteriosclerosis, and decrements in respiratory function. Wessel and Van Huss (1969) documented the fact that physical activity decreases significantly with age. Losses in physiological function were less related to biological aging per se than to long-term decreases in physical activity. Other studies have also shown the clear need for minimum daily physical activity to maintain normal health, suggesting the need to incorporate more activity into the increased leisure time of most middle-aged and older Americans

(Davies et al., 1963; Durnin, 1965; Letunov and Motylyanskaya, 1966).

Other research indicates that regular physical activity and exercise at all ages help individuals retain basic physiological capabilities. A decrease in physiological capabilities can occur gradually over a period of years and may remain largely unnoticed under conditions of normal daily activity. The value of regular exercise and activity for maintaining good health has best been documented in studies that show the sharp loss of physiological functioning when humans are under physical stress (Shock, 1961; deVries, 1970). Physiological dysfunctions that may not appear to be great under conditions of rest or minimal physical exertion have been found to be quite severe when measured at higher levels of activity.

The long-term lack of regular physical activity and exercise, which often characterizes middle and old-age life-styles, is clearly related to greater physiological dysfunction. But this general physiological decline can be avoided or reversed. In a study by deVries (1970) significant improvements were noted in oxygen pulse, minute ventilation, physical work capacity, percent of body fat, and blood pressure among a sample of men aged fifty-two to eighty-eight after six weeks of regular supervised physical activity and exercise. Similar findings with respect to improved aerobic capacity and cardiac function have been documented in other studies (Fischer et al., 1965; Barry et al., 1966).

It is clear, then, that although some decrements in physiological capacity do accompany the aging process, the degree of physiological dysfunction is greatly influenced by the increased inactivity of men and women in the middle and older age groups. Given the findings that significant improvements can be achieved in physiological functioning through regular exercise and physical activity, the participation of older people in various types of athletic activity can be an important factor for their health and general well-being. This chapter, therefore, is oriented toward the question, "What are the sociological aspects and conditions under which older people participate in sports and physical activity?"

Age Stratification and Activity of Older People

Given the clear evidence about the deleterious effects of decreased physical activity among humans, especially those in the middle and older years, it is important to consider the changing trend in sports activity as people age. This chapter purposely does not adhere to the value-free position that others consider requisite for the sport sociologist (see, for example, Kenyon and Loy, 1965). Holding to a value-free position is neither necessary nor advisable in discussing the relative costs and benefits of sports and other physical activities for older people. The fact that this chapter concentrates on older people is itself a value orientation that stresses the unnecessary health problems faced by older people because of long-term physical inactivity. Indeed, the value-free sport sociologist would probably ignore the question of older people's participation in sports *because* of their generally low level of activity.

Rather than ignore older people and consider them unimportant subjects for sport sociology, this chapter will combine an analytic approach with one advocating the need for greater participation of older people in sports activity. The author's role, then, is twofold: as sociologist/gerontologist and as advocate of better health for the elderly. The analytic approach will emphasize the sociology of age stratification and the developmental life cycle, while the advocacy position will use an empirical example as a model for changing the attitudes and behavior of older people regarding physical activity.

Theories of Aging

Two conflicting social gerontological theories about the social integration of the aged have been developed over the last two decades. Both theories embody value orientations leading to the position that the aging process should involve successful social and psychological adjustment (often tritely called "successful aging"). One of these is disengagement theory (Cumming and Henry, 1961), which states that there is a mutual withdrawal or disengagement between older people and the rest of society. The other theory is called, appropriately, activity theory. Like disengagement theory, this model also takes as given certain behavioral changes that accompany the aging process, particularly decreased social interaction in both primary and secondary relationships. But activity theory posits an optimum pattern of aging based on the need of the older individual to contiunue a life pattern of integrated activity within the major subsystems of the social order. Should mandatory withdrawal occur, as best exemplified by occupational retirement, activity theory calls for continued participation in ego-sustaining endeavors that serve as substitutes for the lost activity.

Thus, we have two theories of optimum aging that agree that sociocultural forces in contemporary American society lead to a decrease in activity and social participation as people age. But in one model the older person is seen as a cooperating participant in a process of mutual withdrawal, while in the other he or she is viewed as an unwilling victim of these forces. These differences are akin to those surrounding functionalist theory and conflict theory, the former stressing the social forces of equilibrium in a system, and the latter emphasizing system stress through competing power subgroups in the social order.

These broader macrolevel theories have not been well integrated into social gerontology. One might explore the use of exchange theory (Homans, 1950; 1961; Dowd, 1975; 1980) in understanding the forces of old-age segregation in American society (see, for example, Riley et al., 1969), or the literature on social inequality and social stratification to provide a bridge for understanding the similarities and the complementarity of age and class stratification (Riley, 1971; Gulliver, 1968; Sorokin, 1959).

The social-structural theories that concentrate on macrolevel processes of aging can be integrated with theories concerning attitude formation and change over the life cycle. Both theoretical approaches are useful for an understanding of the factors that lead to the decline in physical activity associated with aging in contemporary American society. The life-cycle developmental approach of social psychology has been widely applied in social gerontology, as exemplified in the works of Neugarten (1966; 1968) and numerous other researchers, the large majority of whom conclude that basic orientations toward activity and social participation are formed throughout the adolescent and adult years through middle age (Maddox, 1966; Rose, 1964; Filsinger and Sauer, 1978). Wilensky (1961) also noted in relation to aging that orderly careers among urban males were the key determinants of activity level, participation in formal organizations, and maintenance of primary informal social interaction.

It seems clear, then, that life history is a crucial factor for the degree of physical and social activity that occurs in the later stages of the life cycle. Except in those cases where poor health or physical disability clearly limit the activity level of older people, it seems that significant age-related reductions in activity are strongly associated with past inactivity, especially in combination with normative expectations and behavioral responses among older people. The problem then becomes one of understanding the patterns of socialization that are based upon negative values and orientations toward old age. This issue has been well documented by Riley et al. (1969), who note similar problems of status inconsistency and role strain generated by differences in chronological and non-chronological orientations toward status in American society (see also Eisenstadt, 1956; Cutler, 1979).

Contemporary American society includes an age status system of role sequences and accompanying norms—i.e., institutionalized ageism. For example, Neugarten et al. (1965) found a high degree of consensus on age-related norms and expected life-cycle characteristics among a sample of middle-aged men and women. These norms were usually considered more binding for others, especially those in another age group (see also Turk, 1965). But it was also discerned that the personal acceptance and internalization of age norms increases noticeably among older people.

A possible explanation for this greater acceptance of age norms among older people is found in the age normative system itself. As age increases the number of possible roles that are available and socially approved tends to decrease. At the same time, the specificity of those roles that do remain tends to decrease. Havighurst and Albrecht (1953) noted the lack of well defined or explicit norms for old age, as did Kuypers and Bengtson (1973) some twenty years later. The ascriptive nature of age stratification has changed little in the last two decades.

Evidence from Survey Data

More recent data on the attitudes of the general American public aged eighteen and over regarding old age have been gathered in a poll by Louis Harris and Associates, which was conducted for the National Council on the Aging (NCOA, 1975). Using a nationwide representative sample of 4,254 people aged eighteen and over, the Harris organization found both distinct differences and similarities between the population age eighteen to sixty-four and that age sixty-five, and over regarding numerous aspects of aging. In general, the greatest differences between these two age groups are found in the images they hold about the age sixty-five and over population. When asked what were the "best things" about being over age sixty-five the highest percent of responses by the total public related to the general theme of increased leisure time and freedom, as expressed by the following responses (the proportion of the total public so responding is in parentheses): increased leisure time (50 percent); freedom from responsibility (33 percent); retirement (29 percent). But among those respondents age sixty-five and over, smaller proportions reported these characteristics as the "best things." The greatest difference was in the orientation toward occupational retirement, where only 18 percent of the older group responded positively (NCOA, 1975, p. 9).

It is interesting to note that both age groups showed congruence (within one to three percentage points) on most other items, all of which had distinctly lower percentages of response. Included in these characteristics cited by the total public were the following: being wiser or more experienced (5 percent); satisfaction with life (1 percent); sense of accomplishment (1 percent). These items, which have much lower frequencies of response, can be interpreted as general characteristics related to the personality of older people and the value or esteem associated with old age. On the other hand, the characteristics with the much higher percentages of response are ones related to structural aspects of life-cycle stage. We can infer from these data that the total public's perceptions of the "best things" about old age relate far more to role changes in life-style (i.e., to structural characteristics), rather than to old-age personality characteristics, esteem, or positive status orientations (i.e., to cultural characteristics).

These discrepancies between the types of orientations toward old age held by the total public, as well as the differences between the younger and older age groups, exemplify the overly negative perceptions of old age and old people in American culture (see also Pierce and Chiriboga, 1979). The overall impression conveyed by these data is one which depicts the older population as a group with much leisure time, but also not much ability, personal resources, or individual worth to adjust to or constructively exploit this increased freedom. One possible result of these negative orientations is the reluctance of younger people to include older people in structured physical activities such as sports.

Moreover, pervasive old-age stereotyping is found in both the younger and the older age groups. But despite the overall negative impressions held *by* most older people about *other* older people, the responses of this age group in terms of actual experience show far lower frequencies on the same items. Turk's (1965) contention that age-related normative expectations are directed largely toward

Table 1

"Very Serious" Problems Attributed to "Most People over 65"
by Public Age 18–64 and Age 65 and Over

| | "Very Serious" Problems Attributed to Most People Over Age 65 (in percent) | |
Problem	By Public Aged 18–64	By Public Aged 65 and Over
Not having enough to live on	63	59
Loneliness	61	56
Not feeling needed	56	40
Fear of crime	50	51
Poor health	50	53
Not enough job opportunities	47	32
Not enough medical care	45	36
Not enough to do to keep busy	38	33
Poor housing	35	34
Not enough friends	28	26
Not enough education	19	25
Not enough clothing	16	17

Source: Adapted from *The Myth and Reality of Aging in America*, a study for The National Council on the Aging, Inc., Washington, D. C., by Louis Harris and Associates, Inc. April 1975, p. 36.

"others" and not toward oneself is strongly borne out by the NCOA study. Table 1 shows the responses of the age eighteen to sixty-four and age sixty-five and over publics concerning "very serious" problems attributed to most older people.

Strikingly clear in these data are the slight discrepancies between the two age groups in the frequency with which very serious problems are attributed to older people. Only the items concerning not feeling needed, not having enough job opportunities, and not having enough medical care are noticeably different, with older people citing these old-age problems less than the public aged eighteen to sixty-four. More important, however, are the large discrepancies between the older public's responses about problems they *attribute* to other older people in general, versus their personal *experiences* with these problems (see Table 2). The large differences in these response types among the older public emphasize the pervasive nature of institutionalized negative images of old age, in spite of the older person's actual experience.

Table 2

"Very Serious" Problems Attributed to "Most People Over 65"
and Felt Personally by Public Age 65 and Over

Problem	"Very Serious" Problems of People Over Age 65 (in percent)	
	Attributed by Public 65 and Over	Felt Personally by Public 65 and Over
Not having enough to live on	59	15
Loneliness	56	12
Not feeling needed	40	7
Fear of crime	51	23
Poor health	53	21
Not enough job opportunities	32	5
Not enough medical care	36	10
Not enough to do to keep busy	33	6
Poor housing	34	4
Not enough friends	26	5
Not enough education	25	8
Not enough clothing	17	3

Source: Adapted from *The Myth and Reality of Aging in America*, a study for The National Council on the Aging, Inc., Washington, D.C., by Louis Harris and Associates, Inc. April 1975, pp. 36 and 37.

Older people, in general, are themselves the victims of generalized old-age stereotyping in American society. The degree to which these negative images are internalized is severe when contrasted with the personal experiences of the older population itself (again, note the immense differences in Table 2). This high degree of internalization of negative old-age stereotypes among older people is akin to the "slave mentality" induced for decades among black Americans. The self-fulfilling prophecy, which for so long worked to severely inhibit the development of a positive self-image among most blacks in American society, may also be operating in a similar manner for older people in our society. If an older person believes that the majority of his or her old-age peers have very serious problems associated with this stage in the life cycle, two responses can be hypothesized. One response is to personally accept these negative images and problems as inevitable correlates of old age. The data in Tables 1 and 2 indicate that this response is quite common. The self-fulfilling prophecy is certainly at work in shaping the generally negative self-images that older people have. A second response, which is not generally supported by these data, would entail a concerted effort to deny these negative orientations and to act against them.

Because here the concern lies with the physical activities of older people, the analysis will be limited to this issue. Other data from the NCOA study provide information about the public's expectations regarding older people's use of leisure time and the experiences of older people themselves. Table 3 once again shows the

Table 3

Images Held by Total Public Regarding Leisure Time Activities of "Most People over 65" and Actual Experiences of Public Age 65 and Over

	"Most People over Age 65 Spend a Lot of Time" (in percent)	
Type of Activity	Total Public's Image	Personal Experience of Public Age 65 and Over
Socializing with friends	52	47
Gardening/raising plants	45	39
Reading	43	36
Watching television	67	36
Sitting and thinking	62	31
Caring for members of the family	23	27
Participating in recreational activities and hobbies	28	26
Going for walks	34	25
Participating in fraternal or community organizations/ clubs	26	17
Sleeping	39	16
Just doing nothing	35	15
Working part-time or full-time	5	10
Doing volunteer work	15	8
Participating in political activities	9	6
Participating in sports, like golf, swimming, or tennis	5	3

Source: Adapted from *The Myth and Reality of Aging in America*, a study for The National Council on the Aging, Inc., Washington, D.C., by Louis Harris and Associates, Inc. April 1975, p. 59.

discrepancies between the total public's image of older people's leisure activity and the actual experience of the elderly. The essentially negative stereotype of the sedentary, isolated, and unstimulated old person that is held by the total public does not correspond with old people's actual experiences. These differences are particularly great with respect to the high proportion of the public who view older people as spending a lot of time "watching television," "sitting and thinking" (the "rocking chair" stereotype), "sleeping," or "just doing nothing."

Although the public considerably exaggerates the amount of time old people spend in sedentary activities, older people are not very active as a whole. Approximately one-fourth of them spent a lot of time walking or participating in recreational activities and hobbies. A much smaller proportion (only 3 percent) regularly participated in the more physically demanding sports such as swimming, tennis, or golf. The public's image of older people as nonparticipants in sports activity is one of the most accurate they hold, with only 5 percent expecting the elderly to spend a lot of time in sports. It is clear that at least in the area of older people's participation in sports activity, the normative expectations of the public and the actual behavior of older people are in close agreement. Again, the vicious circle of the self-fulfilling prophecy is complete. Two questions remaining are whether this low degree of sports activity among the elderly is a pattern that has persisted over time and to what extent it is related to aging per se.

Other Research on Physical Activity among Older People

Little research exists on older people's physical activity or on the relationship between age and degree of activity. Most gerontological studies, whether cross-sectional or longitudinal, have been concerned with patterns of social participation and their change in relation to aging. Only a few studies have concentrated on the physical activity and recreational habits of old people. These studies corroborate the recent NCOA findings of low participation among older Americans in sports.

Bailey (1955) conducted a cross-sectional study of recreational activity among a sample of men aged twenty to fifty-nine who were divided into two-year age groups. He found that the various types of recreational and sports activities tended to maintain their frequency distribution across age groups. Within this pattern of consistency, however, there was also a distinct drop in the proportion of men aged fifty to fifty-nine who participated in sports. In another study, survey data collected by the Opinion Research Corporation in 1957 showed that only 2 percent of the respondents aged sixty and over had engaged in sports activity the day before the survey was taken, in contrast to an average of 8 percent for all respondents aged fifteen and over.

Cunningham et al. (1968) found similarly low rates of participation among older men in physically demanding leisure time activities. Most notable was the considerable increase between ages forty and sixty-nine in the proportion of men who spent only a very small amount of time (one hour/week/year) in active leisure pursuits. While differences in activity level were very small between any of the younger age intervals, the major changes occurred between the fifty to fifty-nine and sixty to sixty-nine age intervals. Notable, too, was the fact that decreases at every age level were greatest for the more strenuous activities.

More direct information on the relationship between aging (as opposed to age) and sports activity is provided in a study by Zborowski (1962), who used the debate between disengagement and second activity theory as the framework for his investigation. His sample of over 200 men and women aged fifty-one to ninety-two was characterized by higher than average levels of education and income. There was a notably higher proportion of women who were single and who had been active in the labor force. Zborowski listed ninety-three recreational activities, which seemed to be ordered in terms of degree of physical stress involved. The first twenty-five to thirty activities listed were ones that are generally regarded as sports, ranging from football, hockey, and baseball to horseshoes, billiards, and table tennis. In order to estimate the direct effects of aging, Zborowski asked the respondents to note which of the activities had been pursued at age forty and "currently." Appropriate scores were assigned according to the number and type of activities pursued at both ages.

Despite reservations some researchers might have about the reliability of the anamnestic method of data collection, these comparative data showed a clear relationship between chronological age and physical activity. The most important change was an average 60 percent decrease in reported levels of participation in sports and athletic activities between age forty and "current age." Zborowski posited that this decrease is partly a function of normative expectations rather than aging per se (1962, p. 306), a conclusion that supports our self-fulfilling-prophecy contention. His explanation is based on data that showed a statistically significant decrease in the mean scores for *group* activities requiring physical exertion, while changes in the mean scores for *solitary* sports activities requiring similar physical exertion were not statistically significant.

Similar to the earlier discussion of life-cycle pattern consistency, this study found a general tendency in older men and women to retain patterns of physical activity that had existed at an earlier age. Despite this constancy, it was shown that group-centered physical activity decreased noticeably with age, suggesting the influence of age-related negative expectations and corresponding restrictions on behavior. The continual pattern of physical activity in solitary sports appears to be one mode of the older person's adaptation to negative stereotypes and sanctions imposed in our age-caste society.

Current Research

Before discussing the initial results of the research which was recently undertaken, the demographic potential for sports activity among the older population can be specified. This potential population of older sports participants can be estimated from national survey data on the health and disability status of the older population. Table 4 provides data on activity limitation due to chronic conditions from the 1973 Health Interview Survey (Public Health Service, 1974). There was a very slight increase from 1972 to 1973 in both minor and major activity limitation within the total population as well as for the older population in the United States (Public Health Service, 1973). Nevertheless, in 1973 more than 50 percent of all people age sixty-five and over reported no activity limitation, with women faring somewhat better than men. Over 40 percent of the men age sixty-five and over reported limitation in some major activity, such as the physical ability to work. The corresponding proportions for 1973 differ little from those reported for 1968–1969, when 54 percent of the older men and 60 percent of the older women had no activity limitation from chronic illnesses (Public Health Service, 1971).

More recent public survey data indicate that these activity levels have changed only slightly in the most recent years. When one includes the approximately 5 percent of older people who are institutionalized, these data show that a total of about one-seventh (14

Table 4

Percent Distribution of Persons with Limitations in Activity
due to Chronic Conditions,[1] by Degree of Limitation, by Sex, and by Age:
United States, 1973

Sex and Age	Total Population	With No Activity Limitation	With Minor Activity Limitation[2]	With Limitation in Major Activity[2]
Both sexes				
All ages	100.0	86.5	3.3	10.2
45–64	100.0	76.7	4.9	18.4
65 and over	100.0	55.9	6.4	37.7
Males				
All ages	100.0	86.5	3.3	10.2
45–64	100.0	75.7	5.2	19.1
65 and over	100.0	53.7	4.5	41.8
Females				
All ages	100.0	86.6	3.3	10.1
45–64	100.0	77.5	4.7	17.8
65 and over	100.0	57.4	7.8	34.8

1. Chronic conditions are those that were known to exist three months prior to the date of the health interview.

2. Major Activity Limitation: refers to ability to work, keep house, etc. Minor Activity Limitation: refers to all other activities not included above, such as recreation and sports.

Source: Adapted from U.S. Public Health Service, National Center for Health Statistics. "Current Estimates from the Health Interview Survey: United States 1973:, Series 10, No. 95 (Washington, D.C.: United States Government Printing Office), October 1974.

percent) of the elderly consider themselves in poor health. Moreover, while over 80 percent of noninstitutionalized older persons reported some type of chronic condition or impairment, less than 18 percent of these persons had any limitation on mobility (Brotman, 1980).

It can be seen from these data that there is no serious activity limitation from chronic conditions for over two-thirds of all older Americans. Yet, from the studies referred to earlier, it is known that less than 5 percent of the older population are active participants in sports. Thus, there exists a demographic potential in

1980 for over 16 million Americans age sixty-five and older who could conceivably be active participants in some form of sports.

In an attempt to verify the findings of the research discussed earlier, we have sampled a group of older people in a coastal community of over 70,000 people in southern California to determine their degree of physical and sports activity at earlier stages in their life cycles.[1] A second, smaller sample, using the same survey instrument, was taken from a high aged-density neighborhood in Los Angeles. The ninety-six respondents from these combined samples ranged in age from sixty to ninety-five, of whom thirty-eight percent were men (slightly below the national average of 42 percent). The median age of the women was seventy-six while for the men it was seventy-four. The sample represented a variety of living arrangements. Almost 60 percent of the respondents were living in residential group quarters, in this case middle- and upper-income private retirement hotel complexes. Another twenty-five percent lived in private quarters (the Los Angeles group). The remaining sixteen percent lived independently, but were also participants in a county nutrition program at a senior citizens center in the coast community.

The survey questionnaire elicited information on the respondent's age and date of birth, sex, marital status, highest education level attained, major lifetime occupation, current labor-force status, and any health or physical impairments that limited his or her activity or mobility. A list of various sports and physical activities was provided in the questionnaire for each of four age-related life-cycle stages: current (i.e., age sixty and over), during ages forty to fifty-nine, during ages twenty to thirty-nine, and during high school and/or college years. Physical activities included types of dancing, conditioning exercises, bicycling, walking, and gardening. Sports activities included golf, swimming, tennis, bowling, skating, volleyball, basketball, baseball, football, etc. There was room to specify types of activities other than those provided in the list. For each activity respondents were asked to report the average amount of time per week per year that it occurred, and whether or not it was undertaken as an organized group activity.

Because the degree of physical exertion is an important consideration in determining whether old people desire and are able to participate in various sports, an estimate of the energy cost for each reported activity was made. In the first section of this paper it was noted how conditions of physical stress can have important bearing on a person's physiological ability to participate in various activities. It is assumed here that inadequate physical conditioning, which is strongly linked to the absence of regular physical activity during earlier life-cycle stages, will militate against the older person's ability to participate in sports. Each activity was given a score on energy cost, which was estimated by the ratio of the work metabolic rate (wmr) to the basal metabolic rate (bmr). The wmr/bmr scores can range from a low of 1.0 to a finite higher number, depending on the type of activity involved. A score of 1.0 indicates that an activity consumes no more energy than the basal metabolic rate.

Reiff et al. (1967) have documented these scores for most physical activities and their measures have been used for this study. Because the energy cost measure is a ratio, it controls for individual differences in body weight and eliminates the need to account for differences in caloric expenditure. Thus, two individuals with notably different body weights will nevertheless have the same relative energy expenditure for a given activity, when measured by the wmr/bmr ratio. The Reiff et al. tables show, for example, that bowling requires an average energy expenditure (i.e., physiological stress) that is three times the individual's basal metabolic rate, while more strenuous activities like football and handball require twelve times the basal metabolic rate.

The incidence of chronic conditions that limited physical activity in our sample was compared with that of the older population in general. The total sample in this study closely mirrored the national older population in terms of activity limitation, with 56 percent reporting no minor or major activity limitation due to chronic conditions (but not including two respondents who specified "old age" as a limitation). However, distinct differences by sex were noted. Among the older women in the sample, 53 percent reported no limitations to activity (slightly below the national average). For the men, only 28 percent reported activity limitations due to chronic conditions, as opposed to the national average of 46 percent in 1973. The men in this sample are far less afflicted with limitations due to chronic conditions than are their age peers in the country as a whole. There has been no attempt to estimate the bias that this difference may have introduced into the findings.

The data from the different sample subpopulations were grouped to create a sufficiently large number of cases for statistical analysis. Because the number of activities reported at each life-cycle stage by each respondent was quite low, this initial part of the research dichotomized the life cycle into a younger age level (i.e., below age sixty) and a current or older age level (i.e., age sixty and over). Because it was necessary to rely on the respondents'

memories, it is suspected that some loss occurred in data on activities reported for the earlier age categories. Despite this problem,
the grouped data revealed higher frequencies of physical and sport
activity for the group when they were younger.

Among those questionnaires that were complete (N = 89), a total
of 126 activities were mentioned for the older-age category and 169
for the younger-age category. Table 5 shows the proportion of
respondents reporting particular activities. It is clear that walking,
conditioning exercises, and gardening comprise the bulk of
physical activities at the older ages. Indeed, when the number of
responses for these three types of activity are omitted from the
total number of mentions, only thirty-five responses remain (see

Table 5

Percent of Respondents Reporting Physical Activity,
by Type of Activity and by Age Group

Type of Activity	Age 60 and Over	Under Age 60
Walking	56.2	9.6
Conditioning exercises	36.9	6.8
Gardening	31.5	11.0
Dancing (all forms)	17.8	12.3
Swimming	12.3	30.1
Bicycling	5.5	4.1
Hiking/climbing	2.7	20.5
Golf	2.7	15.1
Outdoor bowling	2.7	0.0
Indoor bowling	1.4	5.5
Putting green	1.4	0.0
Volleyball	1.4	12.3
Fishing/canoeing	0.0	5.5
Track	0.0	6.8
Baseball	0.0	16.4
Basketball	0.0	21.9
Football	0.0	5.5
Handball	0.0	4.1
Tennis	0.0	31.5
Skating (all forms)	0.0	2.7
Hockey	0.0	1.4

Table 6). Thus, after excluding walking, conditioning exercises, gardening, and dancing, the remaining reported activities in older age accounted for only 17.5 percent of the total, as compared to 82.8 percent in the under age sixty category. As seen in Table 5, all of these other activities represent sports activities requiring various degrees of physical exertion and group participation.

The respondents mentioned a total of 169 physical and sports activities in their younger years. In order to avoid artificial inflation of the number of activities in this earlier age period, no activity was counted more than once for each respondent, even if it was listed in each of the three earlier life-cycle stages. For example, if tennis was listed in all three stages from high school/college through age forty to fifty-nine, it was recorded only once as an activity in the younger age category. Tennis, swimming, basketball, and hiking/climbing had the highest proportion of responses for the younger age level.

As expected, this sample of older people, not unlike the elderly in general, have low participation rates in traditional sports that are associated with younger age. Except for swimming, the activities they do undertake require the lowest levels of physical exertion. The decrease between the two age levels in total activities per se is just over 25 percent.

When walking is eliminated from both sets of responses, however, the decrease in activity between the two age periods is over 45 percent. When conditioning exercises, gardening, and dancing are also eliminated, the decrease in the more strenuous types of activity and sports becomes 84.3 percent (see Table 6). It is interesting to note that most of the strenuous sports listed in earlier ages did not even appear once in the older-age category and that most of these are group participation sports.

These data confirm the findings of the studies noted earlier. The sharp decrease with age in strenuous sports activity, especially those requiring group participation, is a consistent pattern among older Americans. Physiological restrictions seem to be operating along with sociocultural barriers in limiting the activity of these older people. For the small proportion of the elderly who remained active in sports such as swimming, bicycling, and golf, there was almost universal agreement in the reason for doing so—to keep fit and maintain one's health.

In this initial stage of the study, two hypotheses were tested:

Table 6

Number, Proportion, and Percent Change in Mentions of
Selected Physical Activities, by Life Cycle Age Category

| | Age Group | | | | Percent Change |
| | Age 60 and Over | | Under Age 60 | | Percent Change |
	Number	Percent Remaining	Number	Percent Remaining	Under 60 to 60+
Total frequency of mentions	126	100.0	169	100.0	−25.4
Frequency of mentions remaining after elimination:					
Walking	85	67.5	162	95.9	−45.6
Conditioning Exercises	58	46.0	157	92.9	−63.1
Gardening	35	27.8	149	88.2	−76.5
Dancing	22	17.5	140	82.8	−84.3

(1) that despite the large average decrease in physical activity between the younger and older-age levels, those who were physically active during the earlier life-cycle stages were more likely to be so in the later stage; and

(2) that there is a positive relationship between socioeconomic status and consistency in lifetime physical activity.

To test these hypotheses the energy costs measured by the wmr/bmr scores were assigned for each of the specified activities, based on the average hours/week/year that the respondent reported for each of the two age categories.

Spearman rank order correlation coefficients were computed, using ranked pairs as measured by the energy expenditure for each individual in his or her activities at the two age levels. Subjects were also grouped into educational and occupational categories as indicators of socioeconomic status. Because of the small sample size, these groupings were dichotomized into non-college versus college educational level (at least one year of college) and blue-collar versus white-collar occupational level.

The analysis bore out both hypotheses. Spearman's rho for the relationship between the ranked pairs of energy-level expenditures among the respondents was 0.2765, which is significant at the .025 level for a one-tailed test (Student's distribution). Thus, there is a positive relationship between levels of physical activity in the younger (under age sixty) and older (age sixty and over) life-cycle stages. The second hypothesis of a positive relationship between socioeconomic status and consistency in level of physical activity was also accepted, with Spearman's rho at 0.1660 (significant in a one-tailed test at the .05 level). That is, subjects who had the highest rates of continuous lifetime physical activity were slightly more likely to have had white-collar occupations and to have achieved high levels of education (i.e., at least one year of college).

If one were to ignore the wmr/bmr scores in analyzing the subjects' physical-activity-level differences between the two age periods, the information would be less precise. Nevertheless, other socioeconomic differences can be discerned by considering whether or not some type of change occurred in activity level between the two age periods. Although the small sample size limits the ability to generalize from these data, some instructive information can be gleaned concerning the socioeconomic characteristics related to activity-level changes among this group of older people.

One intriguing question concerns the extent to which activity existed in old age when no physical activity was reported for the younger age period. In only five cases out of ninety-six did this phenomenon occur. When the sample was broken down into the four combinations for low-high educational level and blue-collar/white-collar occupation, three of these five cases were white-collar/high-education subjects. Another respondent in this activity change group had a blue-collar/low-education background. The physical activities undertaken by these four respondents were more strenuous than walking, gardening, or conditioning exercises. It appears that this special minority of older respondents put forth a concerted effort to attain a high level of sports and physical activity in old age; one that had been missing in earlier periods of their lives. The fifth respondent in this group had a white-collar/low-education background, but undertook only the less strenuous activity of conditioning exercises.

Other evidence indicates differences within socioeconomic groups between those who maintained a continuous activity sequence over the life cycle and those who did not. Because the sample here is not representative of the older population as a whole, the activity pattern differences within the social class groupings in the sample can only be described for this group. Table 7 provides data on the number and proportion of respondents within each class category who were either continuously active or not continuously active across the two age categories (under sixty and age sixty and over). Subjects who reported physical or sports activity during the earlier period, but none at all in old age, are defined as "not continuously active." Those who reported activity during both age periods are defined as "continuously active." This group is further distinguished by the level of activity pursued in old age. Those with "low-level" activity are respondents who reported only walking, gardening, and/or conditioning exercises. Respondents reporting more strenuous sports and physical activities such as tennis, golf, swimming, jogging, etc. fall into the "high level" group. Those respondents who were active only in the older-age period or who were never physically active (three respondents fall into the latter category) are excluded from these data.

Table 7 indicates that among our sample of older people, those with blue-collar/high-education backgrounds would be most likely to maintain high levels of physical and sports activity, while white-collar/low-education subjects were by far the least likely to have maintained any regular physical activity in old age (42 percent were

Table 7

Percent of Respondents Reporting Continuous and Non-Continuous Activity Patterns, by Occupational and Educational Background and by Level of Old-Age Activity (number of respondents in parentheses)

	Continuously Active[1]		Not Continuously Active[2]	Total
	High Level[3]	Low Level[4]		
Blue-Collar/Low Education	$50_{(8)}$	$38_{(6)}$	$12_{(2)}$	$100_{(16)}$
White-collar/Low Education	$32_{(6)}$	$26_{(5)}$	$42_{(8)}$	$100_{(19)}$
Blue-Collar/High Education	$63_{(5)}$	$25_{(2)}$	$12_{(1)}$	$100_{(8)}$
White-Collar/High Education	$44_{(20)}$	$38_{(17)}$	$18_{(8)}$	$100_{(45)}$

1. Continuously Active: regular physical activity continued into old age.

2. Not continuously Active: no regular physical activity undertaken in old age.

3. High Level: those activities that are more strenuous than walking, gardening, or conditioning exercises.

4. Low Level: includes only walking, gardening, and/or conditioning exercises.

not continuously active). Blue-collar respondents in both educational levels had the highest overall proportion reporting continuous activity. The white-collar/high education group also remained quite active in old age, but were less likely than either of the blue-collar groups to have pursued more strenuous types of activities.

Discussion and Implications

Our study and the findings of other sociological and physiological studies allow us to better understand the low degree of participation among older people in sports and other physical activities. For the large majority of those older people who remain at least partially active, there is a distinct trend toward substituting less strenuous, solitary activities for the more strenuous and group-oriented physical and sports activities of the earlier years. In the study reported here the most frequently cited of these less strenuous activities were walking, conditioning exercises, and gardening. Except for the somewhat strenuous activities of swimming, jogging, tennis, and golf, older people do not generally pursue sports into the later years of life, especially group-oriented sports. For the few older people who do, a consistent pattern of lifetime physical activity is a key factor.

There are a number of implications that can be drawn. The physiological decrements that occur with age due to decreases in physical activity over the life cycle have been documented. But it is known, too, that these physiological decrements need not occur to the degree that they do. If one's goal is to improve the general health and well-being of people in old age, it is clear that higher levels of consistent physical activity should be fostered during young adult and middle ages. One deterrent to this effort is found in the negative value orientations placed upon aging in our society, especially through the disengagement perspective of "successful aging." The self-fulfilling prophecy based upon these negative orientations can be altered by redefining our cultural perspectives on aging and the role prescriptions associated with the aging process. Moreover, the physiological studies revealed in this paper have shown that physical decrements that severely limit activity as age increases need not exist to such a degree.

It seems, then, that the potential exists for increased participation by older men and women in sports activity, perhaps best exemplified by swimming, golf, softball, volleyball, tennis, handball, track/field, bicycling, and hiking (i.e., non-contact sports that nevertheless require medium to high levels of physical activity). Even contact sports such as touch football, soccer, and field hockey are feasible sports for older people, given appropriate rules of play and medical standards for participation. Regardless of which kind of sports activity is involved, it is known that over sixty percent of the older population in general are not hampered in activity by chronic illnesses, creating a potential pool of over 15 million people age sixty-five and over from which to draw. For the advocate of increased physical activity among the elderly, the most likely candidates in this pool would be those middle-aged and older people with blue-collar occupational backgrounds or white-collar/high education backgrounds. Their consistency has been shown in pursuing sports and physical activity into the older years. A more concerted effort would seem to be needed to foster greater continuity in physical activity for those with white-collar/low-education backgrounds.

A promising view of the future changes that could occur can be found through a cohort developmental approach. Because schooling tends to expose people to regular physical activity, there is a strong association between activity level and educational background. A cursory study of current and future cohorts of older people provides encouraging prospects in this regard. As the general population becomes better educated, so too will succeeding five-year age cohorts who enter the middle- and older-age categories (known as the cohort effect). In 1970 the population aged sixty-five and over contained just under 12 percent who had completed one or more years of college and 28 percent who had one to four years of high school education. By 1979, 8 percent of the older population were college graduates. Cohort projections of the old population in the future indicate that in 1980 15 percent will have had some college and 44 percent will have had one to four years of high school. By 1990 these proportions will be approximately 18 percent and 50 percent, respectively (United States Bureau of the Census, 1972). The combination of this growing number and proportion of higher educated older people with a concerted effort to reduce and eliminate age-caste values and roles could yield a far more sports oriented, physically active, and healthy older population.

An empirical example of this process currently exists. It is aptly called the Senior Olympics, a non-profit organization based in Santa Monica, California. Founded in 1969, it held its first competition in 1970 in three sports (diving, swimming, track/field), and was open to people age forty and over. It has grown tremendously in the short period since its inception. Its 200 participants in 1970 grew to over 2,500 in 1975, with competition in over thirty sports categories for anyone age twenty-five and over. In 1979 there were close to 5,000 participants in almost fifty sports categories. All competitive events are stratified into five-year age groups and every event is open to both men and women. In 1980 the twenty to twenty-four age group will be added to the roster of eligible participants.[2]

There are now more than 135 subevents within the broad categories of sports competition. Some of the major sport categories are archery, bowling, softball, bicycling, basketball, decathlon, gymnastics, ice skating, fencing, handball, racquetball, soccer, tennis, sailing, swimming and diving, skiing, and numerous track and field events. Of the 135 subcategories in 1979, competitors aged sixty and over participated in 88 of them (65 percent of all event types). Moreover, in the first year of competition approximately 5 percent of the participants were age sixty-five and over, but this proportion had risen to approximately 13 percent by 1975 (still lower than the 18.5 percent of the age twenty-five and over population that the elderly represent). In 1979 the age sixty-five and over group increased its proportion to 15 percent of all participants (age twenty-five and over). The cohort effect appears to be working along with the Senior Olympics' strong advocacy and publicity program to attract greater numbers and proportions of older men and women (Blaney, 1979). The Senior Olympics now has its own dues paying membership as an association. Given the demographic potential that exists, there is reason to believe that these increases will continue well into the future.

Extensions of our research are planned during the coming year in cooperation with the Senior Olympics staff. The population of active sports participants provides an excellent opportunity to test the hypotheses used here for the initial study. It is expected that this much larger sample will provide greater information and confidence in our research results. This knowledge will not only pertain to life-cycle consistency in physical activity and its relation to sports activity in old age, but will also provide social psychological data on differences in attitudes toward aging. It is expected that most older sports participants will mirror one of the slogans of the Senior Olympics: "Creating the New Adult Image." With each succeeding cohort of older Americans this improved image of aging and old age should become dominant. And along with these new attitudes should follow greater physical and athletic activity among the older population.

Notes

1. I am indebted to Ms. Marcy Stanley for organizing the data collection in this community.
2. I am indebted to Mr. Warren Blaney of the Senior Olympics for providing much of the information on the Senior Olympics participants.

Works Cited

Baley, J. A. "Recreation and the Aging Process." *Research Quarterly of the American Association of Health* 27 (1955): 1–7.

Barry, A. J., et al. "The Effects of Physical Conditioning on Older Individuals. I. Work Capacity, Circulatory-Respiratory Function, and Work Electrocardiogram." *Journal of Gerontology* 21 (1966): 182–91.

Blaney, W. W. *Keep Healthy and Happy Always*. Los Angeles: Senior Sports International, 1979.

Brotman, H. B. "Every Ninth American." Report to the United States Senate Special Committee on Aging. Washington, D.C.: United States Government Printing Office, 1980.

Cumming, E., and Henry, W. *Growing Old: The Process of Disengagement.* New York: Basic Books, 1961.

Cunningham, D. A., et al. "Active Leisure Time Activities as Related to Age Among Males in a Total Population." *Journal of Gerontology* 23 (1968): 551-56.

Cutler, N. E. "Age Variations in the Dimensionality of Life Satisfaction." *Journal of Gerontology* 34 (1979): 573-78.

Davies, C. T., et al. "Does Exercise Promote Health?" *Lancet* 2 (1963): 930-32.

deVries, H. A. "Physiological Effects of an Exercise Training Regimen Upon Men Aged 52-88." *Journal of Gerontology* 25 (1970): 325-36.

Dowd, J. "Aging as Exchange: A Preface to Theory." *Journal of Gerontology* 30 (1975): 584-94.

Dowd, J. "Exchange Rates and Old People." *Journal of Gerontology* 35 (1980): 596-602.

Durnin, J. V. G. A. "Exercise." Pp. 301-26 in O. G. Edholm and A. L. Bacharch, eds. *The Physiology of Human Survival.* London: Academic Press, 1965.

Eisenstadt, S. N. *From Generation to Generation: Age Groups and Social Structure.* Glencoe: Free Press, 1956.

Filsinger, E., and Sauer, W. J. "An Empirical Typology of Adjustment to Aging." *Journal of Gerontology* 33(1978): 437-45.

Fischer, A., et al. "The Effect of Systematic Physical Activity on Maximal Performance and Functional Capacity in Senescent Men." *Internationale Zeitschrift Fuer Angewandte Physiologie Einschliesslich Arbeitsphysiologie* 21 (1965): 269-304.

Gulliver, P. H. "Age Differentiation." Pp. 157-61 in D. L. Sills ed, *International Encyclopedia of the Social Sciences,* Vol. 1. New York: Macmillan Company and The Free Press, 1968.

Havighurst, R., and Albrecht, R. *Older People.* New York: Longmans, Green, 1953.

Homans, G. C. *The Human Group.* New York: Harcourt, Brace, 1950.

―――. *Social Behavior: Its Elementary Forms.* New York: Harcourt, Brace, and World, 1961.

Kenyon, G. S., and Loy, J. W. "Toward a Sociology of Sport." *Journal of Health, Physical Education, and Recreation* 36 (1965): 24-69.

Kraus, H., and Raab, W. *Hypokinetic Disease.* Springfield, Illinois: Charles C. Thomas, 1961.

Kuypers, J. A., and Bengtson, V. L. "Social Breakdown and Competence." *Human Development* 16 (1973): 181-202.

Letunov, S., and Motylyanskaya, R. "Preventative Significance of Exercise Training in Elderly Adults." Pp. 316-20 in W. Raab, ed., *Prevention of Ischemic Heart Disease.* Springfield, Illinois: Charles C. Thomas, 1966.

Maddox, G. L. "Persistence of Life Style among the Elderly: A Longitudinal Study of Patterns of Social Activity in Relation to Life Satisfaction." *Proceedings of the Seventh International Congress of Gerontology* 6 (1966): 309-11.

National Council on the Aging. *The Myth and Reality of Aging in America.* Washington, D.C.: The National Council on the Aging, 1975.

Neugarten, B. L. "Adult Personality: A Development View." *Human Development* 9 (1966): 61-73.

―――. "Adult Personality: Toward a Psychology of the Life Cycle." In E. Vinacke, ed., *Readings in General Psychology.* New York: American Book Company, 1968.

―――. "Age Norms, Age Constraints, and Adult Socialization." *American Journal of Sociology* 70 (1965): 710-17.

Opinion Research Corporation. "The Public Appraises Movies." *Survey Report.* Princeton: Motion Picture Association of America, 1957.

Pierce, R. C., and Chiriboga, D. A. "Dimensions of Adult Self-concept." *Journal of Gerontology* 34 (1979): 80–85.

Reiff, G. G., et al. "Assessment of Physical Activity by Questionnaire and Interview." Pp. 336–71 in M. J. Karvonen and A. J. Barry, eds., *Physical Activity and the Heart.* Springfield, Illinois: Charles C. Thomas, 1967.

Riley, M. W. "Social Gerontology and the Age Stratification of Society." *The Gerontologist* 11 (1971): 79–87.

Riley, M. W., et al. "Socialization for the Middle and Later Years." Pp. 951–82 in D. A. Goslin, ed., *Handbook of Socialization Theory and Research.* Chicago: Rand McNally, 1969.

Rose, A. M. "A Current Theoretical Issue in Social Gerontology." *The Gerontologist* 4 (1964): 46–50.

Shock, N. W. "Physiological Aspects of Aging in Man." *Annual Review of Physiology* 23 (1961): 97–122.

Sorokin, P. A. *Social and Cultural Mobility.* Glencoe: Free Press, 1959.

Turk, H. "An Inquiry into the Undersocialized Conception of Man." *Social Forces* 43 (1965): 518–21.

United States Bureau of the Census. *Current Population Reports.* Series P-25, No. 478. "Demographic Projections for the United States." Washington, D.C.: United States Government Printing Office, 1972.

United States Public Health Service. National Center for Health Statistics. *Health in the Later Years of Life.* Washington, D.C.: United States Government Printing Office, 1971.

———. National Center for Health Statistics. "Current Estimates from the Health Interview Survey: United States 1972." Series 10, No. 94. Washington, D.C.: United States Government Printing Office, 1973.

———. National Center for Health Statistics. "Current Estimates from the Health Interview Survey: United States 1973." Series 10, No. 95. Washington, D.C.: United States Government Printing Office, 1974.

Wessel, J. A., and Van Huss, W. D. "The Influence of Physical Activity and Age on Exercise Adaptation of Women Aged 20–69 Years." *Journal of Sport Medicine* 9 (1969): 173–80.

Wilensky, H. L. "Orderly Careers and Social Participation: The Impact of Work History on Social Integration in the Middle Mass." *American Sociological Review* 26 (1961): 521–39.

Zborowski, M. "Aging and Recreation." *Journal of Gerontology* 17 (1962): 302–9.

PART III
Differentiation in Specific Sports

8
Introduction to Part III

The first two chapters of this part of the book treat some of the facts of social differentiation that result from the socialization process as it responds to an organizational environment. The third chapter in this part, using the medium of baseball, examines explanations of various social phenomena including social differentiation. These chapters depart from the focus in part II where the concentration was on stages in the life cycle and the processes of socialization at each of those stages that lead to social differentiation. In this part, the focus shifts to the examination of specific sports. D. Stanley Eitzen and Norman R. Yetman update their important work on discrimination in major team sports in the United States. James D. Davidson breaks new ground using a classical sociological analysis of social stratification factors to examine golf. Leon H. Warshay focuses his attention on baseball using it to test various sociological theories; first inductively and then deductively.

Eitzen and Yetman begin by indicating that much of the early impetus for studies in the sociology of sport came from interest in race relations. They note that, at this time, there are proportionally more blacks participating in the three major team sports than there are in the general population. People believe that this indicates black progress in the U.S. while critics say it masks racism.

Eitzen and Yetman look at three factors to determine whether racism and discrimination are still a factor in sports: the assignment of playing position, performance differential, and reward and authority structures. They begin by reviewing the phenomenon of stacking; i.e., blacks and whites compete for the same positions but not against each other. They conclude that stacking still exists because blacks are kept out of central positions that involve more interaction and outcome control of games. This phenomenon occurs because blacks are stereotyped by whites who make position placement decisions. Black stereotyping by whites has an effect on choices made by blacks as was indicated in chapter 6. This position is supported when we see that blacks move from central to noncentral positions as they go from high school, to college, and to the pros. This phenomenon, however, is no longer present in professional basketball due to black player dominance of that game. In spite of this, managerial positions in professional basketball are still predominantly white although the players are predominantly black.

In terms of rewards, with performances held constant in the major team sports, blacks are paid less than whites. They get less off-season pay and fewer endorsements. When officiating is examined, it is disproportionately white and stacked so that blacks are not head officials but are supplementary. There are no black head coaches in the National Football League or black managers in baseball (Maury Wills and Frank Robinson, at this writing, had just been hired to manage), and only 9 percent of National Basketball Association head coaches are blacks. In the history of major league baseball there have been only two permanent black managers, one temporary black manager, and a few coaches who are usually found on the first base lines.

In the colleges there are few black coaches. There has been some improvement, however, in adding black head coaches in basketball. The lack of black coaches is primarily due to the stacking phenomenon among players. Coaches are chosen from those who played central positions involving outcome control during their careers. Since few blacks get into those positions few are likely to be chosen for coaching or managerial positions after they retire. The one area of general improvement for players and coaches is in college basketball, which seems to be providing more equal opportunity based on ability. This is associated with the decline in stacking and the addition of black coaches.

Davidson's classic piece of sociological analysis looks at race, religion, gender, education, occupation, and income as they effect golfing behavior. The aspects of behavior that are examined are: who plays regularly, who plays where, and who plays with whom. This chapter fills a gap in the literature by helping to clarify relationships between socioeconomic status variables and dimensions of sports participation. Race, religion, and gender are mediated through socioeconomic status in their effect on golfing behavior.

Education has an indirect effect, but occupation and income have direct effects, and these are partially determined by education.

Davidson describes the game of golf and where it is played, on private and public courses. Then he turns to the question of who plays and indicates the structural characteristics of occupations that are important. While starting to play golf is largely a product of the financial resources of one's family, those most likely to continue to play have flexible working hours, are in occupations that need community contact, and fall primarily into middle-status categories. Women, for example, are not found playing golf as much as men because of traditional role differences and their typically low social status.

Blacks in general are not as likely to play golf as whites because of their relatively low socioeconomic standing. Moreover, golf is not viewed as a means of upward mobility for blacks.

People in high social strata *may* play on private courses where they have memberships, or they may choose to play on public courses. People in lower social strata *must* play on public courses because they cannot afford to belong to the private clubs. Higher education's contribution to higher income produces these players at the private courses. Occupational members who need good contacts can find them at private clubs and are likely to be found playing there. It follows that blacks are excluded from private clubs because of socioeconomic and educational standing in addition to out-and-out discrimination. There are very few black private golf clubs.

Golf is more in the cultural tradition of Protestants, but with the increasing secularization of society all religious groups tend to play. "Liberals" among religious groups are more likely to play while "conservatives" are not. Davidson points out that there are many more Jewish than Catholic private golf clubs. Catholics who have been more interested in social assimilation than Jews have tended to join Protestant clubs. It is liberals in all religions, however, who are most likely to belong to private clubs.

Women belong to private clubs because membership is on a family basis. Men and women do not generally play together, however, because of dissimilar ability and possible sexual overtones. People of similar abilities play together as do people who have compatible occupational interests. Davidson concludes that, on the basis of his analysis, golf legitimates and perpetuates social divisions while reflecting the same social divisions that already exist in society.

Warshay starts his chapter by pointing out that baseball is a game suited to contemplation. In Durkheimian terms, baseball has a mechanical, rural image. Among the other unique social features of baseball that are detailed, the most important is that baseball depends on the mass or a general public rather than on a compact crowd. One does not have to attend a game or even watch baseball on television to be interested. The information is readily available and can be discussed without first-hand experience.

Differentiation factors are also discussed in this chapter. Blacks were admitted to baseball before they were admitted to any other major team sports but discrimination still exists and black players react. For example, one pattern is for them to relate to blacks (not whites) both inside and outside of the game. Warshay points out once again that blacks are accepted where individual performance skills are valued but not where interaction skills are important. In those positions and managerial roles that deal with outcome control we find few if any blacks. In addition, women are not included in major league baseball because of the surrounding structure of a sexist society.

There are additional stratification factors to be accounted for besides the class origins of players and spectators. Research should account for stratification along the following dimensions: position, stars and ordinary ball players, who owns clubs, cliques and statuses on teams, what happens to players after they retire, and various styles of play (e.g., the hustler versus the more casual approach). These are all suggestions that could be applied to any sport.

After outlining the micro and macro social factors involved in baseball, Warshay turns to the various social theories to see what they might contribute to the analysis of baseball as a set of social structural arrangements and processes. Interactionism could explore actual interaction, unexpected outcomes, focus on the expressive aspect, and in terms of collective behavior focus on the audience of baseball.

Functionalism could look at baseball from the perspective of society. It would deal with value reinforcement and how minorities are assimilated through baseball. Functionalism would deal with the various functions and disfunctions of baseball perhaps emphasizing instrumental and expressive dimensions. Finally, functionalists would look at baseball as fulfilling functional imperatives inside and outside of baseball.

Exchange theorists could look at baseball as a process of

bargaining and negotiation in a competitive framework. They would point out that minorities and women have fewer exchange values and get fewer bonuses and endorsements, and that women in fact are kept out. The functional conflict tradition would look at the political aspects of baseball and its scarcity and look at baseball in terms of interest groups.

The Marxist tradition would see baseball as part of the superstructure of the society in helping people to develop false consciousness. Marxists would point out that baseball is a privately owned game and would criticize other theories. Baseball from a Marxist perspective would be seen as part of a dialectical process involving many other aspects of social structure.

In the last chapter of this book an attempt will be made to integrate the factors discussed in this part with the factors discussed in part II, using the theoretical materials that were developed earlier.

9

Racial Dynamics in American Sports: Continuity and Change

D. STANLEY EITZEN and NORMAN R. YETMAN

Introduction

No other aspect of sport in America has generated more socio-logical interest than race relations. Indeed, a strong case could be made for the thesis that the salience of race in organized sport in American society has been instrumental in generating much of the burgeoning interest in the sociology of sport.[1] While there have been attempts to use organized sports as a laboratory in which to test broader issues concerning race relations theory (see Blalock, 1962; McClendon and Eitzen, 1975), such studies have, unfortunately, been the exception rather than the rule. The primary sociological interest in race and sport has been the general issue of racism in American sport. Not fortuitously, this research interest undoubtedly has been influenced by the racial turmoil of the late 1950s and 1960s, which generated increased academic and critical attention to all phases of black life in America. This interest was enhanced by the fact that since the early 1960s the percentages of black competitors in each of the major professional team sports (football, basketball, and baseball) have exceeded their proportion (11 percent) of the total United States population.[2] By 1979, 71 percent of all professional basketball players were black, while they comprised more than 47 percent of all professional football and 17 percent of major league baseball players.[3] The disproportionate presence of blacks by itself should raise important sociological questions, especially when black prominence in sports is compared to the relative underrepresentation of members of other American ethnic and racial groups.

The larger proportion of blacks and the prominence of black superstars such as Kareem Abdul-Jabbar, Jim Rice, and Earl Campbell have led many Americans—black and white—to infer that collegiate and professional athletics have provided an avenue of mobility for blacks unavailable elsewhere in American society. Sports, thus, seem to have "done something for" black Americans. Many commentators, however—social scientists, journalists, and black athletes themselves—have argued that black visibility in collegiate and professional sports has merely served to mask the racism that pervades the entire sports establishment. According to these critics, the existence of racism in collegiate and professional sports is especially insidious because the promoters of, and commentators on, athletics have made sports sacred by projecting an image of it as the single institution in America relatively immune from racism.

In previous papers (Yetman and Eitzen, 1971, 1972, 1977), we have examined the phenomenon of racial discrimination in American sports—in particular, collegiate basketball. This chapter examines three aspects of the athletic world that have been alleged to be racially biased—the assignment of playing positions, performance differentials, and reward and authority structures. The analysis will be limited primarily to three major professional team sports (baseball, basketball, and football) where blacks are found most prominently. In addition to describing and explaining the current situation in these sports, the attempt in this chapter will be to determine whether any substantial changes have occurred or can be anticipated in the future.

Stacking

One of the best-documented forms of discrimination in both the college and the professional ranks is popularly known as *stacking* (Loy and McElvogue, 1970; Brower, 1972; Eitzen and Sanford, 1975; Madison and Landers, 1976; Eitzen and Yetman, 1977; Eitzen and Tessendorf, 1978; Schneider and Eitzen, 1979). The term refers to situations in which minority-group members are relegated to specific team roles and excluded from competing for others. The consequence is often that intra-team competition for starting roles is between members of the same race (e.g., those competing as running backs are black, while those competing as quarterbacks are white). For example, Rosenblatt (1967) noted that while there are twice as many pitchers on a baseball team as there are outfielders, in 1965 there were three times as many black outfielders as pitchers.

Examination of the stacking phenomenon was first undertaken by Loy and McElvogue (1970), who argued that racial segregation in sports is a function of centrality—that is, spatial location—in a team sports unit. To explain positional racial segregation in sports, they combined organizational principles advanced by Hubert M. Blalock and Oscar Grusky. Blalock has argued that:

> 1. The lower the degree of purely social interaction on the job, the lower the degree of (racial) discrimination.
> 2. To the extent that performance level is relatively independent of skill in interpersonal relations, the lower the degree of (racial) discrimination (Blalock, 1962:246).

Grusky's notions about the formal structure of organizations are similar:

> All else being equal, the more central one's spatial location: 1) the greater the likelihood dependent or coordinative tasks will be performed, and 2) the greater the rate of interaction with the occupants of other positions. Also, the performance of dependent tasks is positively related to frequency of interaction. (Grusky, 1963: 346)

Combining these propositions, Loy and McElvogue hypothesized that "racial segregation in professional team sports is positively related to centrality." Their analysis of football (where the central positions are quarterback, center, offensive guard, and linebacker) and baseball (where the central positions are the infield, catcher, and pitcher) demonstrated that the central positions were indeed overwhelmingly manned by whites, while blacks were over-represented in the peripheral (noncentral) positions. Examining the data for baseball in 1967, they found that 83 percent of those listed as infielders were white, while 49 percent of the outfielders were black. The white's proportion was greatest in the catcher (96 percent) and pitcher (94 percent) positions, the most central in baseball. Our data analysis from the 1975 major league baseball season showed little change from the situation described by Loy and McElvogue in 1967. In 1975 the percentage of infielders who were white had declined slightly to 76 percent, but the outfield was still disproportionately manned by blacks (49 percent). Moreover, catcher (95 percent) and pitcher (96 percent) remained overwhelmingly white positions.[4] These percentages remained virtually the same through the 1979 season (Simons, 1980:51).

Table 1 compares the racial composition of positions in football for the 1960 and 1975 seasons. The conclusions from these data are clear. While the proportion of black players has increased dramatically during this fifteen-year period, central positions continue to be disproportionately white. One difference between 1960 and 1975 is that blacks have increasingly supplanted whites at noncentral positions. In other words, as black entry into professional football has increased, they have increasingly come to occupy primarily noncentral positions. Blacks, however, appear to have made some inroads in the central offensive positions, for example, a shift from 97 percent white to 87 percent white from 1960 to 1975.

The effects of stacking are more devastating than just limitation to noncentral positions. Peripheral positions in football depend primarily on speed and quickness, which means in effect that playing careers are shortened for persons in those positions. For example, in 1975 only 4.1 percent of the players listed in the *Football Register* in the three predominantly black positions—defensive back, running back, and wide receiver (sixty-five percent of all black players)—had been playing in the pros for ten or more years, while 14.8 percent of players listed in the three predominantly white positions—quarterback, center, and offensive guard—remained that long. The shortened careers for noncentral players have two additional deleterious consequences—less lifetime earnings and limited benefits from the Players' Pension Fund, which provides support on the basis of longevity.

The Loy and McElvogue interpretation of these data rested primarily upon a position's spatial location in a team unit. Edwards has argued, however, that the actual spatial location of a playing position is an incidental factor in the explanation of stacking. The crucial variable involved in positional segregation is the degree of outcome or leadership responsibilities found in each position. For example, quarterbacks have greater team authority

Table 1

The Distribution of White and Black Players by Position in
Major League Football: 1960 and 1975 (in percentages)

Playing Position	1960*		Percent Black by Position**	1975		Percent Black by Position
	White	Black		White	Black	
Kicker/Punter	1.2	0	0	9.0	.2	1.3
Quarterback	6.3	0	0	9.7	.5	3.5
Center	5.3	0	0	6.7	.5	4.9
Linebacker	11.5	3.7	4.2	17.4	8.6	26.0
Off. guard	8.0	1.8	3.1	8.7	4.5	26.9
Off. tackle	8.3	24.1	28.3	8.6	5.7	31.8
Def. front four	11.0	14.8	15.4	12.3	15.7	47.6
End/flanker	22.6	3.7	2.2	11.6	20.2	55.3
Running back	16.5	25.9	17.5	8.1	21.1	65.2
Def. back	9.3	25.9	27.5	8.1	23.2	67.3
Totals	100.0	99.9		100.2	100.2	
N =	(1991/2)	(27)	11.9	(870)	(620)	41.6

*The 1960 data are taken from Brower (1972), who obtained them from the media guides published annually by each team. Whenever a player was listed at two positions, Brower credited him as one-half at each position. Nineteen-seventy-five data are taken from the 1975 *Football Register* published annually by the *Sporting News*. Since both the media guides and the *Football Register* are published before each season, they include only information on veterans.

**Since blacks were 11.9 percent of the player population in 1960, those playing positions with the percentage black less than 11.9 percent were underrepresented. In 1975 those positions less than 41.6 percent black were underrepresented.

and ability to affect game outcome than do individuals who occupy noncentral positions (Edwards, 1973: 209).

Thus, the key is not the interaction potential of the playing position but the leadership and degree of responsibility for the game's
outcome built into the position that account for the paucity of
blacks at central positions. This is consonant with the stereotype
hypothesis advanced by Brower (specifically for football but one
that applies to other sports as well):

The combined function of centrality in terms of responsibility
and interaction provides a frame for exclusion of Blacks and

constitutes a definition of the situation for coaches and management. People in the world of professional football believe that various football positions require specific types of physically—and intellectually—endowed athletes. When these beliefs are combined with the stereotypes of Blacks and Whites, Blacks are excluded from certain positions. Normal organizational processes when interlaced with racist conceptions of the world spell out an important consequence, namely, the racial basis of the division of labor in professional football. (Brower, 1972: 27; see also Williams and Youssef, 1975)

From this perspective, then, it is the racial stereotypes of blacks' abilities that lead to the view that they are more ideally suited for those positions labeled "noncentral." For example, Brower compared the requirements for the central and noncentral positions in football and found that the former require leadership, thinking ability, highly refined techniques, stability under pressure, and responsibility for the outcome of the games. Noncentral positions, on the other hand, require athletes with speed, quickness, aggressiveness, "good hands," and "instinct"—primarily physical attributes (Brower, 1972: 3-27).

Evidence for the racial stereotype explanation for stacking is found in the paucity of blacks at the most important positions for outcome control in football (quarterback, kicker, and placekick holder). The data from Table 1 for 1975 show that of the eighty-seven quarterbacks in the league, only three were black; of the seventy punters and placekickers mentioned in the *Football Register* only one was black; and (3) of the twenty-six placekick holders not one was black.[5]

It is inconceivable that blacks lack the ability to play these positions at the professional level. Placekick holders must, for example, have "good hands," an important quality for pass receivers, two-thirds of whom were black, but not one was selected for the former role. Kicking requires a strong leg and the development of accuracy. Are blacks unable to develop strong legs or master the necessary technique? The conclusion seems inescapable that blacks are precluded from occupying leadership positions (quarterback, defensive signal caller) because subtle but widely held stereotypes of black psychological, intellectual, and leadership abilities still persist in the sports world. As a consequence, blacks are relegated to those positions where the requisite skills are speed, strength, and quick reactions, not thinking or leadership ability.

Another explanation for stacking has been advanced by

McPherson (1975), who has argued that black youths may segregate themselves into specific sport roles because they wish to emulate black stars. Contrary to the belief that "stacking" can be attributed to discriminatory acts by members of the majority group, this interpretation holds that the playing roles to which black youths aspire are those in which blacks have previously attained a high level of achievement. Since the first positions to be occupied by blacks in professional football were offensive and defensive backs and defensive linemen, subsequent imitation of their techniques by black youths has resulted in blacks being overrepresented in these positions today. Although the small sample makes his findings tentative, Brower has provided some support for this hypothesis (1972). He asked a sample of twenty-three white and twenty black high school football players what athletes they admired most and what position they would most like to play if they had the ability and opportunity. The overwhelming majority of blacks (70 percent) had only black heroes (role models) whereas whites chose heroes from both races. A important consideration is the finding that black high school athletes preferred to play at the "noncentral" positions now manned disproportionately by blacks in the pros. Brower concluded that "since the young Blacks desire to perform at the 'standard' Black positions, these findings make plain the impact and consequences of the present football position structure on succeeding generations of professional football players" (Brower, 1972: 28). Although the role-model orientation does not explain the initial discrimination, it helps to explain why, once established, the pattern of discrimination by player position tends to be maintained.

Since McPherson produced no empirical support for his explanation, Eitzen and Sanford (1975) sought to determine whether black athletes changed positions from central to noncentral more frequently than whites as they moved from high school to college to professional competition. Their data from a sample of 387 professional football players indicated that there had been a statistically significant shift by blacks from central positions to noncentral ones.[6] That blacks in high school and college occupied positions that are occupied primarily by whites in professional football casts doubt on McPherson's model. Athletic role models or heroes will most likely have greater attraction for younger individuals in high school and college than for older athletes in professional sports, but professional players were found distributed at all positions during their high school playing days. The socialization model also assumes a high degree of irrationality on the part of the player—it assumes that as he becomes older and enters more keenly competitive playing conditions, he will be more likely to seek a position because of his identification with a black star rather than because of a rational assessment of his own unique athletic skills.

It is conceivable, however, that socialization variables do contribute to the racial stacking patterns in baseball and football as noted above, but in a negative sense. That is to say, given discrimination in the allocation of playing positions (or at least the belief in its existence), young black males will consciously avoid those positions for which opportunities are (or are believed to be) low (e.g., pitcher, quarterback) and will select instead those positions where they are most likely to succeed (e.g., the outfield, running and defensive backs). Gene Washington, an all-pro wide receiver for the San Francisco Forty-Niners and the Detroit Lions, was a college quarterback at Stanford University through his sophomore year, then switched to flanker. Washington requested the change himself. "It was strictly a matter of economics. I knew a Black quarterback would have little chance in pro ball unless he was absolutely superb . . ." (quoted in Olsen, 1968a: 29; see also Pascel and Rapping, 1970; Scully, 1974; and chapter 6 for further explanation).

A final hypothesis for the existence of stacking has been suggested by Medoff (1977). His "economic hypothesis" posits that blacks are underrepresented at "central" positions because of the differences in requisite skills and costs of training for these positions compared to those for peripheral positions. Although some doubt has been cast on Medoff's interpretation (Curtis and Loy, 1978), it does represent another possible facet of discrimination, for it emphasizes how racism in society is manifested in sport.

Social scientists have extensively examined the stacking phenomenon in football and baseball but have neglected basketball. They have tended to assume that it does not occur because, as Edwards has put it:

> In basketball there is no positional centrality as is the case in football and baseball because there are no fixed zones of role responsibility attached to specific positions. . . . Nevertheless, one does find an evidence of discrimination against black athletes on integrated basketball teams. Rather than stacking black athletes in positions involving relatively less control, *since*

this is a logistical impossibility, the number of black athletes directly involved in the action at any time is simply limited. (Edwards, 1973:213; italics added)

However, Eitzen and Tessendorf (1974) reasoned that positions in basketball do vary in responsibility, in leadership, in the mental qualities of good judgment, decision making, and recognition of opponents' tactics, and in outcome control. To confirm this judgment, they undertook a content analysis of instructional books by prominent American basketball coaches to determine whether there were specific responsibilities or qualities attributed to the three playing positions—guard, forward, and center—in basketball. They discovered surprising unanimity among coaches on the attributes and responsibilities of the different positions. The guard was viewed as the team quarterback, its "floor general," and the most desired attributes for this position were the mental qualities of judgment, leadership, and dependability. The center was pictured as having the greatest amount of outcome control because that position is nearest the basket and because the offense revolves around it; the center was literally the pivot of the team's offense. Unlike the traits for other positions, the desired traits mentioned for forwards stressed physical attributes—speed, quickness, physical strength, and rebounding—even to the point of labeling the forward the "animal."

Given this widespread agreement that there are varied zones of responsibility and different qualities expected of guards, forwards, and centers, Eitzen and Tessendorf hypothesized that blacks would be overrepresented—stacked—at the forward position, where the essential traits required are physical rather than mental, and underrepresented at the guard and center positions, the most crucial positions for leadership and outcome control. Using data from a sample of 274 NCAA basketball teams from the 1970–71 season, they found that blacks were, in fact, substantially overrepresented as forwards and underrepresented at the guard and center positions. Whereas 32 percent of their total sample of players were black, 41 percent of forwards were black. But only 26 percent of guards and 25 percent of centers were. Eitzen and Tessendorf found that this pattern held constant regardless of whether the players were starters or second-stringers or whether they played for college or university division teams.

While these data provide substantial support for the thesis that racial stacking has occurred in collegiate basketball, it was found that in 1979 this pattern was not present in professional basketball, which was then 71 percent black. It would be interesting to see whether such a pattern may have occurred earlier in the history of professional basketball, since Berghorn and Yetman (1980), utilizing data from the 1974-75 and 1979-80 collegiate seasons, found that the races were relatively evenly distributed by positon and that the pattern of stacking detected by Eitzen and Tessendorf for 1970-71 had not persisted. Thus, although stacking has remained in football and baseball, the situation in basketball, which, of the three major sports considered in this paper is most heavily black in racial composition, would appear to have undergone substantial change during the 1970s.

Rewards and Authority

Discrimination in professional sports is explicit in the discrepancy between the salaries of white and black players. At first glance such a charge appears to be unwarranted. Black players rank among the highest paid in professional baseball (four of five superstars being paid more than $700,000 in 1979 were black). However, Scully (1974) reanalyzed data employed by Pascal and Rapping (1970) in an earlier study and found that although the mean salaries of black outfielders, infielders, and pitchers exceeded those of whites, there was still substantial salary discrimination against blacks when performance levels were held constant. Blacks earned less than whites for equivalent performance. Moreover, Dubois (1974: 55-56) has noted that the central positions in football are those where the salaries are the greatest.

An obvious case of monetary discrimination becomes apparent if one considers the total incomes of athletes (salary, endorsements, and off-season earnings). Pascal and Rapping, for instance, citing the Equal Opportunity Commission Report of 1968, related that black athletes appeared in only 5 percent of the 351 commercials associated with New York sports events in the fall of 1966 (1970:40). Our own analysis of the advertising and media program slots featuring starting members of one professional football team in 1971 revealed that eight of eleven whites had such opportunities while only two of thirteen blacks did. Neither do blacks have the same opportunities as whites when their playing careers are finished. This is reflected in radio and television sportscasting, where black sportscasters have seldom had any job other than providing the "color."

Officiating is another area that is disproportionately white.

Baseball has had only three black major league umpires in its history; in 1979 only *one* of sixty full-time umpires was black (for the experience of black umpires see Williams, 1978; and Gutkind, 1975). Professional basketball has only recently broken the color line in officiating, although by 1979 nearly one-fifth of NBA officials were black. Blacks comprised only eight percent of the officials in pro football, which provides another example of racial stacking: blacks are typically found in the head linesman role—and never in the role of head referee (Kirshenbaum, 1979).

Although the percentage of black players in each of the three most prominent American professional team sports (baseball, football, and basketball) greatly exceeds their percentage of the total population, there is ample evidence that few opportunities are available to them in managerial or entrepreneurial roles. For example, in 1980, nearly three decades after all three major professional sports were racially integrated, until the middle of the baseball season, *none* of the twenty-four major league field managers and twenty-eight National Football League head coaches was black. Nor has there ever been a black general manager in either of these two professional sports. And, despite the fact that blacks comprise more than two-thirds of all pro basketball players, only two of the twenty-two NBA head coaches (9 percent) were black.

Assistant coaches and coaches or managers of minor league professional teams also are conspicuously white. In 1979 there was but one black field manager in all of baseball and he managed Gastonia in the Class A Western Caroline League. During that same year, despite the disproportionate representation of blacks in major league baseball, only six coaches (5 percent) were black (6 percent were Hispanics). Of 290 coaches in the National Football League in 1979, less than ten were black in a league where nearly half the players were black. Moreover, black coaches are relegated to the less responsible coaching jobs. Baseball superstar Frank Robinson, who was appointed the first black major league field general after the conclusion of the regular 1974 season, has pointed out that blacks are excluded from the most important roles.[7] "You hardly see any Black third-base or pitching coaches. And those are the most important coaching jobs. The only place you see Blacks coaching is at first base, where most anybody can do the job" (quoted in Axthelm, 1974: 57). Similarly, in the National Football League there were no offensive or defensive coordinators among the assistant coaches in 1979 (Garvey, 1979:76)

The dearth of black coaches in professional sports is paralleled at the college and high school levels. Although many predominantly white colleges and universities have, in response to pressures from angry black athletes, recently made frantic efforts to hire black coaches, they have been hired almost exclusively as assistant coaches, and seldom has a coaching staff included more than one black. As of this writing, only a single major college—Wichita State—has a black head football coach, only a handful of Division I colleges (e.g., Arizona, Georgetown, Alcorn A&M, Illinois State, San Diego State, Eastern Michigan, and Washington State) have head basketball or track coaches who are black.

It should be noted that, paralleling other changes that will be discussed more fully below, blacks are increasingly found on the coaching staffs of college basketball teams. This phenomenon was noted by Leonard and Schmidt, who reported that the number of black head coaches increased from two in 1970 to twenty-one in 1973. Their data, however, are misleading since they failed to restrict their analysis to major (NCAA Division I) schools. Nevertheless, Berghorn and Yetman (1980) did detect an appreciable change between 1970 and 1980, during which the percentage of black head basketball coaches at major colleges increased from 0 to 5.5 percent while the percentage of major colleges with black members on their coaching staffs had increased from 14 percent in 1971 to 52 percent in 1980.

The pattern of exclusion of blacks from integrated coaching situations also has characterized American high schools. Historically, blacks have found coaching jobs only in predominantly black high schools. It would appear that the movement toward integration of schools during the 1960s has had the effect of eliminating blacks from coaching positions, as it has eliminated black principals and black teachers in general. Edwards has contended that between 1954 and 1971 more than 2,000 black coaches at formerly all-black schools lost their jobs (1979:126). So anomalous is a black head coach at a predominantly white high school in the South that when, in 1970, this barrier was broken, it was heralded by feature stories in the *New York Times* and *Sports Illustrated* (see Jordan, 1971). And the situation appears to be little different outside the South, where head coaches are almost exclusively white.

The paucity of black coaches and managers could be the result of two forms of discrimination. Overt discrimination occurs when owners ignore competent blacks because of their prejudices or because they fear the negative reaction of fans to blacks in leadership positions. The other form of discrimination is more subtle, however. Here blacks are not considered for coaching positions because they did not, during their playing days, play at positions requiring leadership and decision making. For example, Scully has shown that in baseball, 68 percent of all the managers from 1871 to 1968 were former infielders (1974: 246). Since blacks have tended to be "stacked" in the outfield, they do not possess the requisite infield experience that traditionally has provided access to the position of manager.

Blacks are also excluded from executive positions in organizations that govern both amateur and professional sports. In 1979, only three predominantly white major NCAA colleges had black athletic directors. On the professional level, there was no black representation in the principal ownership of a major-league franchise. Only former black superstar Henry Aaron held a high executive capacity in any of baseball's twenty-four teams, although two blacks did serve as assistants to Baseball Commissioner Bowie Kuhn. Nor have there been any black general managers in pro football. Professional basketball's management structure is most progressive in this regard, although it must be recalled that ownership remains overwhelmingly white. Two of seventeen NBA clubs had black general managers in 1979. It was a noteworthy event, when in 1970, former NBA star Wayne Embry was named general manager of the NBA Milwaukee Bucks, thereby becoming the first black to occupy such a position in professional sports.

Ability and Opportunity

Another form of discrimination in sport is unequal opportunity for equal ability. This means that entrance requirements to the major leagues are more rigorous for black players; therefore, they must be better than white players to succeed in the sports world. Rosenblatt was one of the first to demonstrate this mode of discrimination. He found that in the period from 1953 to 1957 the mean batting average for blacks in the major leagues was 20.6 points above the average for whites. In the 1958-to-1961 time period the difference was 20.1 points, while from 1962 to 1965 it was 21.2 points. He concluded:

> Discriminatory hiring practices are still in effect in the major leagues. The superior Negro is not subject to discrimination because he is more likely to help win games than fair to poor players. Discrimination is aimed, whether by design or not, against the substar Negro ball player. The findings clearly indicate that the undistinguished Negro player is less likely to play regularly in the major leagues than the equally undistinguished white player. (1967: 53)

Since Rosenblatt's analysis was through 1965 it was extended to include the years 1966–1970. The main difference between blacks and whites persisted; for that five-year period blacks batted an average of 20.8 points higher than whites. Updating this analysis, it was found that in 1975 the gap between black and white batting averages was virtually identical (21 points) to what it had been previously (the mean black batting average was .267 while the average for whites was .246).[8]

The existence of racial entry barriers in major league baseball was further supported by Pascal and Rapping, who extended Rosenblatt's research by including additional years and by examining the performance of the races in each separate position, including pitchers. They found, for instance, that the nineteen black pitchers in 1967 who appeared in at least ten games won a mean number of 10.2 games, while white pitchers won an average of 7.5. This coupled with their findings that blacks were superior to whites in all other playing positions, led them to conclude that "on the average a Black player must be better than a White player if he is to have an equal chance of transiting from the minor leagues to the major" (1970: 36). Moreover, Scully's elaborate analysis of baseball performance data has led him to conclude that "not only do Blacks have to out perform Whites to get into baseball, but they must consistently out perform them over their playing careers in order to stay in baseball" (1974: 263). Similarly, Johnson and Marple's analysis of professional basketball revealed that black marginal players are less likely to continue to play after five years than are white marginal players (1973).

The most dramatic increases in the numbers of black professional football players occurred during the middle sixties and early seventies. Table 2 shows the increasing percentages of blacks in professional football (compare these date with the corresponding basketball data in Table 3). Moreover, Brower (1973) found that, as in baseball and basketball, "Black . . . players must be superior in athletic performance to their White counterparts if they are to be accepted into professional football." His data revealed statistically significant differences in the percentages of black and white starters and non-starters. Blacks were found disproportionately as starters, while second-string status was more readily accorded to whites. Whereas 63 percent of black players were starters in 1970, 51 percent of white players were. Conversely, 49 percent of white players, but only 37 percent of black players, were not starters in that year. These findings led Brower to conclude that "mediocrity is a white luxury" (1973: 3).

Table 2

Percentages of Blacks per Year in
Professional Football

Year	Percentage of Black Players
1950	0
1954	5
1958	9
1962	16
1966	26
1970	34
1975	42

Whether black athletes are disproportionately overrepresented in the "star" category and underrepresented in the average, or journeyman, athletic category on collegiate and professional basketball teams was the subject of our earlier research (Yetman and Eitzen, 1971; 1972; Berghorn and Yetman, 1976; Eitzen and Yetman, 1977). This research also provided a historical dimension by investigating whether the racial distribution on basketball teams had changed over time. The investigation showed that the black predominance in basketball is a relatively recent phenomenon and that basketball, like football and baseball, was largely segregated until the late 1950s and early 1960s. There are records of black basketball players on teams from predominantly white colleges as far back as 1908, but such instances were rare during the first half of the century. In professional sports, the National Basketball Association remained an all-white institution until 1950, three years after Jackie Robinson had broken the color line in modern major league baseball, and four years after blacks reentered major league football after having been totally excluded since the early 1930s.

The racial composition of basketball has changed dramatically since 1954. From the immediate post-World War II situation (1948), when less than 10 percent of collegiate squads were integrated, to 1980, when over 90 percent contained members of both races, substantial and impressive progress was made toward integration. Not only were more schools recruiting blacks, but the number of black players being recruited at each school increased dramatically. The most substantial increase among collegiate teams was during the period between 1966 and 1975, which can be partly attributed to the breakdown in previously segregated teams throughout the South (Berghorn and Yetman, 1976).

Therefore, although blacks comprise approximately one-tenth (11 percent) of the total U.S. population, by 1975 they accounted for more than one-third (33.4 percent) of the nation's collegiate basketball players. The percentage composition of black players on college basketball teams is even more striking when it is considered that in 1976 blacks comprised only 10.4 percent of undergraduate students at four year colleges and universities and more than one-third (36 percent) attended historically black institutions (National Advisory Committee, 1979:21).

The change in the professional game is even more marked, for blacks have clearly come to dominate the game. As previously noted, in 1979 blacks comprised seventy-one percent of the players in the National Basketball Association. Black dominance was statistical as well as numerical. Simons found that, in 1979, 92 percent of leaders in all of the important categories (e.g., scoring, assists) were black (Simons, 1979: 47). Therefore, as contrasted to the situation two decades ago, organized basketball—on both the collegiate and professional levels—has eliminated many of the barriers that once excluded blacks from participation. The changes in professional baseball and football, while not so dramatic, have also occurred primarily during the middle sixties.

Having determined that black players are disproportionately overrepresented on collegiate and professional basketball teams relative to their distribution within the general population, the roles they played were systematically examined. Specifically, we wanted to determine whether blacks have been found disproportionately in the first five ranks (starters), and whether their average position ranking on the team has been higher than that of whites.

In order to determine whether the positional patterns had changed significantly in the years during which the percentage of black players had increased so dramatically, it was necessary to examine the distribution of blacks by scoring rank over time.

Operationally defining the top players according to their offensive productivity as measured by their scoring average, the same situation of unequal opportunity for equal ability that Rosenblatt, Scully, and Pascal and Rapping found in professional baseball was discovered (Yetman and Eitzen, 1972; Berghorn and Yetman, 1980). Using data from 1958, 1962, 1966, 1970, 1975, and 1980 collegiate records, demonstrated that during each year the higher the scoring rank, the greater the likelihood that it would be occupied by a black player. This was most marked in the distribution of black players who were leading scorers and poorest point producers. While black players comprised no more than 29 percent of all the members of integrated teams during the years 1958-1970, in each of these years nearly half—and in some years, more than half—of the leading scorers were black. Conversely, blacks were disproportionately underrepresented in the lowest scoring position. Moreover, our data revealed that between 1958 and 1970 no less than two-thirds—and in some years as high as three-fourths—of all black players were starters.

The 1975 and 1980 data obtained by Berghorn and Yetman indicated that although blacks continue to be overrepresented in starting positions, there has been a steady and substantial decline in this relationship from 1962, when 76 percent of all black college basketball players were starters, to 1975, when the percentage had dropped to 53 percent. These changes are shown in Table 3. In other words, black basketball recruits are no longer restricted to those likely to be starters. Thus, unlike the situations in professional baseball and football, which have demonstrated little change throughout the past two decades, collegiate basketball appears increasingly to provide equal opportunity for equal ability. Moreover, these changes parallel the decline in positional stacking and the increase in black coaches in collegiate basketball previously noted.

In professional basketball, where they have come to dominate the game, blacks were slightly overrepresented in starting roles until 1970, when equal numbers of blacks were starters and nonstarters. Following Rosenblatt's approach in comparing white and black batting averages, the scoring averages of black and white basketball players were compared for the five years (1957-58,

1961-62, 1965-66, 1969-70, 1974-75) of our analysis. Although scoring averages were identical for both races in 1957-58, blacks outscored whites in the remaining years by an average of 5.2, 3.3, 2.9, and 1.5 points, respectively. Although there remains a slight gap between the scoring averages of whites and blacks, the magnitude of these differences has declined as the percentage of black players in the league has increased. This is a contrast to the situation in professional baseball, where the mean batting average for blacks has remained twenty points greater than the average for whites for more than two decades.

Table 3

Percentages of Blacks in the First Five Scoring Ranks

Year	Percentage of Black-Players
1958	69
1962	76
1966	72
1971	66
1975	61
1980	53

Summary and Conclusions

In the preceding analysis we have sought to provide a comprehensive examination of the role of race in several aspects —allocation of playing position, authority structure, and opportunity structure—of three American team sports: football, basketball, and baseball. The data presented here suggest both continuity and change in traditional patterns of race relations.

Perhaps the most striking fact is that black prominence in intercollegiate and professional sports—especially football and basketball—continues to increase.[9] Several possible explanations for this phenomenon—the genetic, the structural, and the cultural—have been advanced. First, it has been suggested that blacks are naturally better athletes and that their predominance in American professional sports can be attributed to their innate athletic and/or physical superiority. Sociologists are inclined to reject interpretations of black athletic superiority as genetically or physiologically based, especially since racial categories in any society, but particularly in the United States, are socially defined phenomena. The fallacy of those assuming genetic differences between black and white is, as Berreman has pointed out, that they have

> selected for investigation two socially defined groupings in American society which are commonly regarded as innately different in social worth and which as a result are accorded widely and crucially divergent opportunities and life experiences. Upon finding that they perform differentialy . . . , [they] attribute that fact to assumed but undemonstrated and uninvestigated biological differences. Thus, socially defined populations perform differently on socially defined tasks with socially acquired skills, and this is attributed . . . to biology. (1972: 391)

It is also relevant to note that, despite their prominence in the major team sports, blacks are virtually absent from participation in other American sports such as hockey, golf, tennis, swimming, automobile racing, and soccer. The anomolous dearth of blacks in these sports (as well as the relative recency of their dominance in baseball, basketball, football, and track) is a major stumbling block for any genetic interpretation. For if blacks are inherently athletically superior, why do they not also dominate these sports in a manner comparable to their dominance of basketball, football, and baseball?[10]

Another explanation that has been advanced to explain the disproportionate number of blacks in professional and collegiate sports resides in the structural limitations to which black children and adults are subjected. Since opportunities for vertical mobility by blacks in American society are circumscribed, athletics may become perceived as one of the few means by which a black can succeed in a highly competitive American society; a male black child's and adolescent's primary role models are much more likely than a white's to be athletic heroes. And the determination and motivation devoted to the pursuit of an athletic career may therefore be more intense than for the white adolescent whose career options are greater. Jack Olsen, in *The Black Athlete*, quotes a prominent coach:

> People keep reminding me that there is a difference in physical ability between the races, but I think there isn't. The Negro boy practices longer and harder. The Negro has the keener desire to excel in sports because it is more mandatory for his future op-

portunities than it is for a white boy. There are nine thousand different jobs available to a person if he is white. (1968b: 41)

One of the tragic consequences of this single-minded pursuit of athletic success is, of course, that the actual opportunities are exceedingly small—less than 300 athletes play each year in the National Basketball Association, for example. The combined total of all blacks involved in professional team sports—as major and minor league players, coaches, and trainers—numbers about 1,500, or about one of every 6,000 black males ages eighteen to sixty-four years (Coakley, 1978: 295—96). Thus a black athlete's professional aspirations are likely to be frustrated and the energies expended in quest of the goal of athletic success to be futile.

> The impact of what would otherwise be personal career tragedies reverberates throughout black society both because of the tremendous proportions of black youth channeled into sport and the fact that serious sports involvement often dictates neglect of other important spheres of development. Further, the skills cultivated through sport are utterly worthless beyond the sport realm, unlike the skills one would develop while pursuing a career in, say, medicine, politics, education, or any one of a multitude of other areas. (Edwards, 1979: 119)

A final explanation of the disproportionate black prowess in major sports emphasizes the extent to which the cultural milieu of young blacks positively rewards athletic performance. James Green has questioned whether the lure of a professional career completely explains the strong emphasis on athletics among blacks. He has argued that the explanation that a black manifests a "keener desire to excel . . . because it is mandatory for his future" simply reflects the commentator's own future orientation. An alternative explanation of strong black motivation, according to Green, is the positive emphasis in black subculture that is placed on the importance of physical (and verbal) skill and dexterity. Athletic prowess in men is highly valued by both women and men. The athletically capable male is in the comparable position of the hustler or the blues singer; he is something of a folk hero. He achieves a level of status and recognition among his peers whether he is a publicly applauded sports hero or not (Green, 1971).

Nearly as dramatic as the proportion of blacks in player roles is the dearth of blacks in administrative, managerial, and officiating positions. Although there have been significant advances for black athletes in the past quarter of a century, there has been no comparable access of blacks to decision-making positions. With the exception of professional basketball, the corporate and decision-making structure of professional sports is nearly as white as it was in 1946, before Jackie Robinson entered major league baseball. The distribution of blacks in the sports world is, therefore, not unlike that in the larger society, where blacks are admitted to lower-level occupations but virtually excluded from positions of authority and power (see Yetman and Steele, 1975: 37).

Because black participation in the major team sports continues to increase, many observers have incorrectly concluded that sports participation is free of racial discrimination. As the analysis here has demonstrated, stacking in football and baseball remains pronounced. Blacks are disproportionately found in those positions requiring physical rather than cognitive or leadership abilities. Moreover, while the data indicate that although the patterns have been substantially altered in collegiate and professional basketball, black athletes in the two other major team sports have been found and continue to be disproportionately located in starting roles and not often in journeymen positions. The three interpretations previously considered—the genetic, the structural, and the cultural—appear inadequate to explain these patterns. A genetic interpretation cannot explain the prevalence of blacks in starting roles or their relegation to playing positions defined as not requiring qualities of leadership or outcome control. Even if blacks possessed genetically based athletic superiority, they should not be systematically overrepresented in starting positions or "stacked" in "black" positions, but should still be randomly distributed throughout the entire team. As Jim Bouton (a former major league baseball player who has challenged the racial composition of major league baseball teams) has written, "if 19 of the top 30 hitters are Black, then almost two-thirds of all hitters should be black. Obviously it is not that way" (1970: 302). Similarly, explanations emphasizing the narrow range of opportunities available to blacks, or the emphasis upon athletic skills in black subculture, fail to adequately explain the distribution of blacks by position and performance.

Despite some indications of change, discrimination against black athletes continues in American team sports; sport is not a meritocratic realm where race is ignored. Equality of opportunity is not the rule where race is a variable. These conclusions have implications that extend beyond the sports world. If discrimination occurs in so public an arena, one so generally acknowledged to be discrimination free, and one where a premium is placed on individual achievement rather than upon ascription, how much more subtly pervasive must discrimination be in other areas of American life, where personal interaction is crucial and where the actions of power wielders are not subjected to public scrutiny?

We would like to thank John Daggett, Cindy Kemper, Barb Moore, Red Miller, Gary Ozello, and John Schneider for their assistance in the preparation of this chapter.

Notes

1. For a general review of the literature on this subject, see McPherson (1974) and Coakley (1978: 274-312).
2. In baseball, for example, the 1957-58 season was the year that blacks achieved a proportion equivalent to their percentage in the U.S. population (Scully, 1974: 233). The watershed year in professional football was 1960 (see Table 1); in professional basketball it was 1958 (see Table 3).
3. Data from 1974 showed that 16 percent of major league baseball players were Latin Americans (Leonard, 1977: 87).
4. Although stacking occurs for blacks in baseball, it does not for another minority—Latins (Freischlag and Strom, 1978).
5. Data from the 1979 *Football Register* show that the proportion of blacks for these positions had not changed at all from 1975.
6. A similar study was conducted by Madison and Landers (1976) comparing the shift in position by race as athletes moved from the college to the professional level. As in the Eitzen and Sanford study, blacks were found to be much more likely than whites to have changed from central positions to non-central ones.
7. Robinson's appointment, coming more than twenty-seven years after the entrance of another Robinson—Jackie—into major league baseball, was the exception that proves the rule. So historic was the occasion that it drew news headlines through the nation and a congratulatory telegram from President Ford. Robinson was subsequently fired as manager of the Cleveland Indians. In 1978 Larry Doby was hired briefly as field manager of the Chicago White Sox. In 1979, however, there were no black managers. While in 1980 Maury Wills, the first ex-infielder among blacks to do so—became field manager of the Seattle Mariners in mid-season.
8. For an extension of this analysis, including adding Latins, see Leonard (1977).
9. There are indications that black participation in baseball has begun to decline, however (Kirshenbaum, 1979; Edwards, 1979: 127).
10. For an incisive critique of the "racial superiority" interpretation of differences in athletic performance, see Edwards (1973a).

Works Cited

Axthelm, Pete. "Black Out." *Newsweek* (15 July 1974): 57.

Berghorn, Forrest J., and Yetman, Norman R., "Racial Participation and Integration in Inter-Collegiate Basketball, 1958–1980." Unpublished paper, 1980.

Berreman, Gerald, D. "Race, Caste, and Other Invidious Distinctions in Social Stratification." *Race* 13 (April 1978): 385–414.

Blalock, H. M., Jr. "Occupational Discrimination: Some Theoretical Propositions." *Social Problems* 9 (Winter 1962): 240–47.

Bouton, Jim. *Ball Four*. New York: World Publishing Company, 1970.

Brower, Jonathan J. "The Racial Basis of the Division of Labor Among Players in the National Football League as a Function of Stereotypes." Paper presented at the annual meetings of the Pacific Sociological Association, Portland, 1972.

———. "The Quota System: The White Gatekeeper's Regulation of Professional Football's Black Community." Paper presented at the annual meetings of the American Sociological Association, New York, 1973.

Coakley, Jay J. "Blacks in Sport: Opportunities or Dreams?" *Sport in Society: Issues and Controversies*. St. Louis: C. V. Mosby, 1978, 274–312.

Coleman, James S. Equality of Educational Opportunity. Washington, D.C.: U.S. Government Printing Office, 1966.

Curtis, James E., and Loy, John W. "Positional Segregation and Professional Baseball: Replications, Trend Data and Critical Observation." *International Review of Sport Sociology* 13 (1978): 5–23.

Dougherty, Joseph. "Race and Sport: A Follow-up Study." *Sport Sociology Bulletin* 5 (Spring 1976): 1–12.

Dubois, Paul E. "Sport, Mobility and the Black Athlete." *Sport Sociology Bulletin* 3 (Fall 1974): 40–61.

Edwards, Harry. *The Revolt of the Black Athlete*. New York: Free Press, 1969.

———. "The Black Athletes: 20th Century Gladiators for White America," *Psychology Today* 7 (1973): 43–52.

———. *Sociology of Sport*. Homewood, Ill.: Dorsey Press, 1973.

———. "Sport Within the Veil: The Triumphs, Tragedies and Challenges of Afro-American Involvement," *Annals of the American Academy of Political and Social Science* 445 (September 1979): 116–27.

Eitzen, D. Stanley, and Tessendorf, Irv. "Racial Segregation by Position in Sports: The Special Case of Basketball." *Review of Sport and Leisure* 3 (Summer 1978): 109–28.

Eitzen, D. Stanley, and Yetman, Norman R. "Immune from Racism: Blacks Still Suffer From Discrimination in Sports." *Civil Rights Digest* 9 (Winter 1977): 2–13.

Eitzen, D. Stanley, and Sanford, David C. "The Segregation of Blacks by Playing Position in Football: Accident or Design?" *Social Science Quarterly* 55 (March 1975): 948–59.

Freischlag, Jerry, and Strom, Brent. "Dimensions of Racial Discrimination in Organized Baseball," *Review of Sport and Leisure* 3 (Winter 1978): 42–53.

Garvey, Ed. "Proposed Press Release." *Boston Globe*, November 15, 1979, p. 76.

Grusky, Oscar. "The Effects of Formal Structure on Managerial Recruitment: A Study of Baseball Organization." *Sociometry* 26 (September 1963): 345-53.

Gutkind, Lee. *The Best Seat in Baseball, But You Have to Stand!* New York: The Dial Press, 1975.

Jacobson, Robert L. "Black Enrollment Rising Sharply, U.S. Data Show." *Chronicle of Higher Education* (4 October 1971).

Johnson, Norris R., and Marple, David P. 1973 "Racial Discrimination in Professional Basketball." *Sociological Focus* 6 (Fall 1973): 6-18.

Jordan, Pat. *Black Coach*. New York: Dodd Mead, 1971.

Kirshenbaum, Jerry. "Baseball's Enduring Color Line." *Sports Illustrated* (8 October 1979): 21.

Leonard, Wilbert M., II. "Stacking and Performance Differentials of Whites, Blacks and Latins in Professional Baseball." *Review of Sport and Leisure* 2 (June 1977): 77-106.

Leonard, Wilbert M. II, and Schmidt, Susan. "Observations on the Changing Social Organization of Collegiate and Professional Basketball." *Sport Sociology Bulletin* 4 (Fall 1975): 13-35.

Lipsyte, Robert. "Al McGuire Was in Town Last Week." *New York Times* (1 March 1971): 37.

Loy, John W., and McElvogue, Joseph F. "Racial Segregation in American Sport." *International Review of Sport Sociology* 5 (1970): 5-24.

McClendon, McKee J., and Eitzen, D. Stanley. "Interracial Contact on Collegiate Basketball Teams: A Test of Sherif's Theory of Superordinate Goals." *Social Science Quarterly* 55 (March 1975): 926-38.

McPherson, Barry D. "The Segregation by Playing Position Hypothesis in Sport: An Alternative Explanation." *Social Science Quarterly* 55 (March 1975): 960-66.

―――. "The Black Athlete: An Overview and Analysis." *Social Problems in Athletics*, Daniel M. Landers, ed. Urbana: University of Illinois Press, 1976, 122-50. 122-50.

Madison, Donna R., and Landers, Daniel M. "Racial Discrimination in Football: A Test of the 'Stacking' of Playing Positions Hypothesis." *Social Problems in Athletics*, Daniel M. Landers, ed. Urbana: University of Illinois Press, 1976, 151-56.

Medoff, M. H. "Positional Segregation and Professional Baseball." *International Review of Sport Sociology* 12 (1977): 49-56.

National Advisory Committee on Black Higher Education and Black Colleges and Universities. *Access of Black Americans to Higher Education: How Open Is the Door?* Washington: U.S. Government Printing Office, 1979.

Olsen, Jack. "The Black Athlete—a Shameful Story." *Sports Illustrated* (22 July 1968): 28-41.

―――. *The Black Athlete*. New York: Time-Life Books, 1968.

Pascal, Anthony H., and Rapping, Leonard A. *Racial Discrimination in Organized Baseball*. Santa Monica, California: Rand Corporation, 1970.

Rosenblatt, Aaron. "Negroes in Baseball: The Failure of Success." *Transaction* 4 (September 1967): 51-53.

Schneider, John, and Eitzen, D. Stanley. "Racial Discrimination in American Sport: Continuity or Change?" *Journal of Sport Behavior* 2 (August 1979): 136–42.

Scully, Gerald W. "Discrimination: The Case of Baseball," Government and the Sports Business, Robert G. Noll, ed. Washington, D.C.: The Brookings Institution, 1974, 221–73.

Simons, Bill. "We Shall Overcome (Eventually)." *Professional Sports Journal*, February 1980, pp. 46–52.

Williams, Art. "Interview," *Referee* 3 (July 1978): 8–15, 45.

Williams, R., and Youssef, Y. "Division of Labor in College Football along Racial Lines." *International Journal of Sport Psychology* 6 (1975): 3–13.

Winkler, Karen J. "Black Youths' Share of Enrollment Grows," *The Chronicle of Higher Education* 15 (December 1975): 4.

Yetman, Norman R., and Eitzen, D. Stanley. "Black Athletes on Intercollegiate Baseball Teams: An Empirical Test of Discrimination." *Majority and Minority: The Dynamics of Racial and Ethnic Relations.* Norman R. Yetman and C. Hoy Steele, eds. Boston: Allyn and Bacon, 1971, 509–17.

———. "Black Americans in Sports: Unequal Opportunity for Equal Ability," *Civil Rights Digest* 5 (August 1972): 20–34.

Yetman, Norman R. and Steele, C. Hoy. *Majority and Minority: The Dynamics of Racial and Ethnic Relations.* 2d ed. Boston: Allyn and Bacon, 1976.

10

Social Differentiation and Sports Participation: The Case of Golf

JAMES D. DAVIDSON

Introduction

This chapter discusses the effects that race (black and white), religion (denominational affiliation), gender (male and female), and socioeconomic status (education, occupation, and income)[1] have on three dimensions of golfing behavior: who plays regularly and who does not; the places people play (at private clubs or public courses); and who plays with whom at these different kinds of courses.

These issues are important because understanding the effects these factors have on golf extends knowledge of how and why group membership affects human behavior in general. Exploration of these issues also provides some insights concerning the effects "elite" sports such as golf have on social inequalities based on race, religion, gender, and socioeconomic status.[2]

The theoretical framework used here has been derived from the sociological literature on social differentiation and sports participation. Data have been gathered from previous research; information published in "popular" sources such as *Golf* magazine, *Sports Illustrated*, *Ebony*, and the *Washington Post*; and observations that the author has made while playing golf at private clubs and public courses in different parts of the country.[3]

The Problem

People differ in many ways. Some differences—such as race and gender—are inherited; others—such as religious affiliation and

181

socioeconomic status—are socially acquired. Not all differences are socially significant, but race, religion, gender, and socioeconomic status are. Previous research on socioeconomic status has shown that education, occupation and income affect a variety of behaviors relating to people's life-styles and life chances (e.g., Tumin, 1967; Heller, 1969; Thielbar and Feldman, 1972; Matras, 1975; Abrahamson, Mizruchi, and Hornung, 1976; Vanfossen, 1979). Studies also have demonstrated the existence of a racial structure that gives white Americans numerous advantages over blacks (e.g., Blauner, 1972; Bromley and Longino, 1972; Himes, 1973; Yetman and Steele, 1975; Pettigrew, 1975; Burkey, 1978). The differential effects of being Protestant, Catholic, or Jewish and belonging to different denominations within these three faiths have been documented by Lenski (1961), Parenti (1967), Glock (1973), Faulkner (1973), Johnstone (1975), and Wilson (1978). And the advantages that males have over females have been summarized in works by Epstein (1970), Amundsen (1971), Huber (1973) and Dworkin (1976).

Given the effects that these factors have on many other aspects of people's lives, one also might expect them to affect participation in sports. Some research supports this expectation, but the evidence—especially relating to golf—is limited and ambiguous.

Socioeconomic Status

Several studies have suggested there is a positive, linear relationship between socioeconomic status and sports participation: the higher one's socioeconomic status, the more one tends to participate in sports generally (Snyder and Spreitzer, 1974) and individual sports in particular (Eitzen and Sage, 1978: 211–12). Some writers, however, have noted exceptions to this generalization. Kenyon (1966) found that education was positively related to "primary" or behavioral involvement in sports, but was not highly related to "secondary" involvement (i.e., viewing or listening to sports events and having positive attitudes about sports). Occupational status was not related to primary involvement or viewing and listening to sports events, but was associated with positive attitudes towards sports. Snyder and Spreitzer (1973) reported a positive relationship between socioeconomic status and sports knowledge but found no relationship between socioeconomic status and people's feelings about sports or their behavioral involvement in sports activities. In short, the relationships among socioeconomic status components and their association with particular sports participation dimensions remain unclear.

The literature on golf does not shed much light on these issues. Virtually nothing is known about the effects of education and income on people's golfing behavior. Several researchers have reported data on the relationship between occupational status and participation in golf but their results have not been very consistent. These studies will be reviewed in more detail later and some observations concerning new directions for research will be offered.

Race

It is often assumed that sports, due to their emphasis on universalistic criteria such as performance, encourage racial integration and equal participation more than do most other aspects of society. But, research over the last fifteen years has revealed unequal treatment of minority athletes, even in sports where they constitute a substantial percentage of all participants (Rosenblatt, 1967; Olsen, 1968; Edwards, 1969; Yetman and Eitzen, 1975; Loy, McPherson, and Kenyon, 1978; and chapter 6 of this book). Golf certainly has an image of being "a white man's game," and some evidence that will be reviewed here supports this image. The relationship, however, between race and various aspects of golfing behavior remains largely unknown.

Religion

Though research has shown that religious affiliation can affect many aspects of people's lives, this factor has received very little attention in the literature on sports participation. The fact that it has not been considered suggests that researchers feel it may have little or no effect on this aspect of people's lives. Yet, Baltzell's (1958 and 1964) analyses suggest that being Protestant, Catholic, or Jewish affects one's chances of being a private golf club member. And Deford's (1976) articles in *Sports Illustrated* indicate that religion *is* a force among athletes in many sports, including golf, although the effects of religious affiliation on various aspects of people's golfing behavior have yet to be determined.

Gender

Finally, research has shown that men tend to participate in most sports more than women; they also tend to derive more benefits from their participation than women do. There are well-known differences in the annual earnings of professional men and women golfers—Tom Watson, the leading money winner on the men's tour in 1979, earned twice as much ($462,636) as Nancy Lopez ($197,488), the leading money winner on the women's tour. These differences suggest that gender also plays some role in golf; but its effects on various aspects of golfing behavior have not been examined in any systematic fashion.

In short, there is enough evidence in the existing literature suggesting that race, religion, gender, and socioeconomic status *can* affect people's golfing behavior, but these effects are not fully understood.

Perspective

Since the concern here lies with social differentiation and golfing behavior, some preliminary observations about each of these phenomena and their probable interrelationships will be a good starting point.

Social Differentiation

It is assumed that race, religion, gender, and socioeconomic status can have separate effects on people's golfing behavior. Each factor can affect golfing behavior, even after the effects of the other factors have been controlled. This approach is outlined in Figure 1 and discussed briefly below.

Socioeconomic Status. The literature on sports participation in general suggests that some socioeconomic variables can have more effects on golfing behavior than others and those which are most influential can affect participation in different ways. To explore these possibilities, education, occupation, and income will be treated separately. Figure 2 summarizes our perspective regarding the general relationships among these variables as they effect golfing behavior. It is likely that education has few direct consequences, but it does affect occupation and income, which have separate and important effects. The specific nature of these outcomes will be discussed later.

Race. A variety of formal and informal mechanisms (e.g., laws and hiring practices) have maximized whites' access to higher education, better jobs, and higher incomes, while limiting blacks' access to these, and other, resources. Some racial differences have been reduced in recent years. For example, the educational gap between younger blacks and whites today (i.e., the median number

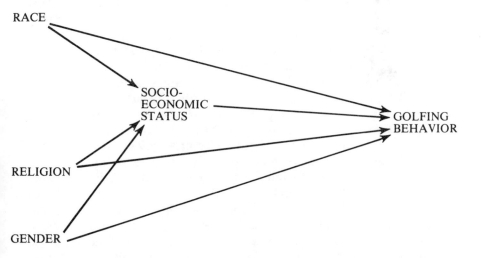

Figure 1. Effects of race, religion, gender, and socioeconomic status on golfing behavior.

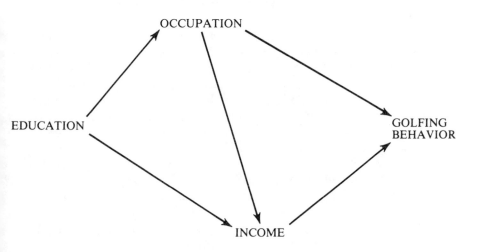

Figure 2. Relationships among socioeconomic variables as they relate to playing golf.

of years completed by each race) is smaller than it was between blacks and whites of the same age several decades ago. But, other differences between blacks and whites are as large today as they were ten, fifteen, or twenty years ago. For example, the ratio of unemployed blacks to unemployed whites is as large today (two to one) as it was in the mid-1950s and the ratio of black income to white income is about the same today as it was fifteen years ago (with blacks earning less than two-thirds of what whites earn). In short, there has been some racial progress in the past two decades, but whites continue to have greater access to most socioeconomic resources than blacks do. These differentials give whites numerous advantages over blacks in access to sports participation.

Even if blacks and whites were equal in terms of education, occupation, and income, blacks still would not possess many of society's privileges to the same degree as whites. Other factors having little or nothing to do with socioeconomic circumstances probably would limit blacks' access to these privileges (Blauner, 1972; Himes, 1973; Eitzen and Sage, 1978: 240-43). Cultural traditions developed in response to historical discrimination may cause many blacks to participate in leisure and sports activities other than the ones (e.g., golf) that white society has defined as socially attractive. And blacks who do pursue "white man's games" may encounter racial restrictions and prejudices limiting their participation. How these factors apply specifically to golf will be shown.

Religion. Religious affiliation can also affect socioeconomic status and, consequently, participation in many aspects of society, including sports. Jews outrank Protestants and Catholics on all dimensions of socioeconomic status. Historically, Protestants have outranked Catholics, but in the last two decades, Catholics have achieved parity with Protestants and now outrank them on some status dimensions (e.g., income; see Glenn and Hyland, 1967; *Time*, 1975; Greeley, 1977; Wilson, 1978; Burkey, 1978). Moreover, Reform Jews and mainline Protestants enjoy higher status than members of more "conservative" groups within their respective faiths (Stark and Glock, 1968; Goldstein and Goldscheider, 1969). Consequently, religious affiliation may affect people's golfing behavior because it affects their access to the socioeconomic resources needed to play golf.

Religious affiliation can also affect people's golfing behavior for other reasons. For example, throughout American history, Protestants (particularly mainline Protestants) have enjoyed more social respectability than Catholics or Jews (Lenski, 1961). Although Protestant hegemony has been challenged in recent years (Schrag, 1971; Marden and Meyer, 1978), Protestants' superior social respectability persists (Baltzell, 1958 and 1964; Gaustad, 1968). This respectability differential may give Protestants (even some with fewer socioeconomic resources than white Jews and Catholics) unequal access to a sport with a high status reputation.[4] The fact that golf was brought to this country from Scotland and England and is associated with WASP country clubs in this country (Loy, McPherson, and Kenyon, 1978), further enhances the likelihood of Protestants being more inclined toward the sport than Catholics or Jews.

The values and beliefs of various denominations within the three major faiths also might be a factor. Betts (1974: 352–55) has observed that "liberal" denominations have been more tolerant of "Sunday sports" than "conservative" denominations, and the ideologies of "liberal" groups are tolerant of the behaviors that are associated with golf (e.g., drinking and gambling), while the orientations of more "conservative" groups define such activities as sinful. As a result, people's religious affiliations can affect their golfing behavior for ideological reasons that are quite separate from the matter of socioeconomic status.

Gender. Research has shown that men have higher socioeconomic status than women. Indeed, Knudsen (1969: 192) reported that, contrary to conventional wisdom concerning greater gender equality, since 1940

women have experienced a gradual but persistent decline in status [relative to men] as measured by occupation, income, and education. The sources of this lowered status included diminished efforts by women and institutionalized discrimination. . . . Women, ambivalent about careers and convinced that they will face discrimination, make lesser efforts than men, permitting employers to justify discrimination by appealing to evidence of lower achievement and commitment to employment.

These socioeconomic differentials are likely to affect the extent that men and women participate in golf.

Even if men and women were equal in status, there still would be differences in their sports participation. As Snyder and Spreitzer (1974: 476) have observed:

Traditional sex role definitions either do not legitimate athletic pursuits for females or they narrowly define the range of appropriate physical activities (Griffin, 1973; Harris, 1971, 1973; Hart, 1972). In this regard, women are clearly at a disadvantage in terms of opportunities and resources available for physical expression of the self in the form of sport.

Traditional sex roles continue to exert considerable influence on the behavior patterns of most men and women, leading to our expectation that gender affects the degree and nature of golf participation.

Golfing Behavior

Comparing golf with other sports may aid readers who are not familiar with sport, and may help all readers interpret some of the later parts of this chapter.

Golf and Other Sports. Golf is played on a piece of land known as a "course." Most courses have eighteen holes and are between 6,000 and 7,000 yards long; some courses have only nine holes and are only about half as long. A "typical" eighteen-hole course consists of four short holes (i.e., under 250 yards), four long holes (i.e., over 470 yards), and ten medium-length holes (i.e., between 250 and 470 yards). Each hole consists of a "tee," where the first shot is hit and a "green," where the hole ends. In between, there usually are a number of obstacles (e.g., lakes, sandtraps, trees, and gullies). Some holes are straight; others are "doglegs" (i.e., they bend to the left or right). The object is to get the ball from the tee into a small cup on the green in as few strokes as possible. The general expection (i.e., "par") on short holes is three strokes: one shot from the tee to the green and two "putts." Par on medium length holes is four: two shots to the green and two putts. And on long holes, par usually is five: three shots from tee to green and two putts. Players hit the ball with clubs known as "woods" and "irons." In general, woods are for longer shots and irons for shorter ones.

Table 1 summarizes some of the similarities and differences between golf and other sports. Like most other sports, golf is played according to a set of rules that are administered by a national governing body (the United States Golf Association, the USGA). The Professional Golf Association (PGA) governs the teaching of the rules and "the mechanics" of the game. Participants rely on basic equipment that is manufactured, advertised, and sold by independent business groups. As we have observed, the contest takes place within a limited geographical area. And, in golf—as in most other sports—the outcome of the contest (i.e., whether one wins or loses) usually depends not only on one's own performance but also on how well or badly others play.

In other respects, golf is more similar to some sports than to others. Teams are essential for football, basketball, and baseball but are not essential for golf and tennis. Body contact does not occur in golf or tennis but is normal in some other sports. A violation of the rules in golf is assessed against the individual (e.g., a two-stroke penalty), as it is in tennis (e.g., loss of points). In basketball and baseball violations are assessed against individuals and teams at the same time; in football penalties are against the team (except on the rare occasions when a player is ejected from the game).

Golf is quite unique in some respects. Individual play is possible in golf but not in most other sports as no one else is needed to begin a round of golf.[5] In golf, an individual's performance is not necessarily related to any other participants' performance (though the outcome of a match depends on the result of that performance in comparison to other performances). Amateur golfers must pay each time they play (or must have paid a membership fee in some club), whereas amateur participants in other sports do not necessarily have to pay each time. It also takes more time to play eighteen holes of golf—three to five hours—than it usually takes to play a complete game in other sports; the "action" in golf is slower paced than in other sports.[6]

Dimensions of Golfing Behavior. One dimension of golfing behavior concerns the distinction between "golfers" and "nongolfers." "Golfers" play regularly, whether as amateurs or professionals; "nongolfers" never play or play only infrequently. Twelve and one-half million people (about seven percent of the U.S. population aged fourteen and over) played at least fifteen rounds of golf in 1978 (Statistical Abstract, 1979: 242). These people are responsible for a majority of the 300 million rounds of golf played each year. (Another fourteen million people play at least one round of golf but do not play regularly enough to be considered golfers.)

Golfers, as a rule, are very attached to their sport. Nelson (1956: 57) once said, "Golf is more than a game, it is a way of life."

Table 1

Similarities and Differences Between Golf and Several Other Prominent Sports

Similarity/Difference	Golf	Tennis	Football	Basketball	Baseball
LIKE MOST OTHER SPORTS					
Play by formal rules	Yes	Yes	Yes	Yes	Yes
National governing body	Yes	Yes	Yes	Yes	Yes
Formalized instruction by professional teachers, coaches	Yes	Yes	Yes	Yes	Yes
Basic equipment	Ball, Clubs	Ball, Racket	Ball, Goal Posts	Ball, Hoop	Ball, Bat, Glove
Equipment manufacturers, publishers, other auxiliary groups	Yes	Yes	Yes	Yes	Yes
Play in limited geographic area	Yes	Yes	Yes	Yes	Yes
Outcome dependent on performance of others	Sometimes	Yes	Yes	Yes	Yes

LIKE SOME OTHER SPORTS

Team play	Sometimes	Sometimes	Essential	Essential	Essential
Body contact among participants	Not Normal	Not Normal	Normal	Normal	Sometimes
Amount of violence permitted	None	None	Some	Little	Very Little
How penalties assessed against	Individual	Individual	Team	Individual, Team	Individual, Team
QUITE DIFFERENT					
Individual play	Possible	Impossible	Impossible	Impossible	Impossible
Number of others needed to play	0	1	Several	Several	Several
Individual performance dependent on performance of others	No	Yes	Yes	Yes	Yes
Cost of amateur to play	Each Time	Varies	None	None	None
Hours needed to play	4 – 5	1 – 2	2 – 3	1 – 2	2 – 3
Pace of action	Slow	Fast	Fast	Fast	Intermediate

Houghton (1959) and Updike (1973) have described their love for golf as an addiction. Kieran (1941: 171-72) described the power of this addiction in a poem that most golfers can relate to:

> On, yesterday, flushed high with hope, I stood upon the tee.
> My drive I hooked behind a rock; my second hit a tree;
> And all the dreadful afternoon I flubbed in misery.
> But tomorrow, by the gods of golf! I'll try the game again!
>
> Oh, yesterday my heart was torn with top and slice and hook;
> The wayward path I followed led by rough and trap and brook;
> And as I missed the tenth short putt, my soul in anguish shook.
> But tomorrow, by the Great Horn Spoon! I'll try the game again!
>
> Oh, yesterday I drenched the course with bitter scalding tears, and what I said of golf I hope will never reach your ears.
> I swore I wouldn't touch a club for years and years and years.
> But tomorrow—you can bet on this!—I'll try the game again.

Though they may curse a blue streak after blowing a two-foot putt, most golfers would agree with McCarthy's (1976) quip that "Providence [has] singled us out for pleasure denied the rest of mortal man."

A second dimension of golfing behavior concerns the places where golf is played. The earliest golf courses in the United States began to appear in the 1880s and were private clubs.

> The popularity of golf grew rapidly in the United States and by 1900 there were approximately 400 clubs; by 1920 there were over 4,500 clubs, and in 1930 at the peak of private golf club activities, there were about 5,700 clubs. In the years following the depression, many clubs found it necessary to relax membership restrictions and were taken over by county and city governments and incorporated in public park systems. By the 1960's, there were over 6,000 golf courses in the United States. Of these, about half were private; the rest were either public or semi-public. (*Collier's Encyclopedia*, 1967, Vol. II: 212)

These observations are substantiated by the evidence in Table 2. In 1931, 78 percent of all golf courses in the United States were private. (In Westchester County, New York, where Lundberg,

Table 2

Private and Public Courses in 1931, 1950, 1960, 1970, and 1978

(Number and Percents)

	1931[a]	1950[b]	1960[b]	1970[b]	1978[c]
Total	100%	100%	100%	100%	100%
	(N = 5,691)	(N = 4,931)	(N = 6,385)	(N = 10,188)	(N = 12,684)
Private	78%	62%	51%	45%	41%
	(N = 4,448)	(N = 3,049)	(N = 3,236)	(N = 4,619)	(N = 5,168)
Public	22%	38%	49%	55%	59%
	(N = 1,243)	(N = 1,882)	(N = 3,149)	(N = 5,569)	(N = 7,516)

[a]Source: Golf, June 1976, p. 14.
[b]Source: Statistical Abstracts, 1972, p. 208.
[c]Source: Statistical Abstracts, 1979, p. 242.

193

Komarovsky, and McInery [1934] did their classic research on leisure at about this time, 92 percent of the sixty-three golf courses were private). In 1950, only 62 percent of all courses were private. By 1960, just over half (51 percent) were private. The number of private courses fell below the number of public courses for the first time in 1963 (Dey, 1976). In 1970, 55 percent of all courses were public, and by 1977 that figure was up to 59 percent. Of the 12 million golfers in America, about 10 million (83 percent) play on public courses (*Golf*, June 1976: 13).

There are several important differences between private clubs and public courses.[7] Membership in private clubs is based on social considerations, not golfing ability. Old members invite new members to join and they in turn are carefully screened by a committee. Families are usually the basic membership unit, a fact that results in clubs being "status groupings" as well as places where people play golf. This is evident in the number of club activities that have little or nothing to do with golf (e.g., dinners, dances, swimming for the kids, and wedding receptions). Some families join for these reasons more than for golf (Lundberg, Komarovsky, and McInery, 1934).

Nonmembers cannot play golf at private clubs unless they are introduced, and usually accompanied, by a member. There are seldom limits on the number of guests any member can have, but the number of times any local resident can be a guest at the club is often limited (e.g., not more than once a month). There are policies that encourage members with guests to play at certain times of the day rather than others. For example, some private clubs charge guests more to play before 3 P.M. (when members are most likely to prefer playing) and less to play after 3 P.M. (when club "traffic" is slower). These policies stress the members' right to play undisturbed whenever they want to and nonmenbers' "right" to play only when they are granted that "privilege" by club members.

Public courses are not exclusive. Some people have "season memberships" that entitle them to unlimited use of the course; others pay a daily admission price or "greens fee." No screening process is involved; anyone who can pay can play. Families sometimes play at public courses, but use, generally, is on an individual basis. As a result, public courses are not the same kind of social "unit" as private clubs. Social events are not common and extra facilities such as swimming pools usually are not provided. "Social memberships" are seldom found at public courses.

Private clubs and public courses are structurally quite separate. Members of private clubs can play at public courses any time they wish, but they seldom do. On the other hand, people who play at public courses cannot play at private clubs whenever they want to; they must be invited. Moreover, the golfing abilities of people who play at public courses have virtually no bearing on their chances for membership in private clubs. Consequently, there is little or no movement of people between private clubs and public courses.

Private clubs and public courses have unequal reputations among golfers. As a rule, private clubs have more prestige than public courses. For one thing, they are thought to have—and probably do have—more difficult and better-kept courses. They tend to have well-kept tees and greens; watered fairways; large, strategically-placed sandtraps; many trees; and picturesque creeks and lakes. While some public courses have many of these features, as a rule, they are easier to play and are not as well kept. They are more likely to have bumpy or scarred tees and greens; parched fairways; and few sandtraps, trees, and water hazards. These differences tend to result from the greater wear and tear on public courses, and the more limited resources they have for maintenance and repair.

Private clubs are more likely to have rich golfing traditions. On a local level, they are more likely to host "invitational" tournaments involving prestigious golfers from a given state or region. They also are more likely to be the sites of national tournaments such as the Masters, the U.S. Open, and PGA. Public courses, on the other hand, tend to have little or no golfing tradition. They may sponsor tournaments of various kinds, but they usually do not draw top golfers. Some excellent local golfers play at these courses, but regionally or nationally known golfers seldom do. They rarely sponsor—or are asked to host—major golf tournaments.[8]

Finally, private clubs are more likely to employ highly visible and prestigious teaching professionals. Many of these "pros" used to play on the professional golf tour; some still do. Touring professionals also are likely to be affiliated with private rather than public courses. Public courses tend to have less well-known teaching pros; some have no pro at all.

A third dimension of golfing behavior concerns the kind of people golfers tend to play with. People are not always free to choose their golfing partners, so the discussion here must include some indication of the role that differentiation factors play in the rules governing who plays with whom under various circumstances. When golfers are free to choose their playing partners, what criteria do they use? Do race, religion, gender, and socioeconomic status enter into their choices and, if so, how and why? Do these factors have the same effects at private clubs and public courses?

The discussion here of these questions is based on several assumptions about the reasons people play golf and the implications these reasons have for the kinds of criteria people use in selecting their playing partners. Most golfers play to have fun. They play to get away from work and the routine; to get some outdoor exercise with friends; to enjoy the personal challenges inherent in the game.[9] To achieve these goals, they prefer playing with people who are similar to themselves. Under these circumstances, they do not have to play any particular role; they can relax and have enough common bases for some casual conversation (an important ingredient in a sport that takes four to five hours and involves a lot of walking between shots).

Some golfers, however, have ulterior motives for playing. They want to play a particular role and hope that golf will help them to achieve some other end (e.g., business or political success). Some writers (e.g., Clarke, 1956) have suggested this may be a rather prominent motivation, but we believe it applies to a statistical minority of all golfers. When people play for utilitarian reasons, they are likely to play with those whom they consider useful. Utilitarian golfers may choose to play with people who are similar to themselves because these people "having something to offer." For example, a real estate agent may play with a building contractor so they can discuss a business venture that might be "mutually beneficial." Utilitarian motives also introduce the possibility that difference may also be a factor in people's selection of playing partners. For example, a white politician may play a round with a black foreman at a local plant to enhance his credibility in the black community.

In short, "expressive," nonutilitarian motives tend to prevail, fostering an emphasis on similarity as the major factor affecting choice of playing partners. This factor also enters into at least some of the choices made by people who play for more utilitarian reasons. As a rule, then, one should expect that people will tend to play with others who are similar to themselves in terms of race, religion, gender, and socioeconomic status. Golfing ability will also be included in this discussion since it too is likely to affect people's choice of playing partners.

Who Plays Golf and Who Does Not?

Who are the 12 million Americans who play at least fifteen rounds of golf a year? Are these "golfers" different from "nongolfers" in terms of race, religion, gender, and socioeconomic status? If so, how are they different?

Socioeconomic Status

Education. Education per se probably has little or no direct bearing on who becomes a golfer. Most learning in school has little to do with the knowledge and skills required to play golf. While golf requires some ability to reason through difficult situations, advanced education does not seem to be required to master the game's intellectual processes and judgments. Moreover, though golf has a high-status-sport image, education is not as prominent a part of that image as occupational status and income seem to be.

All other things being equal, there would be no particular reason to believe that highly educated persons would be any more likely than less-educated persons would be to play golf. Yet, education is not altogether unimportant because it affects occupational status and income, which have considerable impact on the chances of becoming a golfer.

Occupation. The existing literature contains more evidence on occupational status than the other differentiation variable under consideration. Unfortunately, the evidence is inconsistent.

In his occupational prestige and leisure activities analysis, Clarke (1956: 304) found:

> Several relationships . . . were curvilinear. For example, the number of times a year the respondents played golf increased along with their prestige ratings until the middle status group [comprised of "sales and clerical workers as well as other white-collar employees generally"] was reached. At this point the frequency of participation began to decline with higher occupational scores. Within this middle group the highest degree of participation occurred among those who classified themselves as "salesman."

Burdge (1969) examined the relationship between occupational prestige and leisure activities, and contrary to Clarke found that people in the highest prestige category were most likely to play golf. In their analysis of occupational status and leisure activity, Cunningham et al. (1970: 109–10) found:

In general, little relationship was observed between membership in a specific occupational group and participation in active leisure activities. The main exception to this generalization was found in participation in golf. A significant association was found between golf participation and "white collar" workers for the total of all ages and at age 30 to 49.

There were some differences among white-collar categories (e.g., 27 percent of all "professional" workers reported playing golf compared to 20 percent of people in the "clerical and sales" category), but the most striking pattern was the tendency for white-collar workers to be three to four times as likely to play as blue-collar workers. The authors went on to suggest, however, that "the relationship between golf participation and occupation may disappear" due to the increased opportunities for blue-collar workers to play at public courses.

We disagree with the speculation that occupational differences are likely to disappear. The "democratization of golf" has been going on for several decades now (see Table 2; Lynd and Lynd, 1937: 247–49) and sizable differences remain. Moreover, the "disappearance thesis" acknowledges changes in the structure of golf, but fails to deal with the structural characteristics of various occupations. A closer look at these characteristics suggests some new approaches to studying the effects occupational status can have on people's golfing behavior.

The focus here will be on three job characteristics: the number of hours worked each week; the degree of flexibility in working hours; and the degree that work success requires cultivation of social and community contacts. These three attributes have a single commonality: the extent to which various occupations permit or encourage the inclusion of golf in one's average "work week" (Eitzen and Sage, 1978: 212).

In some occupations, work requires only a limited number of hours per week, thus permitting other pursuits. Other occupations demand long hours and limit non-work-related activity. People in the first type occupations have more hours available for a time-consuming sport. People in the second type occupations have less time available and, as a result, are less likely to play golf.

Occupations also differ in the extent to which working hours are flexible or fixed. People in some occupations can arrange their working hours to make room for golf. Other people cannot; they must work specific hours or lose their jobs. As a result, people in occupations that allow some flexibility in working hours have more opportunities to schedule golf.

Finally, occupations vary in their reliance on social and community relations (i.e., the extent to which the work requires knowledge of local affairs, good public relations, and a willingness to cater to client's interests and needs). Practicing some occupations requires considerable time and energy devoted to knowing the "pulse," keeping abreast of changes, and learning about arrivals and departures in the community. These jobs depend on social involvement. Since playing golf is one way to develop and maintain these community ties, people in occupations requiring such ties are more likely to play. The likelihood of this pattern is greatest when companies are willing to subsidize some portion of their employees' golfing expenses (e.g., club membership). People in jobs not requiring cultivation of community contacts may play golf for other reasons but do not have an occupational incentive for "taking up the game."

Each of these three factors—number of work hours, flexibility, and need for contacts—probably contribute to the likelihood of either playing or not playing golf. Taken together, they suggest occupational profiles of those most and least likely to play. (See Hodge, Seigel, and Rossi [1964] for a ranking of occupations according to prestige.) High-status occupations (e.g., physicians, lawyers, dentists, architects, heads of departments in government, mayors of large cities, and ministers) tend to have flexible hours and require the cultivation of social and community relations, but they also tend to occupy long hours.[10] This means that people in high-status occupations have some, but not all, of the attributes that are conducive to playing golf.

People in middle-status jobs (e.g., undertakers, newspaper reporters, insurance agents, local labor union officials, and traveling salesmen for wholesale concerns) tend to have all three attributes: shorter and more flexible hours and jobs that require social and community relations.

Lower-status jobs (e.g., garage mechanics, truck drivers, cooks in restaurants, janitors, and dock workers) lack most of the occupational characteristics conducive to playing golf. They have somewhat shorter work weeks, but hours tend to be fixed and the work involves things more than people (Kohn, 1969). As a result, these people are probably least likely of all to be golfers.

Income. Some evidence (de Grazia, 1962) suggests that high-income people spend about the same proportion of their income on recreation and leisure activities as low-income people (about 5 percent). But 5 percent of $100,000 is $5,000 while 5 percent of

$5,000 is only $250. This difference in the amount of dollars available for recreation and leisure has direct bearing on the ability to purchase golf clubs, bags and balls, pay greens fees, and rent golf carts. And these expenses are considerable. As Tunis (1958:109) observed: "Golf today, surely one of the most popular of all our participating sports, and one of the fastest growing, is also one of the most expensive." Miller and Russell (1969: 159) note that "Spending by golfers in the United States alone for golf products topped $1 billion in 1969, more than is spent on any other sport." A set of clubs and a bag may cost $100-$750; on the average, a package of three golf balls costs about $4; daily greens fees vary, but average about $5; and the electric carts that have become so popular in recent years cost almost $10 per round. Thus, some rounds of golf may cost about $10 to $20, plus the cost of clubs (and whatever bets, drinks, and food are included). These figures illustrate our major point: financial resources directly affect the extent to which one is able to play golf (Neumeyer and Neumeyer, 1936: 43; Kaplan, 1969: 192).

In short, the three major components of socioeconomic status seem to have different relationships to tendencies to play or not to play golf. Education probably has little or no direct effect. There probably is a curvilinear relationship between occupational status and playing golf, and income probably relates to golf in a positive linear fashion.

Race

Race affects participation in golf through its effects on socioeconomic status. The lower occupational status and income levels of the black community limit the extent to which blacks can even consider playing an expensive and time-consuming sport. Blacks with the same educations, occupations, and incomes as whites probably are not as likely to play golf.

Golf's image as "a white man's game" is fostered by the small number of black players seen on professional tournament television broadcasts. In 1971 there were only two blacks on the women's professional tour (Althea Gibson Darben and Renee Powell). In 1973 there were only seven blacks on the men's tour. Charles Sifford had been on the tour the longest; Lee Elder, Pete Brown, Jim Dent, Curtis Sifford (Charles's nephew), George Johnson, and Chuck Thorpe were relative newcomers (*Ebony*, July 1971; Robinson, 1973).

Not only are there relatively few black professional golfers, those few have encountered racial prejudice and discrimination. Charles Sifford, who was the first black to win a men's professional tournament (the Long Beach Open in 1957) is quoted as saying that "discrimination . . . has kept the black golfer ten to fifteen years behind" (Hoch, 1972 cited in Sage, 1974). Althea Darben, who became the first black to play on the Ladies Professional Golf Association (LPGA) tour in 1963, was not invited to some tournaments because of her race (*Ebony*, July 1971). Lee Elder was the first black man ever to play in the Masters tournament at Augusta National in Georgia in 1975 (Kirschenbaum, 1975; Jenkins, 1975). These circumstances do not do much to enhance golf's popularity among blacks.

Blacks also are not likely to view golf as a means of upward mobility or economic success. For example, an article in *Ebony* (May 1975) on "Who Are the Highest Paid Athletes?" mentioned seventeen blacks: 53 percent (N = 9) were basketball players; 29 percent (N = 5) were baseball players; 12 percent (N = 2) were boxers; one was a football player; and none were golfers.

Finally, as far as leisure activities are concerned, blacks have developed interests other than golf. In his book *The Black Bourgeoisie* (1957), Frazier discussed the sports interests of the black middle and upper classes. These included baseball and football, but not golf.

Religion

Coming to America as it did from Scotland and England, golf was more a part of the cultural tradition and leisure patterns of Protestants than either Catholics or Jews. Moreover, white Protestants were at the heights of power, privilege, and prestige before Catholics and Jews were in America in substantial numbers. Protestant political, economic, and social dominance was well established when the waves of Catholic and Jewish immigration began in the last half of the nineteenth century. Because of their higher socioeconomic status, Protestants were able to afford the time golf required and the expenses it involved (particularly in the 1920s through 1950s when golf courses tended to be private clubs).

The situation has changed in contemporary life because Protestants' socioeconomic status is no higher, in general, than Catholics' and Jews' and golf courses tend to be public not private. We suspect, however, that Protestants still are more likely than Catholics or Jews to be golfers, due to the close relationship between Protestants' social respectability (noted earlier) and the image of golf as a desirable high-status activity. At the same time, there are reasons to believe some of these differences between the three major faiths are lessening.

As Catholics have gained in socioeconomic status, they have expressed considerable interest in assimilation (e.g., Kennedy, 1976; Greeley, 1977). Evidence of this posture has been the Catholic church's elimination of many religious differences that have marked Catholics off from Protestants (e.g., eating fish on Friday; the Latin Mass), the relaxation of many policies that divided Protestants and Catholics (e.g., marriage regulations), and the adoption of many "Protestant ways" (e.g., the democratization of the church through greater lay involvement). As Protestant-Catholic hostilities (Kane, 1955; Stark, 1964) have subsided, some of the blatant discrimination against Catholics has disappeared and Catholic membership in predominantly Protestant private clubs has increased. The growing number of public courses also has made golf more available to Catholics. All of these factors probably have contributed to Catholics being more active golfers today than ever before. This trend is likely to continue as Catholics become even more assimilated.

Like Catholics, Jews were lower-status immigrants through much of the late nineteenth and early twentieth centuries. The Jewish experience after that was quite different, however. Jews achieved high socioeconomic status much sooner than Catholics. They outranked Protestants in education, occupation, and income several decades before Catholics achieved parity and they were more highly concentrated in Northeastern metropolitan areas, giving them more access to golf courses. At the same time, the Jewish experience included more systematic exclusion from private clubs and many other aspects of American society (e.g., hotels and resorts that had golf facilities; see Belth, 1958). This author knows of one private club that did not drop its ban against Jews until the 1960s, a couple of decades after Catholics had been admitted. Jews also have not expressed quite as much overall interest in assimilation as Catholics. They have preferred a posture of cultural and structural pluralism (Gordon, 1964; Sklare, 1971). In short, the Jewish experience in America includes some factors that might foster interest in golf and some that might preclude such an interest.

Jewish involvement in golf seems to be increasing. Postal, Silver, and Silver (1965: 291) report that "for the most part, the Jew was conspicuous by his absence from the links during the early history of the sport in America," but "Jews have turned to golf in ever increasing numbers in the United States and elsewhere." Kaplan (1960: 110) also has noted "the sizable number of second- and third-generation Jews who play golf, a game totally strange to all their grandfathers and to most of their fathers."

In short, Catholics and Jews are more likely to play golf today than ever before, and the historical gap between them and Protestants probably is shrinking. Without more concrete data, however, it is difficult to say whether there is any difference between Catholic and Jewish participation. The suspicion here is that, if there is any difference, it is rather small.

There probably are even greater differences in the golfing behaviors of various subgroups within the three major faiths. For example, within each faith, there are "liberal" groups and "conservative" groups. Reform Jews, mainline Protestants, and "post–Vatican II Catholics" are "liberal." Orthodox Jews, sectarian Protestants, and "pre–Vatican II Catholics" are "conservative." Even after socioeconomic factors are controlled, religious ideologies probably have some effects of their own on golfing behavior. Liberal ideology would seem to be more compatible with playing golf. Liberal groups tend to be less "other-worldly" and more "this-worldly" in their religious orientations. They believe they should be active in their religious groups, but they do not believe religion should consume all of their nonworking hours. Deford's (1976) observation that "the trip out of the house on Sunday is not to visit a church, but to see a game or to play one" probably applies most to members of these liberal groups. They view "this life" as good in its own right—something that they should be involved in. They have positive views of pleasure and leisure. Consequently, they are most likely to tolerate and accept the behaviors that accompany golf (e.g., gambling) and the social activities that are often associated with golf clubs (e.g., drinking and dancing). Conservative groups tend to be other-worldly. They believe their lives should be rooted in religious groups not in "secular" groups. They believe "worldly things" are sinful and should be avoided. As a result, conservative religious groups probably are underrepresented among golfers.[11]

Gender

In 1962, de Grazia reported that men are twice as likely as women to participate in sports (8 percent versus 4 percent). That difference probably has been reduced somewhat in the last fifteen years (Miller and Russell, 1969). Despite the fact that "women are taking to the golf courses in ever-increasing numbers, . . . the ratio of men to women golfers [in 1975 was] about 3 to 1" (*Golf*, June 1976: 14). In other words, of the 12 million golfers in America, only about 3 million are women. The gender difference may be shrinking, but it is still greater in golf than in some other sports.

Some of this gender difference probably can be explained on the basis of socioeconomic differences between the sexes (Knudsen, 1969). Women compared to men with similar educations, occupations, and incomes, are still less likely to play golf. Some of *these* differences can be attributed to the discrepant ways men and women sometimes are expected to perform the same job. For example, saleswomen are not expected to "hustle" potential clients on the golf course. Some of the gender difference can also be attributed to the general social view of how men and women are to use their leisure time. Men are freer to participate in sports activities that take them away from their families. Even if they are working, women are expected to participate in "family activities" (e.g., taking the children to the pool, picnics) or in activities related to their role as housewives (e.g., sewing, gardening). Though some of these gender role differences are being reassessed, many of them still apply to a majority of American men and women. As a result, women—because they are women—are less likely to play golf than men.

Race, religion, and gender influence whether or not people play golf. Some of these effects are the result of socioeconomic status. But even after socioeconomic considerations are "held constant," whites, Protestants in mainline denominations, and men are most likely to play golf. Blacks, Catholics, and Jews—particularly "conservative" Catholics and Jews—and women are least likely to play.

Where People Play: Private Clubs and Public Courses

Now that golfers have been distinguished from non-golfers, the next step is to explore some of the differences between those who play at private clubs and others who play at public courses. How do these two groups compare in terms of race, religion, gender, and socioeconomic status? What seems to account for differences between groups?

Socioeconomic Status

It is widely believed that private clubs are for the rich and public courses are for everybody else (Eitzen and Sage, 1978: 217). While people from higher social strata *may* play public courses, people from lower social strata *must* play public courses. Less affluent people cannot afford the expense of belonging to private clubs—ranging from a few hundred to several thousand dollars a year—and they probably would not be accepted socially even if they could. The result is that people who belong to private clubs tend to be high in socioeconomic status while people who play at public courses are somewhat lower, but also more heterogeneous, in status. The next step is to consider the role that each of the three major components of socioeconomic status plays.

Education. On the average, people who play at private clubs are likely to be better educated than those who play at public courses. But education per se probably has little direct effect on use of these two types of golfing facilities. If everything else were equal (e.g., occupation and income), there would be no reason to expect that highly educated people would prefer private clubs while less educated people would choose, or be relegated to, public courses. The effect of education is indirect through its tendency to increase earning power and access to particular jobs, both of which have more direct bearing on where people play golf.

Occupation. It was noted earlier that people in jobs with shorter work weeks and more flexible working hours would be more likely to play golf than people in jobs with long and fixed working hours. There is little or no reason to believe that these factors have any effect of their own on whether people belong to private clubs or play at public courses. Where people play would seem to be a function of other factors.

The extent to which a job requires involvement in the community would seem to be an important determinant in where people play golf. If a person must establish social networks in the community to perform a job (e.g., business, sales), then it might be in his or her best interest to belong to a private club. Not only are private clubs a good place to meet people, they are a good place to meet the "right kinds" of people (i.e., people with money and connections in the community). This thesis is consistent with Havinghurst and Feingenbaum's (1958: 399) analysis of adult leisure activities in Kansas City:

> Community-centeredness is the favorite leisure style of upper-middle class people. Being successful in business or a profession induces them to join business and social organizations where they interact with each other to form wider circles of social and business contacts. Membership in the country club is part of their proper and accepted style of living.

People in occupations that do not require "staying in tune" with the community are more likely to play public courses. They are less likely to have "ulterior" motives and, consequently, have less "need" to join private clubs.

Income. People with higher incomes are more likely to belong to private clubs and people with lower incomes are more likely to play at public courses. Direct empirical evidence regarding this proposition is limited, but most everything that is known about the behavior of high-income people and the expenses of private clubs suggests that this is a reasonable proposition. For example, Lundberg, Komarovsky, and McInery (1934: 65) observed that

> golf must still be considered a relatively aristocratic pastime. It conforms in a high degree to nearly all the canons of conspicuous waste and offers superior opportunities for advertising one's pecuniary status. Dress, equipment, and other costs can be inflated to very impressive proportions. The heavy demands of golf on space means that great numbers of courses cannot be provided without prohibitive expense. It is extremely time-consuming and in this respect alone suggests one of the main prerequisites of the traditional leisure class. Membership in the "right" golf club would perhaps still be accepted as one of the most impressive single indices of status in the social scale.

Though this statement was made some time ago, it still stands as a fair observation about the expenses associated with membership in private clubs. Lower-income people who can afford to play golf are not as able to afford the luxuries associated with playing at private clubs.

Race

The historical exclusion of blacks by members of private white clubs was referred to earlier, but black exclusion from white clubs is not only historical. Formal racial restrictions have been eliminated for the most part, so racial discrimination is less obvious than it used to be. But the process by which new members are chosen still provides plenty of opportunities for club members to select only those people whom they wish to include among their friends. These mechanisms include having to be asked by a member; needing letters of reference from club members; being "investigated" and interviewed by a screening committee; being voted upon by some body of club members.

As a rule, club members tend to choose people who they know best and who they believe will "fit in" with other club members. Whites are more likely to choose whites for both of these reasons. Social friendships tend to follow racial lines; whites' more intimate social relationships tend to be with other whites, and blacks' tend to be with other blacks. Moreover, whites who are acquainted with blacks may assume that other whites would fit in better than blacks would. The assumption springs from two sources: a belief that people of each race prefer to "be with their own kind" and a belief that white club members would prefer that blacks not be included. Whether or not these beliefs are valid, they are likely to affect club members' behavior and result in whites' being selected more often than blacks. Do black golfers play at predominantly black private clubs, or do they play at public courses? There are a few predominantly black private golf clubs. For example, Renee Powell's father started the "first and only individually black-owned course in America" in the late 1940s (*Ebony*, July 1971: 108). Lies's (1929) survey of Indianapolis's recreational facilities revealed one predominantly black public nine-hole course, but no private black clubs. In his analysis of the black bourgeoisie, Frazier discussed black "social clubs" but he never mentioned golf and country clubs. Robinson (1973: 142) observed that most of today's black men professionals "learned on municipal [i.e., public] courses of far less difficulty than the ones they face when they come onto the professional tour."

Religion

Protestants played a major role in the growth of private golf clubs during the late nineteenth and early twentieth centuries. The exclusion of Catholics and Jews from these clubs suggests that the desire to separate and protect themselves from the lower-status, non-Protestant immigrants was one force in the formation of these clubs. Baltzell's (1958 and 1964) analyses suggest that Protestants are still overrepresented among private club members.

Catholics and Jews who are interested in playing golf have been faced with the choice of establishing private clubs of their own or playing on public courses. Jews probably have been inclined to create their own private clubs more than Catholics. Jewish clubs began to appear in the New York area in 1914. The 1923 U.S. Open championship was held at Inwood, a Jewish club in Glen Head, Long Island (Postal, Silver, and Silver, 1965: 291). By 1931, "there were more than one hundred golf clubs in the United States with a membership predominantly or exclusively Jewish" (Betts, 1974: 333). Baltzell (1964) cited examples of private Jewish clubs in Philadelphia and Pittsburgh.

Catholics have not had the necessary occupational and income resources until quite recently to form private clubs, but, as they have gained in socioeconomic status, they have expressed their preference for assimilation. Catholic membership in predominantly Protestant private clubs has increased as Protestant-Catholic tensions have waned. This pattern and the existence of separate Jewish clubs are apparent in the following example cited by Baltzell (1964: 357):

> In the city of Springfield, Massachusetts, there are three leading country clubs: the oldest, the Longmeadow Country Club, has an exclusive membership of some four hundred Protestant families of solid old-stock ancestry (only a few Catholics); the newer and less exclusive Springfield Country Club has three hundred member families, half of whom are Catholic (mostly Irish); and finally, the newest and most lavish club, the Crest View Country Club, has three hundred members, all of them Jewish."

Though we have not been able to locate any data on this matter, we believe that mainline Protestants, "post-Vatican II Catholics," and Reform Jews are more likely to belong to private clubs than conservative Protestants, "pre-Vatican II Catholics," and either Conservative or Orthodox Jews. The religious values and norms of the more liberal bodies are more compatible with the social expectations and social conduct that are a part of country-club behavior. The religious ideologies and behavioral demands of more conservative groups do not permit participation in many club activities. People from these groups who want to play golf are more likely to be found on public courses.

Gender

Membership in private clubs tends to be a family affair. Some people have "single memberships," but "family memberships" are more common. As a result, women are about as likely to belong to private clubs as men.

For a variety of reasons having to do with their work, their breadwinning role in the society, and their tendency to play golf more often, men probably suggest joining private clubs to their wives more often than women suggest it to their husbands. As a result, many women belong because their husbands do. Women, however, may play an active role in the decision to join a private club as they might view membership as an excellent way to fulfill their mother role. They might believe that their children will be better off associating with the children of other club members than with lower-status children in the community. They also might believe this process of selective association will increase the chances of their children marrying someone from "the right kind of family." Consequently, some men may belong to private clubs mainly because their wives want to join for their children's sake.

Among the men and women who belong to private clubs, men play golf more often than women. At the same time, women in private clubs play golf more than women who play golf at public courses. This pattern results from the socioeconomic advantages of women who belong to country clubs, their greater amount of leisure time, and the family nature of private club membership.

Men are more likely than women to play golf at public courses. Some reasons for this pattern pertain to men's socioeconomic advantages over women. Some reasons, however, have to do with gender and the nature of public courses. Since men are more likely to play golf than women, and public courses are primarily golfing (rather than social) facilities, men are more likely than women are to use them. Some women play golf at public courses, but they are underrepresented in comparison with their proportion in the total population. They also are underrepresented in comparison to their female counterparts at private clubs.

Who Plays Golf with Whom?

Now that some idea of the kinds of people who belong to private clubs and those who play on public courses has been established, one question remains: to what extent do socioeconomic status, race, religion, and gender affect choice of playing partners? Since the people who belong to private clubs are different from the people who play public courses, and the differentiation factors previously considered may play different roles in each place, the format here will be changed and the two facilities will be discussed separately. Golfing ability is also included as a factor that can influence playing partner selection.

Private Clubs

Gender and golfing ability are the two most important determinants of who plays golf with whom at private clubs. Socioeconomic status, race, and religion are not inconsequential, but—at least partly because private clubs tend to be homogeneous in respect to these dimensions—they tend to be less important in choice of playing partners there.

How often do men and women play golf together at private clubs? Seldom. Most of the time, men play with men, and women play with women. Several factors contribute to this gender differentiation pattern.

Private clubs with more than one course usually designate one as the "men's course" and another as the "women's course." The men's course is usually longer, "tougher" and is used as the "championship course" when tournaments are held at the club. Even at clubs where men and women play the same course, they seldom play together. One way that gender differentiation is encouraged is the designation of "ladies' days."[12] This practice concentrates women's play into one or two days a week (usually Monday or Tuesdays), which has the effect of reducing the number of women on the course during most other days of the week (which are not formally designated "men's days" but amount to that). Men and women also are urged to play at different times. The usual pattern is for women to play in the morning and for men to play in the afternoon. From 8 A.M. until noon there are hardly any men on the course except for the grounds crew. Heaven help the woman who appears at the first tee between noon and 2 P.M. when the men are teeing off!

These policies probably originated in, and usually are explained in terms of, three common definitions of the situation. One of these concerns men's and women's stereotypes of each others' golfing abilities. Men generally think of women as poorer golfers who play too slowly. As Colman McCarthy of the *Washington Post* satirically observed, "the point of having separate starting times is to keep the slow-moving hens out of the barnyard so the fast-strut [*sic*] roosters can parade without interference" (McCarthy, 1976). Women, on the other hand, tend to view men as better golfers who play too fast.[13] Second, the occupational factors that have been discussed predispose men toward playing with other men; they can "talk business" with other men more than with women. Women also believe they have more interests in common with other women than with men. Finally, there are some concerns about the romantic implications of men and women playing golf together, though these are not as likely to be articulated by club members. The practice of men playing with men, and women with women, reduces the chance of extramarital affairs and/or rumors that might disrupt the ebb and flow of "normal club activities."

There are certain occasions at private clubs where men and women play golf together. These occasions usually involve a special type of golfing competition (e.g., adult or junior-senior scotch foursomes).[14] These activities are sprinkled throughout club's monthly calendars of events but it is understood that they are exceptions to the rule of the same-sex playing partners. The exceptional character of these events is symbolized by the use of special rules and the lighthearted nature of the "competition" that takes place.

A second determinant of who plays golf with whom is golfing ability. Men of similar ability tend to play together as do women of similar ability. Ability usually is measured in terms of "handicap" (i.e., the difference between par for eighteen holes and a person's average score for eighteen). The lower the handicap, the better the golfer. Because handicaps are posted regularly for all to see, they become one of the factors people use to judge similar ability, and since golf is an "expressive" rather than an "instrumental" activity for most people, they prefer to play with someone with a relatively similar handicap. "Good" golfers prefer to play with other "good" golfers; playing with people who have higher handicaps is thought to be a "drag." High handicappers also tend to choose one another, preferring to "play their own game" rather than slowing down people who are likely to shoot ten, twenty, or thirty strokes less.

Sometimes men of different ability play together, as do women of different calibers. (When this happens, they "make things even" by teaming better golfers with poorer golfers or by giving each other strokes to equalize the competition.) At least some of these pairings of golfers with different competencies may be accounted for in terms of socioeconomic, racial, and religious affinities.

Although people are not likely to make precise distinctions among socioeconomic status components when judging another's overall compatibility with themselves, the occupation component may be particularly salient insofar as "instrumental" motivations affect people's choice of playing partners. Under these conditions, the occupational characteristics discussed earlier—length and flexibility of working hours and the extent of community involvement—may be important. But, the functional relationship between particular occupations may be more important. Most occupations involve work habits, goods, or services that are more closely related to some occupations than they are to others. For example, real estate agents and lawyers may "need each other" more than schoolteachers "need" morticians; schoolteachers may relate to businessmen who are on the school board, while morticians and lawyers may have more professional interests in common. Insofar as instrumental considerations are important, people are most likely to play with others whose occupations are most closely related to their own.

To the extent that a club includes people of different racial and religious backgrounds, these factors may affect people's selection of partners. People may choose, or may feel pressured into playing with, other members of their racial or religious group even if their golfing abilities and socioeconomic status are quite different (though not if gender is different). For example, even though they may belong to predominantly Protestant clubs, Catholics may tend to play with other Catholics and Jews with other Jews. Sendler (1969: 412) reports the following incident involving partner selection along racial lines:

> In Cleveland [black and white professional football players] got into a dispute over a celebrity golf tournament at the Ashland Country Club—a competition promoted by white defensive back Ross Fichtner. Black athletes, present in the past, were not invited in '68 and Fichtner said it was because the Blacks hadn't socialized with Whites at previous tournaments.

Public Courses

The situation at public courses is different. People using public courses are more heterogeneous in terms of socioeconomic status, race and religion. On the basis of the increased variety of people, one might expect more interaction among those from different backgrounds, but this does not seem to be the case. Because public courses are not social units, like private clubs, they do not have the social calendars and special events that foster interaction between men and women, people of different ability, and people from different racial, religious and socioeconomic groups.

One of the few elements that might produce such interaction concerns the "starter's" role when someone goes alone to a public course not knowing anyone or seeing anyone he or she recognizes. The starter—an employee who keeps track of the order and pace at which groups go off the first tee—will put that person in a group with other people. The starter may use a variety of visible factors—race, golf swings, the kinds of bags and clubs (cost and condition), dress—to match people he thinks are similar. In this case, socioeconomic status, race, and ability may play some role in who plays with whom. The starter, however, may not consider these factors and simply assign people to groups according to the openings that are available (e.g., putting a "onesome" with a "threesome" and two "twosomes" together). Under such circumstances, socioeconomic status, race, religion, and golfing ability play little or no role in determining who plays golf with whom. A person could wind up playing with others who are very different on some or all of these attributes and, unless players want to make a scene, they play with whomever they are assigned (though the experience that they have on that round may influence whom they look for or avoid the next time they go out to the course).

Most people go to public courses *with* other people to play rounds that they have scheduled in advance. The chances are that these players know one another quite well from other settings (e.g., neighborhood, work, or church). The socioeconomic, racial, religious, and gender composition of these settings usually are not random; nor are people's selection of friends within these settings. People tend to associate with others who are similar to themselves and, if they have a mutual interest in golf, they probably have some idea of one another's golfing abilities. Consequently, these factors are likely to influence their partner selection.

Though all the people playing at a public course at any given time are quite heterogeneous with regard to socioeconomic status, race, religion, gender, and golfing ability, the smaller groups in which people play tend to be quite homogeneous. The groups on the course look more like a mosaic than a melting pot.[15]

Summary and Conclusions

This chapter has stressed the effects that several differentiation factors have on participation in golf. This type of analysis can be important for at least three reasons: (1) its contribution to our knowledge of the social dynamics of golf; (2) as a model for similar analyses of the roles that these factors play in other sports; and (3) its contribution to our understanding of the role that sports play in terms of social inequality in the society as a whole. Let us consider each of these matters briefly.

Social Dynamics of Golf

The chapter began with a perspective that stressed the possibility that each of the several differentiation components under consideration could have separate effects on golfing behavior. The evidence bearing on these factors remains limited and much more research needs to be done before their effects can be fully understood. But, our analysis suggests this perspective has merit. Not only do people with different socioeconomic, racial, religious, and gender attributes participate in golf differently; it seems that the racial, religious, and gender differences cannot be explained away as socioeconomic differences. In fact, race, religion, and gender may have more impact on at least some aspects of golfing behavior than socioeconomic status does.

Insofar as *education* affects people's occupational status and income, it has indirect effects on golfing behavior. But education per se does not seem to have much direct bearing on whether or not people play golf; where they play; or with whom they play.

Occupation has some indirect effects through its bearing on income as well as important effects of its own. People holding jobs that involve short, flexible working hours and the cultivation of community contacts are most likely to play golf. People in jobs that involve long, inflexible working hours which do not require involvement in the community are least likely to play golf. The length and flexibility of working hours probably have little effect on belonging to private clubs or playing at public courses. People holding jobs that require community contact, however, are most likely to join private clubs. People are likely to play golf with others whose socioeconomic status (including their job) is similar to their own. In some cases, the functional relationships among occupations may also affect the choice of playing partners so that people will tend to play with others whose jobs are most highly related to their own.

The higher a person's *income*, the more likely they are to play golf and to play at private clubs. People are likely to play golf with others whose incomes are similar to their own.

Race probably affects all of the golfing behaviors that have been discussed. Even after socioeconomic factors are controlled, blacks are less likely than whites to play golf and to belong to private clubs. People tend to play golf with people of their own race.

In terms of *religion*, Protestants probably play golf and belong to private clubs more than either Catholics or Jews (though the religious differences probably are smaller today than ever before). People also are more likely to play golf with others who belong to their own faith than they are to play with people of different faiths. Moreover, "liberal" Protestants, Catholics, and Jews are more likely than "conservatives" to play golf and to belong to private clubs; conservatives who play are likely to play with others whose religious values and beliefs are similar to their own.

Finally, with regard to *gender*, men are more likely to play golf than women. Because membership in private clubs tends to be family based (whereas playing golf at public courses is more of an individual phenomenon), women are as likely to belong to private clubs as men but are less likely to play on public courses. At both kinds of facilities, men tend to play with men, and women with women, though gender differentiation probably is greater at public courses than it is at private clubs.

These results suggest that the kind of model outlined in Figure 1 would be a useful framework for future research on social differentiation and participation in golf. Such an approach would permit the testing of the generalizations that have been offered. It also would allow for the inclusion of other differentiation factors—such as age and ethnicity—that have not been discussed here. When the perspective is elaborated to include these variables and more systematic data are collected, significant steps will have been made in the direction of understanding the social dynamics of golf.

Differentiation, Golf, and Other Sports

The focus in this chapter has been on golf, but there has been some attempt to compare golf with several other sports (see Table 1 and note 6). Of the sports considered previously, golf is most similar to tennis. For this reason, the propositions that were offered regarding the role of differentiation factors in golf also might apply to participation in tennis. If the reader were to substitute "tennis" for "golf" in the brief summary provided above, most of the propositions would seem quite reasonable.

If the factors previously considered play similar roles in golf and tennis, then it would be interesting to examine the roles these factors play in other sports, including those which might be quite different from golf and tennis. Such analyses might suggest some new bases for combining and comparing various sports. For example, distinctions might be made between those sports which are affected most by differentiation factors and those which are affected least. Further distinctions might be made between those which are affected mainly by socioeconomic factors and those which are also affected by race, religion, and gender. These possibilities might suggest new sports typologies and research directions on the effects of social structure on different kinds of sports. They might also suggest some new possibilities for examining the roles that different kinds of sports play in maintaining or changing the structure of social inequality in the larger society.

Golf and Social Inequaltiy

What are the implications our analysis for understanding social inequality in society? It has been argued that golfers and nongolfers are different kinds of people. It has also been argued that golfers who belong to private clubs are different from golfers who play at public courses. And it has been argued that golfers tend to play with other people who are similar to themselves in socially significant ways. Golf at nearly all levels involves more association among some people and less association between them and other groups in society.

It has also been argued that the divisions which occur in golf are not divisions among equals; they are divisions among people who are unequal in many socially significant ways. The groups that have   more   access   to   society's   power,   privilege,   and prestige—whites   more   than   blacks;   "liberal"   Protestants,

Catholics, and Jews more than "conservative" Protestants, Catholics, and Jews; men more than women; and high-status people more than low-status people—tend to play golf at different places and in separate groups.

From this point of view, golf is affected by and symbolizes deeper social divisions. But, our analysis suggests that golf, in some ways, legitimizes and actively perpetuates social divisions. Private clubs help to maintain the privileges that their members enjoy over others by means of several mechanisms (e.g., admission policies that foster socioeconomic, racial, and religious homogeneity among club members; involving members in a network of social activities that consume a considerable portion of their free time, thereby making sure their roots are firmly planted in the "proper" social strata; enhancing the chances that one's children marry into families of similar status; providing offspring with a sporting skill that enables them to interact in club circles later in life; automatically transferring parents' membership in that club to their children provided the children fulfill residency or other such club requirements; and providing easy access to people in functionally related occupations).

Golf's bearing on social inequality extends beyond the role private clubs play in perpetuating differences between their members and others. Socioeconomic, racial, religious, and gender differentiation also occur *within* private clubs. Gender differentiation has been stressed because of its prominence in the life of private club members. Club activities reflect and reaffirm the different roles that high-status men and women are expected to play in society. The men play together, are allowed to have the "best" tee times, and tend to make economic and political decisions that affect the club's survival. Women play golf less, have poorer tee times, and are expected to look after the children's activities at the club. These divisions tend to be viewed as "natural" (because they are consistent with men's and women's roles) and desirable (because they help both sexes to perform their social roles more effectively).

Public courses have attracted a more heterogeneous collection of people. One might expect this diversity to foster more egalitarian interaction among people from different backgrounds, contributing to some reduction in the divisions previously discussed. This does not seem to be the case, however. People who play at public courses tend to play with people they know from other settings. Since these associations tend to involve socioeconomic, racial, religious, and gender similarity, choices of golfing partners reflect these affinities. Only when individuals come alone to a public course looking for a "pick up game" is it likely that they will wind up playing with people who are quite different from themselves. Thus, public courses do not seem to play a major role in fostering more interaction between people with different socioeconomic, racial, religious, or gender attributes. Finally, because there are no structural linkages between public courses and private clubs (e.g., membership in the former does not necessarily affect one's chances of playing at or belonging to the latter), people do not "graduate" from public courses to private clubs. In this sense, the "democratization of golf" probably has not contributed much to the upward mobility of golfers from less privileged social groups.

Golf is a reflection of, and active contributor to, deeply rooted racial, religious, gender, and socioeconomic divisions. As long as these divisions remain, golf will continue to be a sport that some Americans enjoy immensely but many others will never get to play. And, as long as golf encourages the socioeconomic, racial, religious, and gender differentiation observed in this chapter, it will continue to contribute to social inequality.

Notes

1. These are not the only differentiation factors that can affect people's golfing behavior. Others include age and ethnicity (Loy, McPherson, and Kenyon, 1978:332–376). Hopefully these factors will be included in future and more comprehensive analyses of the social dynamics of golf. A number of non-differentiation factors that might affect golfing behavior also are not included. Some of these include region; the rural, suburban, or urban characteristics of communities; and whether or not one's parents played golf. More comprehensive analyses of factors that affect golfing behavior should also include these factors.

2. Recent texts in the sociology of sport (e.g., Snyder and Spreitzer, 1978; Coakley, 1978; Loy, McPherson, and Kenyon, 1978; Eitzen and Sage, 1978; Ball and Loy, 1975) include only fleeting references to golf and the research literature includes no systematic studies of golf comparable to studies on sports such as baseball, football, and basketball. The reasons for the lack of attention to golf are not known, but one factor probably is the small number of sociologists who play golf (Jordan, 1956 and 1963). Some of our observations about the effects of religion and socioeconomic status suggest some reasons why sociologists play golf less than members of some other occupational categories, but further research is needed before the sports interests of different occupational groupings are fully understood.

3. My parents enrolled me in golf classes at a private club when I was five or six years old. I took lessons every summer until I was in my teens; played on the high school golf team and won the championship for sixteen to eighteen-year-olds at the private club where I took lessons. Since then I have played at private clubs and public courses in various parts of the country (ranging from championship courses like Medinah in Chicago to nine-hole courses with sand greens in rural Oklahoma). I continue to play regularly and shoot in the upper-

seventies and low-eighties. As a golfer, I have had opportunities to observe first hand many of the patterns we will be discussing. As a sociologist I also have had opportunities to relate these observations to larger bodies of scientific literature in social differentiation and the sociology of sport.

4. Golf's high-status image is implicit in most discussions of the sport and explicit in some. Johnson's (1964) analysis of the relationships among various leisure activities also sustains this image. He found that participation in golf was highly correlated with other middle-class activities such as swimming and skiing, sailing, attending musical events, attending theater, and reading humor.

5. Bowling is like golf in this respect.

6. A comparison of these sports at the professional level reveals other similarities and differences. As in most other sports at the professional level, participants are "sponsored" or supported by some group of financial backers. Spectators are encouraged to attend and are sold programs to facilitate their understanding of the action.

Professional football, basketball, and baseball players are owned and can be traded by their owners; golfers and tennis players—except in the now defunct World Team Tennis—are not owned. This difference is reflected in the participants' incomes. Football, basketball, and baseball players sign contracts for salaries. Golfers and tennis players have no "guaranteed" income; their annual income depends on how well they perform in relation to their peers.

The crowd at a professional golf event (about 20,000 per day) is larger than a crowd at an average tennis match or basketball game, but it is smaller than the crowds at professional football or baseball games. The ticket price for a golf event (about ten dollars) is higher than for basketball and baseball, but comparable to tennis and football. Once "inside," the crowd is expected to be quiet while watching a golf or tennis match; at football, basketball, and baseball games the crowd is permitted—and even encouraged by cheerleaders—to be loud in support of its favorite team or players.

Starting times in golf and tennis are staggered; matches do not all begin at the same time, as football, basketball, and baseball games do. The national anthem and quasi-religious ceremonies do not occur at the beginning of golf and tennis events, as they do in the other sports. Finally, golfers and tennis players are not compelled to wear uniforms as football, basketball, and baseball players are (though certain kinds of clothing—such as bermuda shorts or "golf shirts" or the traditional tennis "whites"—tend to be worn).

Finally, referees in professional golf are called upon by the players to make selected rulings only in situations that the players define as problematic; in the other sports, referees oversee and judge every play.

7. The sociological literature on golf stresses private golf clubs; public courses are seldom mentioned. Our analysis attempts to provide a more balanced view of the two kinds of facilities. We are aware, however that our observations about private and public courses involve many oversimplifications. Private clubs differ from one another in many ways (e.g., some have longer waiting lists than other do). Some municipally owned public courses are different from other public courses because they have access to city or county taxes and, as a consequence, may be similar to some private courses. We acknowledge these differences but cannot deal with them in detail here.

8. Professional tournaments have been played at public courses such as Torrey Pines, Winged Foot, and Pebble Beach, but these courses are exceptions to the rule.

9. Mulvoy and Spander (1977:10) have described these personal challenges in the following way:

Golf is a game of individual achievements and failures. You face the challenge of the course alone; your teammate is the self-indulgent belief that you can beat it. Your opponent, in the last analysis, is yourself—your inadequacies, your poor judgment, your helplessness. Par is an immediate and unrelenting yardstick, you either play well or you don't, and your score leaves no room for doubt . . . a golfer finds out a great deal about himself during an eighteen-hole round, and besides, life itself could be regarded as an equally unwieldy venture. The fact is we must cope or cop out, and there is no finer place to learn that lesson than on the golf course . . . golf allows you a chance to triumph over yourself. It's a game of the ego.

10. Professional, technical, managerial, and administrative positions have the largest proportions of people working fifty or more hours per week (*U.S. News and World Report*, 24 May 1976:76–77). The reference to physicians competes with a popular image of doctors as "always being on the golf course." We suspect, however, that compared to people in other jobs with similar incomes, doctors are less likely to be golfers; and those who are, are likely to play less often.

11. The "liberal" members of these groups also are more likely to play golf than the "conservative" members are. The term "liberal" must be interpreted carefully here. In the broadest sense, it refers to people who do not adhere to conservative standards of religious belief and practice. These people may or may not have "liberal" social or political views. In fact, their social and political views may be quite conservative (Hadden, 1969; Wuthnow, 1973; Quinley, 1974).

12. In light of our discussion of women's subordinate role in golf, it is interesting to note the similarities between "ladies' day" and the "caddies' days" that many clubs used to have and some still do.

13. For some women's views of golf, see Collett (1928) and Suggs (1960).

14. These events call for team members to hit alternate shots instead of every shot. Junior-senior events often involve pairing male children with adult females and female children with adult males.

15. This mosaic was very evident in a recent round of golf I played. I was playing in a threesome with two other white males (one a campus minister, the other a faculty member in the mathematics department). Four white women were playing in front of us, and four black men were playing on the adjacent fairway.

Works Cited

Abrahamson, Mark; Mizruchi, Ephraim H; and Hornung, Carlton A. *Stratification and Mobility*. New York: Macmillan, 1976.

Amundsen, Kirsten. *The Silenced Majority: Women and American Democracy*. Englewood Cliffs, N.J.: Prentice-Hall, 1971.

Ball, Donald W., and Loy, John W. *Sport and Social Order: Contributions to the Sociology of Sport*. Reading, Mass.: Addison-Wesley, 1975.

Baltzell, E. Digby. *Philadelphia Gentlemen*. Glencoe: Free Press, 1958.

———. *The Protestant Establishment*. London: Sacker and Warburg, 1964.

Belth, N.C., ed. *Barriers: Patterns of Discrimination Against Jews*. New York: Friendly House, 1958.

Betts, John Rickards. *America's Sporting Heritage, 1850–1950*. Reading, Mass.: Addison-Wesley, 1974.

Blauner, Robert. *Racial Oppression in America.* New York: Harper and Row, 1972.

Bromley, David G., and Longino, Charles F., Jr. *White Racism and Black Americans.* Cambridge: Schenkman, 1972.

Burdge, Rabel J. "Levels of Occupational Prestige and Leisure Activity." *Journal of Leisure Research* 1 (Summer 1969):262-70.

Burkey, Richard M. *Ethnic and Racial Groups.* Menlo Park, California: Cummings Publishing Company, 1978.

Clarke, Alfred C. "The Use of Leisure and Its Relation to Levels of Occupational Prestige." *American Sociological Review* 21 (June 1956):301-7.

Coakley, Jay J. *Sport in Society: Issues and Controversies.* St. Louis: Mosby, 1978.

Collett, Glenna. *Ladies in the Rough.* New York: Alfred A. Knopf, 1928.

Colliers Encyclopedia. "Golf." 11 (1967):209-17.

Cunningham, David A.; Montoye, Henry J.; Metzner, Helen L.; and Keller, Jacob B. "Active Leisure Activities as Related to Occupation." *Journal of Leisure Research* 2 (Spring 1970):104-11.

Dee, Norbert, and Liebman, John C. "A Statistical Study of Attendance at Urban Playgrounds." *Journal of Leisure Research* 2 (Summer 1970):145-59.

Deford, Frank. "Religion in Sport." A three-part series in *Sports Illustrated,* 19, 26, April, and 3 May 1976.

de Grazia, Sebastian. *On Time, Work, and Leisure.* Garden City, N.Y.: Doubleday, 1962.

Dey, Joseph C. "Chip Shots through a Crystal Ball." *Golf Digest* 27 (February 1976): 14-16, 1976.

Dworkin, Gary Anthony, and Dworkin, Rosalind J., eds. *The Minority Report.* New York: Praeger, 1976.

Dworkin, Rosalind J. "A Woman's Report: Numbers Do Not a Majority Make." In Dworkin and Dworkin, eds.: 373-99, 1976.

Ebony. "Lady Pros Seek Golf Glory." 28 (July 1971):106-11.

———. "Who Are the Highest Paid Athletes?" 30 (May 1975): 33-42.

———. "Black Athletes: Pioneers and Record Holders." 30 (August 1975): 68-74.

Edwards, Harry. *The Revolt of the Black Athlete.* New York: Free Press, 1969.

Eitzen, D. Stanley, and Sage, George H. *Sociology of American Sport.* Dubuque, Iowa: William C. Brown, 1978.

Epstein, Cynthia F. "Encountering the Male Establishment: Sex Status Limits on Women's Careers in the Professions." *American Journal of Sociology* 75 (May 1970): 965-82.

Faulkner, Joseph E., ed. *Religion's Influence in Contemporary Society.* Columbus, Ohio: Charles E. Merrill, 1972.

Frazier, E. Franklin. *Black Bourgeoisie.* Glencoe: Free Press, 1957.

Gaustad, Edwin S. "America's Institutions of Faith: A Statistical Postscript." In William G. McLoughlin, and Robert N. Bella, eds. *Religion in America.* Boston: Beacon Press, 1968, 111-33.

Gerstl, Joel E. "Leisure, Taste and Occupational Milieu." *Social Problems* 9 (Summer 1961):56-68.

Glenn, Norval D., and Hyland, Ruth. "Religious Preference and Wordly Success: Some Evidence from National Surveys." *American Sociological Review* 32 (February 1967):73–85.

Glock, Charles Y., ed. *Religion in Sociological Perspective*. Belmont: Wadsworth, 1973.

Goldstein, Sidney, and Goldscheider, Calvin. *Jewish Americans*. Englewood Cliffs, New Jersey: Prentice-Hall, 1969.

Golf. 18 June 1976.

Gordon, Milton. *Assimilation in American Life*. New York: Oxford University Press, 1964.

Greeley, Andrew M. *The American Catholic*. New York: Basic, 1977.

Griffin, P.S. "What's a Nice Girl like You Doing in a Profession Like This?" *Quest* 19 (July 1973):72–76.

Hadden, Jeffrey K. *The Gathering Storm in the Churches*. New York: Doubleday, 1969.

Harris, D. V. "The Sportswoman in Our Society." In Harris, ed. *Women in Sports*. Washington, D.C.: American Association for Health and Physical Education, 1971, pp. 1–4.

———. "Dimensions of Physical Activity." In Harris, ed. *Women and Sport: A National Conference*. University Park: Pennsylvania State University, 1973, pp. 3–15.

Hart, M. Marie. "On Being Female in Sport." In Hart, ed. *Sport in the Socio-Cultural Process*. Dubuque, Iowa: William C. Brown, 1972, pp. 291–302.

Havinghurst, Robert J., and Feigenbaum, Kenneth. "Leisure and Life-Style." *American Journal of Sociology* 64 (November 1958):396–404.

Heller, Celia S., ed. *Structured Social Inequality*. New York: Macmillan, 1969.

Himes, Joseph S. *Racial Conflict in American Society*. Columbus, Ohio: Charles E. Merrill, 1973.

Hoch, Paul. *Rip Off the Big Game*. New York: Doubleday, 1972.

Hodge, Robert W.; Seigel, Paul M.; and Rossi, Peter H. "Occupational Prestige in the United States: 1925–1963." *American Journal of Sociology* 70 (November 1964): 286–302.

Houghton, George. *Confessions of a Golf Addict*. New York: Simon and Schuster, 1959.

Huber, Joan, ed. *Changing Women in a Changing Society*. Chicago: University of Chicago Press, 1973.

Jenkins, Dan. "You're All Right, Jack." *Sports Illustrated* 42 (21 April 1975):18–22.

Johnson, Charles E. "An Exploratory Study of Individual Patterns of Leisure-Time Activities." Doctoral dissertation, University of Minnesota, 1964.

Johnstone, Ronald L. *Religion and Society in Interaction*. Englewood Cliffs, N.J.: Prentice-Hall, 1975.

Jordan, Millard L. "Leisure Time Activities of Sociologists, Attorneys, Physicists, and People at Large from Greater Cleveland." *Sociology and Social Research* 47 (April 1963):290–97.

———. "Leisure Time Activities of Sociologists and Attorneys." *Sociology and Social Research* 40 (January 1956):176–78.

Kane, John J. *Protestant-Catholic Conflict in America*. Chicago: Henry Regnery, 1955.

Kaplan, Max. *Leisure in America: A Social Inquiry*. New York: John Wiley and Sons, 1960.

Kennedy, Robert E., Jr. "Irish Americans." In Dworkin and Dworkin eds. *Minority Report*, 1976, 353–72.

Kenyon, Gerald S. "The Significance of Physical Activity as a Function of Age, Sex, Education, and Socio-Economic Status of Northern United States Adults." *International Review of Sport Sociology* 1 (1966):41-57.

Kieran, John. *The American Sporting Scene*. New York: Macmillan, 1941.

Kirshenbaum, Jerry. "Long Countdown to Augusta." *Sports Illustrated* 42 (10 March 1975):24-30.

Knudsen, Dean D. "The Declining Status of Women: Popular Myths and the Failure of Functionalist Thought." *Social Forces* 48 (December 1969)183-93.

Kohn, Melvin L. *Class and Conformity*. Homewood, Ill.: Dorsey Press, 1969.

Lenski, Gerhard. *The Religious Factor*. Garden City, N.Y.: Doubleday, 1961.

Lies, Eugene T. *The Leisure of a People*. Indianapolis: Crippin and Son, 1929.

Loy, John W.; McPherson, Barry D.; and Kenyon, Gerald. *Sport and Social Systems*, Reading, Mass.: Addison-Wesley, 1978.

Lundberg, George A.; Komarovsky, Mirra; and McInery, Mary Alice. *Leisure: A Suburban Study*. New York: Columbia University Press, 1934.

Lynd, Robert S., and Lynd, Helen Merrell. *Middletown in Transition*. New York: Harcourt, Brace, and World, 1937.

Marden, Charles F., and Meyer, Gladys. *Minorities in American Society*. 5th ed. New York: D. Van Nostrand, 1978.

Matras, Judah. *Social Inequality, Stratification, and Mobility*. Englewood Cliffs, N.J.: Prentice-Hall, 1975.

McCarthy, Colman. "Parrying Repeated Onslaughts from the Multitudinous Critics of Golf." *Washington Post*, 1 March 1976, Section D.

Miller, Donna Mae, and Russell, Kathryn R.E. *Sport: A Contemporary View*. Philadelphia: Lea and Febiger, 1971.

Mills, C. Wright. *The Power Elite*. New York: Oxford University Press, 1956.

Mulvoy, Mark, and Spander, Art. *Golf: The Passion and the Challenge*. Englewood Cliffs, N.J.: Prentice-Hall, 1977.

Nelson, George. "Down with Housekeeping." *Holiday* 19 (March 1956):54-57, 145, 147-49.

Neumeyer, Martin H., and Neumeyer, Esther S. *Leisure and Recreation*. New York: A.S. Barnes and Company, 1936.

Olsen, Jack. *The Black Athlete*. New York: Time-Life Books, 1968.

Parenti, Michael. "Political Values and Religious Cultures: Jews, Catholics, and Protestants." *Journal for the Scientific Study of Religion* 7 (Fall 1967):259-69.

Pettigrew, Thomas F., ed. *Racial Discrimination in the United States*. New York: Harper and Row, 1975.

Postal, Bernard; Silver, Jesse; and Silver, Roy. *Encyclopedia of Jews in Sports*. New York: Bloch Publishing Co., 1965.

Quinley, Harold E. "The Dilemma of an Activist Church." *Journal for the Scientific Study of Religion* 13 (March 1974):1–21.

Robinson, Louie. "Gold on the Green." *Ebony* 28 (May 1973):132–42.

Rosenblatt, A. "Negroes in Baseball: The Failure of Success." *Transaction* 4 (September 1967):51–53.

Sage, Charles H., ed. *Sport and American Society.* Reading, Mass.: Addison-Wesley; 1974, 380–95.

Schrag, Peter. *The Decline of the WASP.* New York: Simon and Schuster, 1971.

Sendler, Dave. "The Black Athlete—1968." In Pat Romero, ed. *In Black America.* Washington, D.C.: United Publishing Company, 1969.

Sklare, Marshall. *America's Jews.* New York: Random House, 1971.

Snyder, Eldon E., and Spreitzer, Elmer. "Family Influence and Involvement in Sports." *Research Quarterly* 44 (October 1973):249–55.

———. "Sociology of Sport: An Overview." *The Sociological Quarterly* 15 (Autumn 1974):467–87.

———. *Social Aspects of Sport.* Englewood Cliffs, N.J.: Prentice-Hall, 1978.

Stark, Rodney. "Through a Stained Glass Darkly: Reciprocal Protestant-Catholic Images in America." *Sociological Analysis* 25 (Fall 1964):159–66.

Stark, Rodney, and Glock, Charles Y. *American Piety.* Berkeley: University of California Press, 1968.

Statistical Abstracts. Washington, D.C.: U.S. Bureau of Census, 1972.

Suggs, Louise. *Golf for Women.* New York: Doubleday, 1960.

Thielbar, Gerald W., and Feldman, Saul D. *Issues in Social Inequality.* Boston: Little, Brown and Company, 1972.

Time. "American Notes: Who's Ahead," 27 October 1975, p. 8.

Tumin, Melvin. *Social Stratification.* Englewood Cliffs, N.J.: Prentice-Hall, 1967.

Tunis, John R. *The American Way in Sport.* New York: Duell, Sloan, and Pearce, 1958.

Updike, John. *Picked-Up Pieces.* New York: Alfred A. Knopf, 1973.

U.S. News and World Report. "The 40-Hour Week is A Myth for Millions." 80 (24 May 1976):76–77.

Vanfossen, Beth E. *The Structure of Social Inequality.* Boston: Little, Brown and Company, 1979.

Wilson, John. *Religion in American Society.* New York: McGraw-Hill, 1978.

Wuthnow, Robert. "Religious Commitment and Conservatism: In Search of an Elusive Relationship." In Glock, ed. *Religion in Sociological Perspective,* 1973; pp. 117–32.

Yetman, Norman R., and Eitzen, D. Stanley. "Black Americans in Sports: Unequal Opportunities for Equal Ability." In Yetman and Steele, ed. *Majority and Minority* pp. 532–43, 1975.

Yetman, Norman R., and Steele, C. Hoy. 2d ed. *Majority and Minority.* Boston: Allyn and Bacon, 1975.

11
Baseball in Its Social Context

LEON H. WARSHAY

Introduction

> Whoever wants to know the heart and mind of America had
> better learn baseball.
>
> —Jacques Barzun

A sociological analysis of baseball offers a focus that other approaches—for example, psychology, theology, aesthetics, common sense—do not. Such an analysis emphasizes variables including interaction, conflict, culture, functional requisite, and exploitation. It also brings a special set of logical, methodological, and value presuppositions to bear. Among these are regularity of phenomena, spontaneity, participant observation, statistical treatment, objectivity, value immersion, and/or activism. Sociological analysis of baseball is facilitated because baseball has "self-consciously" studied itself over the years; its voluminous quantitative records lend themselves to this. For example, Branch Rickey, a baseball executive for many years with the Cardinals, Dodgers, and Pirates, developed a formula that combined various pitching, batting, fielding, and baserunning records for predicting the order of finish of major league teams in the standings. At about the same time, Frederick Mosteller, a statistician, decided through the use of formulas that the "better" team won the World Series only about 80 percent of the time between 1903 and 1951. (Mosteller, 1952:366–68)

More recently, a computer compared the value of the "best" baseball batting order with the "worst" batting order over a 162-game season: the results indicated a difference of about three victories (Freeze, 1974). Sportswriters frequently turn to records to test or buttress an argument (e.g., Leonard Koppett in his weekly column in the *Sporting News*) and there are countless baseball fans (many of these graduate students and college professors) who make quantitative studies of the game (cf. Sand, referred to in *Sporting News*, 1976c; Holtzman, 1977c).

This chapter will first pick out the salient sociological features of baseball, largely professional, major-league baseball, emphasizing features that distinguish it from other sports. Second, this study will provide a micro-sociological analysis of the concrete game itself played by players and teams but will inevitably find itself turning to a third concern, a macro-sociological analysis (cultural, historical, and social-structural aspects). Fourth, and last, the efficacy of applying sociological theories and schools—such as interactionism, functionalism, and Marxism—to the game will be examined.

The Game: Its Micro and Macro Features

Baseball and Other Sports

> All winter long I am one for whom
>   the bell is tolling;
> I can arouse no interest in basketball,
>   indoor fly casting or bowling;
> The sports pages are strictly no soap,
> And until the cry of Play Ball,
> I simply mope.
>
> —Ogden Nash

Baseball, frequently called the national pastime, though less so recently, is a game suited to relaxation and contemplation (cf. Kahn, 1970; Axthelm, 1972:187). It presents less continuous excitement to spectators, viewers, or listeners than do football, basketball, hockey, and boxing. This is not surprising given the fact that in batting, the most popular part of baseball for most fans, even the best batters fail about two-thirds of the time (cf. Pope, 1979; Biederman, 1979). Originally a daytime game in a setting where the "green grass met the blue sky" (Wallop, 1969; chapter 9), its implied relaxed pace has continued into the nightball era. Almost throughout its history, however, there has been criticism of time delays in the game, of long-warm ups by pitchers, of summit meetings on the pitcher's mound, and of interminable arguments that are said to give the game a dull obsessive quality (cf. Wallop, 1969:99–103; Zurcher and Meadow, 1972:193; Sorrentino, 1978). In 1968, the Baltimore Orioles conducted time-and-motion studies that showed that about one-fifth of the game was "dead time" (Furst, 1971:163). Baseball's one-thing-at-a-time, fixed positions, and high-visible specialization reflect a rural or a *mechanical* age of an earlier industrialism in contrast with the more fluid motion and division of labor of sports as football during the *electronic* age of later industrialism (cf. Lahr, 1972:110; McLuhan, 1976:90; Cavanaugh, 1976).

Yet, delaying and time-consuming features aside, baseball's slow pace can also be an advantage (cf. Craig, 1976d; Young, 1977b). The leisurely pace allows the spectator to look at the fielders, coaches, and/or pitchers in the "bullpen" to *anticipate* who might enter the game to relieve the pitcher, to pinch hit, to pinch run, and when; or, what the possibility or probability is for a stolen base, an intentional walk, or a double play (cf. Kahn, 1970). Anticipation is also found in considering other potential events that may never occur; for example, the visiting pitcher may throw one or two "balls" to the first batter in the last half of the ninth inning and the home crowd anticipates a walk and the beginning of a rally. Thus, baseball is a leisurely, almost pastoral, game punctuated by sudden buildups of tension and excitement, leaving room for relaxed enjoyment (and boredom) at times and for active thought by the (knowledgeable) fan (cf. Wallop, 1969:152; Axthelm, 1972:187; Sorrentino, 1978).[1]

Moreover, there are several other aspects that make baseball unique. One, it is not a *timed* game (cf. Cavanaugh, 1975; Sorrentino, 1978) but is continuous until all "innings" and "outs" have been expended; this aids the fan's anticipation because the team that is behind always has the opportunity to "tie the score" without being concerned about time running out (and has encouraged the proverb that "the game isn't over until the last man is out").[2] Two, it is not a *space, field,* or *territory* game in the sense that football and, to a lesser degree, basketball and hockey are. There is not the military advance and retreat along a front to and from the enemy's and one's own goal. Baseball's circling the bases and "flagging down outfield flies" are symbols with less simple, congruent, or isomorphic spatial references; the road to home plate only partly conquers territory (cf. Cavanaugh, 1976). Three, baseball is played every day during the season, whereas football is played once a week and basketball and hockey two or three times a week. Thus, other sports, particularly football, have up to a week to study the last game and to plan major alterations for the next game and opponent, whereas baseball managers and coaches are more likely to make only minor changes between games (Koppett, 1979b). Baseball relies less for its interest on actual game attendance even though baseball tickets are relatively inexpensive (cf. Isle, 1980). Baseball fans usually keep up with the game through the mass media—radio, television, newspapers, and magazines (through written accounts and the "box scores")—or through "telephone hot lines" (Atkin, 1976). People may rarely or never attend a game and still be "fans" (Lukes, 1979; Kennedy, 1980:36). It is only after the World Series that presidential campaigns capture many voters' complete attention.

A fourth aspect of baseball's uniqueness is that it is probably the most quantified of all sports. Its records on individual, team, and league performances frequently go back for a century; "in few occupations is individual performance so easily calculated" (Blalock, 1969:418). In this respect, it is similar to cricket. Fifth, and related to the fourth point, there appears to be as much interest in the fortunes and careers of individual players (heroes, "superstars," and lesser lights who are sympathetically perceived or even resented or disliked) as in the success of the teams themselves. This undoubtedly is aided by the available quantitative records and the possibility of comparing present and past players (Hecht, 1976) (e.g., Aaron with Ruth, Wills or Brock with Cobb or Carey, and Koufax, Seaver, Ryan, or Richard with Feller, Grove, or Johnson). The strong interest in comparing present records with those of the past—individual, team, and league—may partially explain the fact that fans may want changes in other sports, according to surveys, but not in baseball (cf. Eldridge, 1978b). Sixth, and last, baseball, more than other sports, occupies its fans' time the year round. Its "hot stove league" is kept active during the winter off-season by record publishing and announcements of Most Valuable Player and Hall of Fame winners, by stories about player trades, "holdouts," and signings (and, more recently, potential player and umpires' strikes, court cases, and free agents); and just by the intermittent arguing by fans over the events of the past season(s) and the anticipation of a better season ahead. This is not to deny the role of contrived publicity released throughout the winter by organized baseball, nor the increasing degree to which interest in other sports is maintained during their "off season."

In collective behavior terms one might say that, in contrast with many other sports, baseball depends for its interest more on the *mass* and *public* (i.e., the diffuse macro context) than on the *compact crowd* and the *audience* at the actual event (i.e., the micro context) (cf. Turner and Killian, 1972: chs. 3,5,7–10). Hence, studies of the relative popularity of various sports would need to measure several dimensions; for example, interest at the game itself, interest while listening and watching the game on television or radio, interest while following the game in newspapers and magazines, purchase and trading of baseball (or football, basketball, etc.) cards by mail and at the many sports collectors conventions (cf. Cattani, 1976; Madden, 1976, 1978, and 1980), sale or collection of books (Jares, 1979), and personal participation.

The Players and the Team: A Micro Analysis

The Official Baseball Rules: Interaction. In the Official Baseball Rules (1974), Rule number 1.01 reads as follows:

> Baseball is a game between two teams of nine players each under the direction of a manager, played on an enclosed field in accordance with these rules, under the jurisdiction of one or more umpires (1974: 3).

A sociological analysis of baseball could begin here and focus on the playing rules and the positions' names, for example, batter, fielder, runner, umpire, official scorer. It would be a micro analysis focusing on the game situation. Accordingly, a sociologist might emphasize *interaction*, that is, the players can only play the game by (1) taking others into account (e.g., their own teammates, the opposing team, the umpires, the coaches); (2) anticipating possible and probable strategies and outcomes—for example, batter versus pitcher (and catcher, umpire), baserunner versus pitcher (and catcher, first baseman, other infielders); and thereby (3) engaging in role taking in relation to a "generalized other" and particular others (Mead, 1934:150–63).

It is said that Joe Tinker and Johnny Evers, the shortstop and second baseman, respectively, of the famed Chicago club double-play combination ("Tinker to Evers to Chance") in the early years of this century, went for years hardly saying a word to each other during off hours (Smith, 1970:181), an apparent contradiction of role-taking theories. Yet, their very success belies this because they apparently knew each other's unique baseball movements (the "particular other") very well. It is axiomatic in baseball, and undoubtedly true, that infielders need to work together and even room together for an extended period of time before they learn to anticipate the other's movements and decisions (cf. Elderkin, 1976a). The same is true for the relation between outfielders and also between infielders and outfielders (e.g., relevant to pop flies hit into the outfield), and certainly for catchers and pitchers. Undoubtedly, role taking and empathy research would be useful here, particularly as baseball's class, ethnic, and gender composition becomes more diverse.

Status and Role. The very existence of the Official Baseball Rules is a manifestation of a "generalized other," in this case the more formalized "attitude" of the organized (baseball) community or social group (Mead, 1934:154). The rules are a basis for analyzing the "team" nature of a baseball game. They refer to baseball statuses such as catcher, left fielder, manager, and coach, and they also denote the organization of teams into leagues or conferences, with their own rules and regulations, involving both league officials at a distance and umpires and scorekeepers in the actual game situation.

Status and role studies become relevant at the micro level of baseball. One study of the longevity of major league players showed, perhaps surprisingly, that third basemen have the longest life span, with pitchers and first basemen having the shortest (Metropolitan life, 1975b:7); the shorter life span of pitchers may be explained by their irregular and very intense participation in the game, and by the anxiety at being injured by a line drive (Moore, 1980), but there is no evident explanation for first basemen. Baseball field managers have shorter life spans than players and do not live much longer than the general white male population (Metropolitan Life, 1975a:4). The tensions and uncertainties of being a field manager might explain the last finding, but one would think that the pressure on third basemen would be greater than on other fielders. Other role studies could be made, related to the significance of positions (statuses) on a team—such as pitchers versus other fielders, the expectation that outfielders and first basemen should be heavy hitters, the specialized role of coaches for training pitchers, batters, catchers, or fielders and/or coaching at first or third base and/or giving and transmitting signs, and significance of playing managers versus "bench" managers.

ters," that umpires should "even out" close calls between the contending teams). Moreover, the Official Baseball Rules' very existence implies a macro level, and there is direct reference not only to statuses involved in the game itself—the Umpire (rule 9.00), the Official Scorer (rule 10.00)—but also to more removed macro phenomena. One of these is the Official Playing Rules Committee. A second is the three organizations that underlie that Commitee—the American League, the National League, and the National Association of Professional Baseball Leagues (the first two are major leagues; the third is the representative of the organized minor leagues). A third macro feature is the Office of the Commissioner of Organized (i.e., Professional, North American) Baseball.

Cultural, Historical, and Structural Dimensions: A Macro Analysis

Values and Norms. A characteristic that distinguishes baseball from its major competitors (football, basketball, hockey) is that it is more *individualistic* (less individualistic, however, than some other sports—boxing, wrestling, golf, tennis, bowling, bullfighting). That is, despite the fact that teamwork is required in most game conditions, there still is a premium on individual skills and identity. For example, the offense is built upon a *lineup* where batters take their turn one at a time. The pitcher receives as much attention (despite the importance of the catcher's calling of signals) as the football quarterback and probably more than the hockey and soccer goalkeeper, or the center in hockey or basketball. Moreover, while many team and league records are kept, there is still great emphasis upon an individual's achievements in batting, pitching, fielding, and base stealing. The individualistic thesis does not denigrate the role and necessity of teamwork in the game but helps to relate the longtime popularity of baseball to the individualistic ideology that has long been emphasized in American culture—e.g., economic, religious, and political aspects (Cavanaugh, 1976).

A second focus for normative analysis is contradiction (cf. Edwards, 1973:168-74). On the one hand, norms of sportsmanship or fair play are part of the culture of baseball and of other sports. At the same time, a win at any cost norm (e.g., stealing signs by electronic devices) is prevalent (cf. Hagen, 1979).

Another norm, tied to sportsmanship, is to win without disgracing the other team. Analogous to keeping the score down in football, the principle is that the team with a commanding lead in the late innings of a game should not humiliate its opponent by stealing bases (e.g., Maury Wills, a veteran Dodger player in the late 1950s and 1960s) or bunting (e.g., Dave Winfield, a San Diego player in a game against the Dodgers in 1975). It is, however, considered legitimate for the batters, pitchers, and fielders of the team with such a lead to keep trying to do their best (cf. Tuley, 1979).

A third characteristic of baseball is the abundance of superstition in the game. Examples are stepping over foul lines, but being sure to step on third base or first base on the way into and returning from the outfield, picking up hair pins as a good omen for getting hits; smoothing the dirt on the mound before each new batter; sitting in the same order in the dugout or keeping the bats in the same slot in the rack; and using the same shower and/or not changing socks or underwear during a winning streak (Galloway, 1979). In 1976, the Oakland Athletics hired Laurie Brady to be the team astrologer (Weigel, 1976a; Twombly, 1976c) and the California Angels hired Louise Heubner to do the same the following year (Miller, 1977), as did others for Los Angeles, Baltimore, and Boston (Holway, 1977).

One explanation for superstition, with support from anthropologists such as Frazer, Mauss, and Malinowski, is that it is a form of magic used to try to control events in highly uncertain but important areas of life. Baseball superstition, however, unlike some forms of magic, is used to improve one's own performance more than to hurt someone else's (cf. Gmelch, 1971:54). Baseball, more than most team sports, is variable from game to game; the point of effective contact between a round bat and a round ball is about the diameter of a dime, thereby making batters and pitchers (and, therefore, teams) perform like champions one day and like losers the next. Interestingly, there is more superstitious behavior intended to bring about or maintain good batting and pitching, and team victories, than to bring about or maintain good fielding (Gmelch, 1971:40), perhaps because fielding is less scrutinized and/or less rewarded.

Another example of the role of values and norms in baseball is the presence of "macho" or "machismo" sentiments. Baseball players, predominantly male and exclusively so in organized baseball, reflect the norms of the Americans and Latin Americans who dominate the game; athletics serve as male role models for children (cf. Hoberman, 1976). This may account for the long time that it took for fielders' gloves with more than a minimum of padding to be accepted, not only generally but even for catchers and first basemen. There also was a long-time resistance to the wearing of batting helmets, the Pittsburgh Pirates becoming the first major league team to wear them in 1952 (Garagiola, 1977). Roger Breshnahan, New York Giants' catcher in the first two decades of this century, is said to have introduced shinguards (Broeg, 1977). Even such protection as padded outfield walls and warning tracks required many injuries to outfielders before they were put in effect (the shortening and ruining of Pete Reiser's career is a dramatic example). Today, there is controversy over whether the "duster," the "brushback," and "knockdown" pitches should be permitted against dangerous batters, vulnerable batters, and/or against the first "innocent" batter to come to bat after a home run. All this suggests that macho norms are still potent and/or that the conflict and excitement created by such aggressive playing are "good box office" (cf. Broeg, 1976; Durslag, 1976c), although often contrived.

One last example of baseball's "culture" is formal and informal umpires' norms. Formal norms are exemplified by rule enforcing and official gestures (the latter developed to accommodate a deaf player). At the same time, there are many informal norms. Some examples are the "automatic" or "phantom" out at second base on the first half of a double play, allowing catchers to block home plate before they have the ball, and the reluctance of umpires to call balks or to declare (via an official warning) that a pitcher has deliberately thrown at a batter.

Some Historical Aspects: From "Play" to "Game" to "Work". Early Puritan values inveighed against idleness in both England and the colonies; work and play have been seen as separate dimensions well into the twentieth century. While colonial Americans imported sporting customs from Europe—hunting, fishing, cock-fighting, wrestling, horse racing, and "playing at bowls"—participation in sports was limited by the harsh conditions in the early colonial years and was largely an activity of the nobility and the upper classes, as it had been under feudalism (Eitzen and Sage, 1978:25–27; Lucas and Smith, 1978:chapters 1–4, Benagh, 1976b; Dulles, 1974:64–71; Stone, 1972:53; Huizinga, 1950:196).

The Continental Congress forbade sports by a 1774 resolution (cf. Benagh, 1976b). Limitations and probations such as these, however, were never completely effective and became even less so after the Revolutionary War. In the nineteenth century, old and new sports—including baseball—and sports facilities developed and flourished (Benagh, 1976b; Paxson, 1974). This was undoubtedly stimulated by rapid industrialization and urbanization after the Civil War. Increased economic and physical well being are presumably important for growth and excellence in sports (Novikov and Maximenko, 1972:39).

As America was becoming a mass society, sports, including baseball, were becoming commercial activity. Baseball arose earlier than football, hockey, or basketball, and may best fit an early, pre-electronic industrialism (cf. Lahr, 1972:109–10). Baseball's predecessors in the late eighteenth and early nineteenth centuries include games wherein one struck the ball with a stick or bat and rounded a circle of bases (the medieval English game of "rounders"), or ran to first base and back ("one old cat," or "one-hole cat," or "catapult ball") (Smith, 1970:2, 8). A successor to rounders was "town ball," dating back to Boston in 1831 (Furst, 1971:55), or even to colonial days (Smith, 1970:8, Lucas and Smith, 1978:171), often called "soak ball" or "sting ball" because one could put out base runners by throwing the ball at them (e.g., "soaking," "stinging," "plugging," or "pinging") (cf. Smith, 1977; Lucas and Smith, 1978:173).

A now discredited version of baseball's origin had Abner Doubleday, a Civil War general who reputedly fired the first defensive shot at Fort Sumter (*New Yorker* magazine, 1975:20) laying out the first baseball "diamond" in a cow pasture near Cooperstown, N.Y., in 1839 while attending classes at West Point (Wallop, 1969:24; Koppett, 1969:7). The Doubleday-as-inventor hypothesis permitted the elimination of all hints of foreign influence from baseball's origin and allowed for the celebration of the game's centennial—and the creation of a National Baseball Museum (and Hall of Fame) and National Baseball Library in Cooperstown—in 1939 (Wallop, 1969:24–27; Koppett, 1969:1, Lucas and Smith, 1978:187–89).

Later baseball scholarship, most notably that by Robert W. Henderson of the New York Public Library, reestablished the game's origin as English and the fact of its slow, evolutionary development (Wallop, 1969:26). Its origins may go back at least to England before 1744 (Wallop, 1969:33; Lucas and Smith, 1978:170). The currently accepted "father" is Alexander Joy Cartwright, Jr., a surveyor, civil engineer, and member of the socially elite Knickerbocker Club of New York City in the early 1840s.

Playing a game similar to baseball, the Knickerbockers introduced refinements and innovations. Cartwright, in particular, instituted such features as flat bases instead of posts or rocks; foul lines; about ninety feet between all bases; nine players to a side (including a "shortstop," an innovation); three outs to an inning (although not yet nine innings; instead, the game ended when one team scored twenty-one runs, or "aces," as they were called then); an out when the ball was caught on the first bounce; the dropped third strike; and eliminated the practice of throwing balls at base runners in order to get them out. The first game was played on 19 June 1846, a Sunday, on an opening called Elysian Fields near Hoboken, New Jersey. It was a four-and-a-half-inning game umpired by Cartwright but lost by the Knickerbockers (many of their members went on to influence the game), 23–1, to a pick-up team it had challenged called the New York Nine (Wallop, 1969:28–30; *New Yorker*, 1976; Walter, 1976; Bisher, 1976; Koppett, 1969:7; Lucas and Smith, 1978:172–73; Adams, 1980).

Baseball developed slowly, being played largely by a few high status Eastern private clubs until the Civil War, which brought together many baseball "nines," often during specially arranged North-South truces. This nationalized and massified the game and led to much activity after the war by athletic clubs, town teams, high schools, and colleges. Baseball began to spread to the more "vulgar" river towns of the Midwest such as Louisville, Cincinnati, and St. Louis and was apparently at first strongly influenced by "drunks and gamblers" (Shaw, 1969:7; Wallop, 1969:35–38, 55–56). The first professional all-contract (Koppett, 1969:1) team, the Cincinnati Red Stockings, was formed in 1869 and the first major professional league, the owner-dominated National League of Baseball Clubs—one of whose efforts was to reform the game (Twombly, 1976b:30)—in 1876 (the American League was formed in 1901).[4] Professional baseball, aided by the growth of the railroads (Betts, 1972:119–20; Eitzen and Sage, 1978:31–33), soon became successful as a producer's business in the large cities and as a spectator's sport; by involving the urban as well as the rural populations, baseball became, like cricket in England, but unlike horse racing and boxing in America, a game for everyone (Paxson, 1974:86–87; Cavanaugh, 1976; Lucas and Smith, 1978:176–84, 199–201).

Baseball has moved along a continuum from *play* to *work*, according to Furst (1971:54–57), passing through three stages: *play* (from 1831–1845); *game*, i.e., codification (1845–1869); *work*, i.e., professionalization (1869–present period).[5] Another way of saying this is that it had gone from the spontaneity and carelessness of amateurs and gentlemen to the superior capacity of professionals (Huizinga, 1950:197); from intrinsic to extrinsic reward (cf. Lueschen, 1976b:96), where one's goods or wealth are greater at the end of play than they were at the beginning (Caillois, 1962:10; Weiss, 1962:10; Coakley, 1978:10–12). It had moved from a game for high-status gentlemen in private social and athletic clubs to one of class privilege, with club owners attempting to dominate the players (cf. Wallop, 1969:chapter 5; Twombly, 1976b:30).

Organization Level: Problems of Capital, Labor, and the Courts. There is little doubt that organized baseball is a business, a big business, one worth several hundred million dollars. This fact does not deny its leisure and expressive aspects (i.e., "psychic income") but emphasizes its similarity to other businesses (Brower, 1977; Eitzen and Sage, 1978:179–80; Smith, 1979). The locus of power is in private ownership—individual, partnership, and/or corporations (with some powerful and sober leaders such as the late Walter O'Malley of the Dodgers, and other more deviant, innovative, irrascible, and occasionally influential ones such as Bill Veeck of the White Sox, Charles Finley of the Athletics, and even George Steinbrenner of the Yankees (Hawkins, 1978a; Anderson, 1979). There probably is not a lot of money to be made in the game although local and national television and radio broadcasting revenue, financial returns from parking and "concessions" (food and other items sold at ball parks), and aid from local municipalities (such as building or at least refurbishing ball parks) have made for better recent financial stability. New marketing approaches may increase major league attendance from about 40 million people in 1979 to close to 80 million at the end of the century, according to Bowie Kuhn, the commissioner of professional baseball (Eldridge, 1978b). A further saving is made by calculating the depreciation of the value of the players and, in the case of financial loss (real or nominal), by subtracting this from profits in non-baseball enterprises, thereby lowering individual or corporate taxes (cf. Koppett, 1976e; Scherer, 1976; Eitzen and Sage, 1978:180–83). Moreover, beginning in 1953, there has been little hesitation in moving franchises (ball clubs) from one city to another, although recent law suits have made this more difficult (cf. *Sporting News*, 1976a). Nor have owners been very concerned about expanding the number of teams from sixteen to twenty-four, and then to twenty-six, thereby diluting talent (cf. Hank Greenberg, quoted in Spander, 1976d), a factor supporting the business and politics of baseball (cf. Brown, 1977).

A modicum of power or authority is granted the presidents of the two major leagues and the president of the minor leagues. There is also a high commissioner of organized baseball who may use "extraordinary powers" for the "good of the game." The first commissioner, Judge Kenesaw M. Landis, used these powers with little opposition from 1920 to 1944; Albert "Happy" Chandler, the second commissioner, used such powers to suspend Leo Durocher, the Brooklyn Dodgers' manager, in 1947. The present commissioner, Bowie Kuhn, after a relatively uneventful five or six years in office, began to use these powers more actively. In 1975, he ordered the Atlanta Braves to play Henry Aaron on the "road" (the Braves had wanted Aaron to hit lifetime home runs numbers 714 and 715 before the hometown fans in Atlanta). In 1976 and since, he canceled some sales and trades of ball players. He has also forbidden players, or ex-players employed by ball clubs (such as Willie Mays), but not often owners, from maintaining formal connections with gambling interests (Kirschenbaum, 1979b). Any such powers, however, are limited; effective power, at least since the death of Judge Landis in 1944, has been in the hands of owners who hire and pay the high comissioner and the league presidents.

Until the mid-1970s, baseball's so-called reserve clause was included in the standard contract of each player. It was introduced in 1879 (Koppett, 1969:7; Lucas and Smith, 1978:185) and helped to maintain the owners' power by binding players to the clubs that had originally signed them until and unless the players are sold, released, or retire from the game. Among reasons given by the owners for having continued this clause is that it is a necessary protection for the owners' investment in the players and for the time and expense devoted to train them in the minor leagues. It was further argued that without the reserve clause, the wealthier clubs and/or those in attractive climates or large television markets (New York, Los Angeles, and perhaps Chicago) would buy most of the better players, thereby destroying the competitive balance of the game (cf. Edwards, 1973:280); Eldridge, 1976; Colborn, 1977). Players may also find their playing integrity questioned when playing against possible future employers (Koppett, 1976b).

In contrast, many players, some sports writers and broadcasters, and the Major League Players Association (the players' union, under the leadership of Marvin Miller) have argued that the reserve clause was a form of occupational servitude (therefore a violation of the "free enterprise" espoused by the owners on other occasions) that deprived players of bargaining power and the right to sell their services in the market place. Moreover, managers, general managers, and coaches move around freely without apparent harm to baseball's competitive status. The amount of movement from club to club under a more liberal contractual system was exaggerated since most players prefer to stay where they are (cf. Twombly, 1976a; Colborn, 1977); an expectation not supported by later experience. No ball club could afford more than a few stars in any case. Finally, the owners' concern for competition, never very evident in the past during periods of Giant, Cub, Yankee, and Dodger domination, could better be implemented by subjecting more players to the draft, by reducing the number of players on a club's protected roster, and by limiting the number of years that the reserve clause would bind a player to a club (cf. Twombly, 1976a; Koppett, 1976a).

Baseball's reserve clause was first tested, then protected by law, in 1922 when a Supreme Court decision declared the game not subject to the rules applying to interstate commerce. The Baltimore Terrapins, the last remaining club of the dying Federal League (that had arisen to challenge the major leagues in 1913), sued the American and National Leagues for conspiring to monopolize baseball by buying up some of the Federal League clubs and inducing other clubs to leave (Robinson, 1969: 224; Grant, 1977: 30). A lower court awarded Baltimore treble damages of $240,000 under the Sherman Anti-Trust Act, but the Supreme Court reversed this; Justice Holmes declared that the mere crossing of state lines does not change the fact that baseball games are purely local affairs (Robinson, 1969: 230). Since that time, however, the increase in interstate affiliations (e.g., "farm systems," interstate broadcasting and advertising, connections of ball clubs with other corporate enterprises), inconsistency with the treatment of other sports,[6] the increased tendency of the courts to activism, and the increasing player militancy (with a boycott of spring training in 1969 and a strike in 1972 backed by the Major League Players Association, set up in 1968,[7]) and an owners' lockout in 1976; (cf. Holtzman, 1976b:1) offered ample reason to suggest that baseball's favored status would not last much longer. Law suits, by Danny Gardella in the 1940s and by Curt Flood in the late 1960s and 1970s failed. Arbitration decisions, however, in the Jim "Catfish" Hunter case in 1974–75 (that the terms of his contract were violated by the ball club), and the Andy Messersmith and Dave McNally cases in late 1975 (where the players had played in 1975 without signed contracts, therefore, becoming free agents) created a situation whereby major league players could, by not signing their contract for a given year, be subject to a 20 percent salary reduction for that year but be free to sign with another club after that (cf. Eldridge, 1976; Eitzen and Sage, 1978:192–93; Grant, 1977:30). There was over a 60 percent increase in aggregate player salaries during the first two years of the free agent rule, according to Bowie Kuhn, the professional baseball commissioner (Eldridge, 1978b).

In July, 1976, the reserve clause was greatly narrowed so as to severely modifying the owners' power. Under terms of a four year agreement between Miller of the Major League Players Association and John Gaherin, chief negotiator for the owners, the results of the Hunter, Messersmith, and McNally cases stood, making it easier for players to become free agents. This happened: (1) for players at the end of the 1976 season, if unsigned for that season; (2) for signed players after playing the renewal year(s) of the current contract; and (3) under future contracts, for players with six years' major league service who notify their club in writing (cf. Chass, 1976). There were other conditions and restrictions, particularly on ball clubs, but the balance of power between owners and players had been altered.

This is likely to hasten the already apparent trend away from players spending their career with one team (Warren, 1977). It also makes the age of a player less important on the market since both twenty-five and thirty-year-old players can play out their options in one year (Young, 1977). Ball clubs, therefore, will be inclined to concentrate on becoming "competitors" in the present at the expense of long-range planning (cf. Whiteside, 1977). Although the present performance of some highly paid free agents, particularly pitchers like Don Gullett, Bill Campbell, and Nolan Ryan, has shown such investments to be very risky (Elderkin, 1980). The overall record of free agents, however, remains comparable to that of their last season with the teams they left (Vass, 1980).

Jim Eshoff and Chris Ritz, of the University of Pennsylvania Wharton School of Business, argue that some teams may face bankruptcy from pressures by the majority of players who are not "superstars" (Holtzman, 1978:323). The Wharton report recommends eight major changes, the more far-reaching of which include pay television, eliminating the minor leagues, allowing fans to manage via electronic voting buttons in stadiums, and reducing the number of teams while increasing the number of divisions. Others, however, argue that increased television revenue will enable major league baseball to afford the higher salaries (Holtzman, 1978:323). Despite fan disenchantment with players, according to a 1978 Yankelovich poll (Kennedy and Williamson, 1978), the publicity given the signing of free agents stimulated attendance by 30 percent between 1976 and 1979 (Koppett, 1980b). Finally, postponement of the player strike at the last minute highlights continuing conflict between management and players (Chass, 1980b).

The Mass Media, Sportscasters, and "Spectatoritis". Game broadcasting is important to baseball in its organizational aspect and in its relation to spectators and fans. Radio broadcasting began 21 August, 1921 (Sage, 1974a:11) on Station KDKA, Pittsburgh, for a game against Philadelphia. By the 1930s radio began to rival newspaper coverage as an important source of information and became part of the game's publicity and public relations. Major league television broadcasting (begun in New York City in 1946), however, presented a problem in the post–World War II period, an apparent conflict between television's revenues and its possible effect in decreasing attendance. Solutions ranged from total coverage of games by the Yankees in the top television market to selective telecasting by teams such as the Milwaukee Braves, Kansas City Athletics, and San Francisco Giants, with the greatest negative effect falling on the minor leagues (cf. Opotowsky, 1972:283). In 1976, radio and television revenue was expected to rise to about 50 million dollars (Craig, 1976b). The more recent role of cable television, offering games from anywhere in the United States or Canada, has led to protests by major league baseball and the commercial stations to the Federal Communications Commission, which has ruled in favor of the cable companies (*Sports* magazine, 1979; Craig, 1979b). As yet another extension of sports as an "indoor species of entertainment," cable television is likely both to hurt ball park attendance to a degree and to increase fan participation (Spreitzer in Grossi, 1979).

One problem with televising baseball is that, for the less knowledgeable fan, the spatially diffuse action of the game makes it more difficult to follow than the more spatially focused action in sports such as boxing or tennis. A second problem with television is its influence on baseball schedules, for example, in encouraging more night games (first introduced in Cincinnati in 1935), including playing games of the 1979 World Series on cold and rainy evenings in Baltimore. Other influences are dugout interviews, the planting of microphones on managers, the stationing of cameras in dugouts and on the field, and the emergence of the "television umpire" (cf. Craig, 1976e; Puscas, 1976b; Eldridge, 1978a).

The importance of television and radio raises the question of the credibility of baseball announcers. While announcers on national television are network employees, announcers for local stations and channels are usually hired directly by the ball clubs. This fact makes the question of "objectivity," universalism, and professional "broadcast journalism" standards difficult to maintain for local announcers (cf. Opotowsky, 1972:382; Durslag, 1976a); moreover, the imposition of network "superstars," such as Keith Jackson and Howard Cosell, or Joe Garagiola and Tony Kubek, into broadcasts of league playoffs and the World Series, lowers professionalism further (Bisher, 1977, Craig, 1979a; Isaacs, 1979). Some local announcers have been known as "homers," making little attempt to hide their partiality to the local team (e.g., Harry Carey of the St. Louis Cardinals in the 1940s and 1950s and Chicago White Sox in the 1970s; the late Bert Wilson of the Chicago Cubs in the 1950s; Bob Prince of the Pittsburgh Pirates from the late 1940s through the mid-1970s; and Monty Moore of the Kansas City and Oakland Athletics since the late 1960s). Others, while partial to the local team, have been more professional e.g., Walter "Red" Barber, first for the Dodgers, then for the Yankees, from the 1930s through the late 1960s; Ernie Harwell of the Detroit Tigers and other teams—Brooklyn, Baltimore —since the 1940s; and Al Michaels of the Giants since the 1970s. Many, such as Curt Gowdy and Mel Allen, have tended to exaggerate the differences in ability among players. In contrast, the credibility and critical acumen of baseball writers in newspapers and magazines remains high.

Finally, "spectatoritis" is said to have infected baseball, as it has other sports. Furst (1971:166–67) points to an incompatibility between *sports*, which require gratification through direct participation, and *entertainment*, which requires diverting the spectators. This is an intrinsic-extrinsic distinction of particular relevance to the commercial nature of a mass and organizational society. For the player, the intrinsic and extrinsic aspects of playing the game seem intertwined; for the spectator, intrinsic enjoyment seems stronger.

To management, spectators are an extrinsic value in that they are an important financial resource. Declining or insufficient attendance at games not only affects revenue from ticket sales but also from concessions and parking. Concern about attendance may be responsible for recent attempts to enliven the game by reversing a long term decline in batting.[8] This was attempted after the 1968 season by diminishing the strike zone (that had been broadened after the 1962 season) and by lowering the pitching mound. Another means of raising baseball's batting level, confined to the American League and to most minor leagues (that had introduced it earlier), was the "DH," or Designated Hitter rule, introduced for the 1973 season (and for alternate World Series beginning in 1976); not only did the DH rule enhance American League hitting, it enabled starting pitchers to stay in games longer where, before this rule, they would have been frequently replaced by pinch hitters. An increase in successful base stealing has helped hitters by distracting pitchers and also increased the level of scoring and excitement. Other innovations designed to appeal to spectators include entertainment at games (from Al Schacht to Nick Altrock and Max Patkin), organ music as almost a universal necessity, and fans playing musical instruments in the stands. Also, there are scoreboards that give a variety of information (verbal and pictorial) and explode after a home run by the home team, colorful uniforms, people dressed as animals (such as San Diego's "chicken") to entertain the gathering (Kirschenbaum, 1979a; Director, 1979).

Another worry has been the recent violence by players and fans. Player violence during games is a cyclical phenomenon (Marcin, 1977) and is controlled sooner or later. The 1980 season seemed to be a high point in the cycle (Richmond, 1980; Anderson, 1980). Violence by fans is more serious, however, perhaps reflecting national and worldwide trends (cf. Mike Royko, quoted in the *Sporting News*, 1976b). Ball clubs are ambivalent about spectator violence in that it is often related to profits from the sale of beer at games (cf. *Sporting News*, 1976c; Spander, 1976a, 1977b; Hechter, 1977; Vecsey, 1978).

The Modern Athlete:Increasing Hedonism and Egoism? Emphasis on the personality of the athlete remains despite the corresponding increase in emphasis on the organizational aspects of the game from the "Golden Age" of sports of the 1920s, and the economic depression of the 1930s, to the present. Perhaps, as with the movie star, such emphasis sells tickets. One might also point to the individualism and adulation (cf. Falls, 1976b) inherent in both movies and baseball. Perhaps the athlete is only a "celebrity without power," performing the role long held by the attractive female (cf. Lipsyte, in Spander, 1976b). The image of the *star* athlete, however, has changed somewhat in the public's eye from "hero" to "entrepreneur" (cf. Sifford, 1976; Kennedy and Williamson, 1978:42). It may be that the difference in *behavior* between current and earlier athletes is slight; rather, their behavior is now more subject to public scrutiny. The financial and personal events of the lives of Cobb, Hornsby, Ruth, Dean, and Medwick were less known to the public, at least the unsavory aspects, than those of, say, members of the Oakland Athletics of the early 1970s or the New York Yankees of the late 1970s (cf. Newhouse, 1980:87–89).

There is enormous potential for financial reward, in and out of baseball, for current "superstars." The average salary in 1979 was between $113,000 and $121,000, higher than that of professional hockey ($102,000) or football ($62,500), although below that of professional basketball ($180,000) (Hawkins, 1980);[9] however, it still is below that of entertainers (Jacobson, 1978:52). By the late 1970s, the salaries of some players were over $500,000. The twenty-two free agents of the post-1979 baseball season signed for an aggregate total of over $32 million in the last two months of that year, with Nolan Ryan, a pitcher with the California Angels, signing with the Houston Astros for over $1 million per year (Chass, 1980).

Such rewards may discourage players from spending their spare time enhancing their abilities and correcting their weaknesses.[10] They may be more inclined to concentrate on available and lucrative non-baseball activities and to think earlier about their post-baseball careers than may have been the case a generation or two ago (Furth, 1971: 166). Players are less likely to stay with one team during their careers (Warren, 1977). Another variable in the free-agent situation is signing for huge amounts and creating "relative deprivation," that is, teammates becoming dissatisfied and seeking to renegotiate their own contracts (cf. Durson, 1978).

Other factors, such as the player's higher education level, the unionization movement, and the weakening of the reserve clause have probably increased the tendency of athletes toward greater independence,[11] hedonism, egoism, and an extrinsic view of baseball as work and as an avenue of post-career rewards

(although not as much as the stereotype of athletes as political conservatives would have us believe; Petrie, 1977). The contemporary
situation requires more delicate and "honest" handling of players
by field managers (cf. Holtzman, 1976a:40, Slocum, 1979),
although there also appears to be a recent trend toward more conservative dress and grooming imposed by clubs (cf. *New York
Times*, 1976a; *Detroit Free Press*, 1976). In any case, apart from a
few current heroes, fans have had to look to the past for color.[12]
This fact may explain the increasing charismatic image of Joe
DiMaggio as a reminder to middle-aged Americans of a
presumably more heroic but innocent, or at least more hopeful,
time (cf. Grimsley, 1976; London, 1978).

Race, Ethnicity, and Gender. The assimilation and upward
mobility of immigrants and minorities in American society have
probably been aided by baseball and by sports in general (cf.
Boyle, 1971:259). This has been more true, however, for those
coming from outside the country (e.g., German, Irish, Italian,
Polish) than for some already here (e.g., black), or for women in
general, foreign or domestic.

Race. Except for isolated cases, blacks were not part of professional
American baseball in the nineteenth century and were banned
altogether before the twentieth.[13] Blacks, however, formed their
own teams—the Cuban Giants, Lincoln Giants (and many other
teams named "Giants"), Birmingham Black Barons, Pittsburgh
Homestead Grays, Pittsburgh Crawfords, Memphis Red Sox, and
Kansas City Monarchs—and also the Negro National and
American Leagues (Smith, 1970:317–26; Boyle, 1972:261–63;
Lucas and Smith, 1978:374–76). Baseball and the major professional sports, with the exception of boxing, did not desegregate
until after World War II (Eitzen and Sage, 1978:236–37; Lucas
and Smith, 1978:39–91; Coakley, 1978:276–77). Unlike the more
urban world of entertainment, baseball was more closely attached
to conventional American racism (E. Franklin Frazier, quoted in
Boyle, 1972:277; Voight, 1976; Lucas and Smith, 1978:269–75).
    Black players' entrance into the major leagues came after World
War II when Jackie Robinson, carefully selected and socialized by
the Brooklyn Dodgers President Branch Rickey (in the face of a
15–1 vote against this by the sixteen major league ball clubs, cf.
Smith, 1970:236; Reese, 1977), joined that club in 1947.
    Robinson had broken the "color line" at Montreal of the Inter-

national League, Brooklyn's top minor league affiliate, in 1946 where he had led the league in batting. He became one of Brooklyn's star players for the next decade, leading the National League in batting in 1949. The number of blacks in baseball grew slowly at first (Loy and McElvogue, 1970:15; Edwards, 1973:189; Coakley, 1978:276), but soon became a significant factor in the game, more in the National League (particularly the Dodgers and New York Giants), perhaps accounting for that league's rise to dominance over the American League beginning in the 1950s. The Boston Red Sox of the American League became the last major league team to introduce a black player (Baseball Digest, 1976:11-12); in contrast, in 1976, the Pittsburgh Pirates of the National League became the first major league team to begin a regular season game with black players filling all nine positions.

Blacks soon became the leading stars of the game, first in batting, base running, and fielding,[14] and eventually as pitchers,[15] and materially improved their teams' performance and attendance (Gwartney and Haworth, 1974:875-80). Any current list of the leading major league players tends to be dominated by blacks. Statistical studies of the 1950s and 1960s showed average black performance to be superior overall to that of whites (Rosenblatt, 1967) and by position (Loy and McElvogue, 1972:309; Pascal and Rapping, 1970, Eitzen and Sage, 1978:253-54). However, this may mean that while superior black athletes are used, average to mediocre blacks are not, or they are dropped sooner than mediocre whites (Rosenblatt, 1967:53; Pascal and Rapping, 1970; Scully, 1973; Eitzen and Yetman, 1977; Leonard, 1977).

Moreover, between 1949 and 1979, blacks (including Latin American blacks) have won the Most Valuable Player title twenty-one times out of a possible thirty-one in the National League, and eight times in the American League (the first in 1963) (Official Baseball Guide, 1980:365-66). In the same period, blacks have won the rookie-of-the-year award fourteen times in the National League and seven times in the American League (Official Baseball Guide, 1980:365). Black success in baseball may be a special case of the principle that, where individual performance can be easily measured (unlike social skills or sociable interaction) and works to the advantage of the other group members, there is less discrimination (Blalock, 1969:418-23), although baseball desegregation was slow relative to the proven contribution of black players (Gwartney and Haworth, 1974:880). Finally, while the proportion of blacks in major league baseball far exceeds their proportion in the general population, it does not approach the 62 to 65 percent in the National Basketball Association (Nigro, 1978), or even the 42 percent in the National Football League. The recent trend actually shows a decline on major league baseball rosters from 20 percent black in 1973 to about 18 or 19 percent in the 1976–80 period (Benagh, 1977; Nigro, 1978; Lapointe, 1f,6f 1980b). This decline may be attributed to two factors: (1) young blacks in inner cities tend to play basketball, whereas little league baseball is essentially a white sport (Lapointe, 1980a); (2) black attendance at major league games, which was never too high at about three percent, has fallen to one percent (Lapointe, 1980b:1-f).

This is not to imply that blacks were otherwise integrated into the game. In the early years after Jackie Robinson's breakthrough, separate living accommodations and eating arrangements were used in the South during spring training and in selected major league cities during the regular season (Smith, 1970:329, 337; Sylvester, 1976b:1-D; Reese, 1977). Moreover, bonuses paid black athletes were lower (Boyle, 1971:275) and television endorsements almost absent (Boyle, 1972:274; Edwards, 1972:306). Black athletes also tended to segregate themselves, to support and reinforce one another's status, dress, and deportment, and to take advice about these from older black players such as George Crowe; in fact, white players were more likely to accept social invitations from black players than the other way around (cf. Boyle, 1972:273). Also, black players were supported and idolized by the black community and therefore did not exhibit the hostility toward the Negro world historically found among black entertainers (Boyle, 1972:277n). Hence, they were more likely to concentrate their time and efforts in the black community rather than in society at large.

Even in the game itself, blacks were more likely to be found in team positions requiring less interaction with other team positions (i.e., outfield) than in positions with high interaction (i.e., catcher, infielder). This, called "stacking" by Harry Edwards (Edwards, 1973:205), was found in an analysis of the 1956-67 period (Loy and McElvogue, 1970:8–10, 16–20) that applied Oscar Grusky's "formal structure" view of organizations to baseball and Blalock's explanation of occupational discrimination. Grusky's (1969) own study of baseball managers that showed them most likely to come from high interaction positions suggests one major factor, apart from integration in other facets of the game, that makes black players less likely to become field managers. Grusky's analysis and

Blalock's (1969) theoretical propostions also help to explain why not only the Loy and McElvogue findings about black under-representation in high interaction baseball team positions, but also by extension, theirs is an explanation of baseball's general reluctance and lateness in hiring blacks to be announcers on radio and television, to be club and league officials, and, particularly, to be field managers (cf. Hoch, 1974:382; Spink, 1978a; Edwards, 1979). Medoff (1976b), alternatively, finds more blacks in such positions in 1970 than in 1960 and offers change in black economic circumstances (e.g., improved black income and training facilities that increase black skills) rather than sociological changes (reduced prejudice) for this.

It was not until 3 October 1974, over a quarter century after the breaking of the major league player color line, that Frank Robinson, the first black major league field manager, was hired by the Cleveland Indians (cf. Weigel, 1976b; Elderkin, 1976b).

There appears to be a reluctance to hire other blacks who have potential as managers such as Wills (until the middle of the 1980 season), Aaron, and Elston Howard, although Larry Doby, the first black player in the American League, became the second black manager, hired by the Chicago White Sox in mid-1979 but fired after that season.

Among black penetrations into nonmanaging positions in the major leagues have been Monte Irvin, a star of the old Negro leagues and the New York Giants, hired to be special assistant to the commissioner, and three umpires—Emmett Ashford in the American League from 1966 to the early 1970s and Art Williams beginning in 1973 and Eric Gregg beginning in 1977 in the National League (Holtzman, 1977b; *Detroit Free Press*, 1979b). The Atlanta Braves hired Aaron to direct its farm system and Bill Lucas as director of player personnel. These cases are the exception and it remains to be seen whether black penetration into nonplaying positions in baseball at moderate and high organizational levels will follow the experiences of other immigrant and ethnic "groups" (cf. Edwards, 1973:186–87).

In contrast to the rising consciousness among black players, Latin American players, who had entered the major leagues earlier, have been quiescent. This may be the result not only of the fact that Latins entered organized baseball gradually but also of the fact that many are foreign nationals who return to their native countries between seasons. They face an identity problem, a complaint frequently made by Clemente, Oliva, and Campaneris. The language factor is undoubtedly an important barrier, but so is ethnic prejudice by players and sports writers, with terms such as "hot dog" and "showboat" probably applied to Latins or Hispanics even more than to blacks (Burns, 1979; Lapoint, 1980c).[16]

Ethnicity. While the black example is the most dramatic one, ethnic change in baseball has been the norm rather than the exception.[17] [18] One possible explanation for ethnic (including black) succession in baseball and other sports relates immigrants to upward mobility. Baseball, and sports such as boxing (cf. Weinberg and Arond, 1972:293), offered opportunities for upward mobility to the active or ambitious poor. In the case of immigrants, it would be their male children, the "first American generation," imbued with the ideology and desire for success and full assimilation, who entered competitive sports (cf. Riesman and Denney, 1969:316; Weinberg and Arond, 1972:285; Hock, 1974:380; Voigt, 1976). This explanation not only fits the pattern of baseball's changing European ethnic composition, it may also apply to black entrance into the major leagues if black migration from the rural South into Northern cities is seen as comparable to European immigration into the United States. The color ban in baseball, however, complicates this. The above explanation may or may not be applicable to Latin American players.[19]

Gender

> The typical American male strikes out the Yankee side before going to sleep at night.
>
> —James Thurber

Women have been virtually excluded from sports throughout history. For example, with the exception of Sparta, women were not allowed to participate in sports in ancient Greece and were even barred from viewing the Olympics (Coakley, 1978:245), partly because there were nude male athletes (Hawkins, 1980b).[20] Women were first allowed to compete in Olympic golf and tennis in 1900 (Lucas and Smith, 1978:349-50). They were included in swimming and diving in the 1912 Stockholm games and in track and field in 1928 (Sage, 1974a:286) but are still excluded from Olympic wrestling, judo, boxing, weightlighting, the hammer throw, the longer footraces, high hurdles, and all team games except volley ball (cf. Metheny, 1976:283) and basketball.

Despite the fact that the feminist movement in the United States began before the antislavery and civil rights movements, women have not entered organized baseball as players, not even in leagues or teams of their own (although there are women's professional softball leagues; cf. *Detroit Free Press*, 1976e; Benagh, 1976a). The major leagues' first female executive, Margaret Donahue, who died in January 1978 at age eighty-five, began as corporate secretary of the Chicago White Sox in 1926 and later became a vice president of the club. There have been occasional women in the front office of minor league teams (*Sporting News*, 1977). The first woman sports writer was Mary Garber, who entered this field during the Second World War (Green, 1978; Scott, 1978). More recently, the number of women sports writers has increased, some being allowed grudgingly into locker rooms, although law suits were sometimes necessary (cf. Spander, 1977a; *Detroit Free Press*, 1977c and 1979a; Lincoln, 1979; *N.Y. Times*, 1979); occasionally, a woman appears as part of a sportscasting team.

There have been at least two women umpires in organized baseball, Christine Wren in the Class A Northwest League and Pam Postema in the Gulf Coast League (Holtzman, 1977d). Another, Bernice Gara, successfully sued organized baseball, umpired part of a minor league game in a hostile atmosphere, and retired (Voigt, 1976).

More change has occurred in amateur baseball where occasional court decisions (cf. *Detroit Free Press*, 1978b), laws, and rulings by official bodies have decreed that women can play with men (in non-contact sports), that baseball is a non-contact sport (cf. Title IX, 1972 Education Amendments, U.S.), and/or that schools spend an equal amount of money on both female and male (i.e., segregated) athletics. The application of Title IX has apparently had the twin effect of (1) producing a proliferation of women's athletics from elementary schools through colleges and, (2) causing some panic and turmoil in athletic departments and some retrenching, especially in "minor" and "women's" sports (particularly in junior colleges) (*Sporting News*, 1977b; Merry, 1978).

An obvious explanation for the slowness of women's entry into sports is the sexism of American society. Submission to a sexist structure is ingrained in women as well as in men in many societies, particularly in the lower classes (cf. Lueschen, 1972:241–42) and also among some advocates of racial equality (cf. Edwards, 1972:305; Hoch, 1974:381–82), although the black community is more receptive to active competent women (cf. Edwards, 1973:233–34). The "macho" or "machismo" norms among baseball players are a case in point. There is a wealth of literature on the differential socialization of girls and boys in the family, with girls being raised to be more passive, altruistic, and nurturant and boys being raised to be more aggressive, egoistic, and instrumental (cf. Kagan and Moss, 1960; Maccoby, 1966; Horrocks, 1969; Maccoby and Jacklin, 1974; chapter 4). This kind of socialization encourages and reinforces norms against women's participation in sports (cf. Petrie, 1971; Sutton-Smith, Rosenberg, and Morgan, 1974) requiring bodily contact, overcoming resistance, or projecting one's body through space (cf. Metheny: 1976:282–90).

If girls' early socialization can be interpreted as inculating obedience and responsibility, and boys' early socialization as inculcating achievement, then it is not surprisng that girls play more games of *strategy* (bridge, checkers) and *chance* (dice, craps, bingo), whereas boys play more games of *physical skill* (golf, tennis) (cf. Sutton-Smith, Roberts, and Kozelka, 1969:247; Sutton-Smith and Roberts, 1971:82–86). Today, there are women as well as men who argue that women, as a category, cannot compete equally with men, as a category, because of differential talent or size, because of differential ability to take hard competition and the physical grind, or because of inferior opportunities and facilities (cf. Pezzano, 1976, Craig, 1976; *Detroit Free Press*, 1976b; Spink, 1977a). The foregoing arguments contradict the individualistic ethic that each person's ability be considered regardless of gender, race, age, or other criteria that are less than completely relevant to the activity in question. Billy Martin, the ex-Yankee manager (and successfull manager of Oakland in 1980), apparently has hope for women as competitors (Elderkin, 1978). Paul Weiss, a philosopher, seems content to treat women as an innately less instrumental subspecies and in terms of cultural stereotypes (Weiss, 1969:214–22). A more relevant argument may be that the position of women in baseball is but a more extreme instance of their general place in the occupational structure. That is, whereas women comprise over 40 percent of the American labor force, they are found largely in the lower rungs of the occupational hierarchy where they neither exert power nor gain much intrinsic reward.

The future prospect for women in baseball may be more hopeful. Raised female (and male) consciousness, as a result of women's liberation movements of the 1960s, 1970s, and 1980s, has caused some changes in business and government and encouraged women to go into law, medicine, the executive levels of business and education, and sports. It remains to be seen when, or whether, women will play in organized baseball under universalistic criteria. Baseball's high commissioner, Bowie Kuhn, welcomes women to professional baseball (Cohen, 1977), as does Henry Aaron (Spring, 1977b). Since the lower classes are still a major source of baseball talent, that may first require significant modification of sexism (cf. Lueschen, 1971: 242).

Social Stratification and Mobility. While some disagree (Burdge; 1974: 241-43), judging from the class origins of athletes (cf. Loy, 1972: 9-11) and perhaps fans, baseball is a working-class sport (Clarke, 1956: 304) and Stone, 1969: 8, 11). At the same time it has been a source of player upward mobility (cf. Loy, 1972: 15-19 and in Sage, 1974: 253, 265), as have other sports (cf. Lueschen, 1971: 247-54), although it has probably wasted the time of the more numerous "failures" (cf. Edwards, 1973: 99; Coakley, 1978: 275; Snyder and Spreitzer, 1974: 474-75; Eitzen and Sage, 1978: 224-29). Unresolved, in its relevance to upward mobility, is the question of whether or not athletic participation, particularly in high school, is detrimental to education (cf. Colemen, 1961: 260-66; Loy, in Sage, 1974a: 258; and cf. Schafer and Armer, 1972: 203-23; Buhrmann, 1972: 126-27; Rehberg and Schafer, 1974: 458-64; Phillips and Schafer, 1974). Hauser and Lueptow, in a later study, argue that while an athletes' grade point averages are higher at the end of high school than at the start, they do not gain as much through the high school years as do nonathletes, although other variables may account for these differences (Hauser and Lueptow, 1978).

Unlike tennis, golf, and pool, baseball began as an upper-class sport (Page, 1969: 198; Wallop, 1969: 36-37; Sage, 1974a: 230), as did British football (Elias and Dunning, 1972:77; McIntosh, 1971:7). In time, it came to serve the lower working classes, immigrants, and ethnic minorities, not only as a source of amusement, but also as a source of occupational mobility (cf. Boyle, 1972: 259). Baseball seems to fit Guenther Lueschen's analysis of fashion cycles in sports, that sports tend to have a higher social position when first introduced (Lueschen, 1976b:98); this generalization is apparently far from universal. It also may be that the increase in economic affluence and education after World War II raised the class level of baseball spectators (Furst, 1971:165), though this in itself would not explain the discrepancy between Burdge's findings and those of Clarke and Stone.

A few other study areas related to stratification and mobility are suggested here. For example, one might study the class origins of people who select, or are found in, certain team positions (akin to studies of the race of players); who win batting, pitching, fielding, and base stealing titles; who receive Most Valuable Player, Cy Young, and Golden Glove awards; who become managers and general managers; and even those who buy ball clubs—and whether these have been changing over the years. One might study informal cliques and status relationships on ball clubs, the bases for popularity and isolation, and informal status systems across ball clubs (cf. Bouton, 1970). More attention should be paid to what happens to athletes after their career is over (cf. Furst, 1971:166); that is, under what circumstances do they experience identity crisis, personal disorganization, and/or downward mobility (cf. Wallop, 1969:54–55; Page, 1969:200; Sylvester, 1976b:1-D)? This appears to be a particular problem for black athletes, and probably certain other ethnics such as Latin Americans, whose extrabaseball and postbaseball economic opportunities are fewer, on the average, than those of white players (cf. Edwards, 1972:305; Hoch, 1974:387). Other studies might relate class to favoritism from baseball's authorities, to ability to triumph over adversity, to flexibility in adapting to changing circumstances, and to developing a hedonistic and/or egoistic baseball style.

Finally, stratification also refers to the power hierarchy of baseball. This includes both formal and informal power inherent in the organization of ball clubs. This kind of power and stratification came into the game by the 1880s, succeeding the more amateur and gentlemanly character of the game, and a degree of control by the players, in the 1845–70 period (Wallop, 1969: chapter 2; Lucas and Smith, 1978:178–84). It also includes the structure of baseball's "official family," for example, the power of the commissioner and league presidents. Study also can be made of the informal and pervasive influence of powerful owners, the relative power of the minor leagues, the, perhaps, parallel contemporary power of the players' union and, eventually, of the umpires' union. One may also examine the influence of the players' representatives chosen from each ball club (and selected for popularity more than for than for competence, cf. Bouton, 1970:172) and more likely to be traded, sold, or released than chance would call for (cf. Pepe, 1975). Another area might be the political use of baseball by politicians, as has been the case with the Olympics (Eitzen and Sage, 1978; chapter 9). These are undoubtedly only a few of the areas where research would be desirable.

Some Theoretical Implications: A Deductive Approach

This chapter's approach so far has had an inductive flavor. Beginning with concrete and familiar baseball phenomena, theoretical insights and explanations have been derived, often imposed, and then advanced. Emphasis will now shift to the explicit application of sociological theoretical schools or systems to baseball.

Recent texts about schools and systems of sociology seem to emphasize interactionism, functionalism, exchange, and conflict theories and to a lesser degree, Marxism, social phenomenology, ethnomethodology, organizational and small group theories, and ecological theory (cf. Zeitlin, 1973; Warshay, 1975:chapter 2; Turner, 1978). This analysis will stress interactionism, functionalism, exchange, conflict, and Marxism as most representative of current theory, with the remaining schools being used occasionally and briefly.

The Five Theories Applied

Interactionism. Interactionism, or symbolic interactionism (Mead, 1934; Blumer, 1937 and 1969), has already been used in the preceding micro analysis in its view of players taking one another into account, anticipating possible and probable strategies, and taking the role of the generalized and particular other(s). While relevant on the micro level, an interactionist perspective also brings in the macro level through its use of the generalized other. Moreover, in an interactionist analysis of macro-phenomena, such as cultural values (e.g., "machismo," fair play) and organizational power (e.g., baseball's ownership and corporate structure), there is focus on the *actual* interaction processes between and among players, managers, owners, union leaders, and judges. There is emphasis on emergent properties and unexpected outcomes in these processes rather than on "obvious" and automatic causation between cultural and structural forces, on the one hand, and the behavior of baseball players as individuals and as members of interacting units, on the other (cf. Blumer, 1962:185). Grusky's (1969) study showing that field managers tend to be recruited from high interaction positions would fit here as would studies by Blalock (1969) and Loy and McElvogue (1970).

An interesting extension of symbolic interactionism's focus on actual interaction would be the study of the persisting and changing identities of players, managers, and fans who are participating in the game, actually and vicariously, showing values and expressing moods in the process (Stone, 1962). Here, one might focus on the expressive symbolism and dramaturgical aspects of baseball—as in arguments between umpire and manager, the ritual of changing pitchers, the byplay between players and fans (who alternatively see players as "heroes, villains, and fools"), and the poetry in laying down a bunt, catching a fly ball, or executing a double play (cf. Burke, 1945, 1950; Klapp, 1964, 1969, 1972).

Interactionism's "elementary collective behavior" forms and mechanisms focus on emergent properties and the unexpected in baseball. Examples of these are riots that sometimes arise in the actual playing of games and social movements that develop over a longer period of time (such as the unionization of players, now in an institutionalizing stage, and of the umpires' union and the strike at the beginning of the 1979 season).[21] Another application of interactionism within the elementary collective behavior framework is the fact that, in contrast with professional football, basketball, and hockey, baseball depends less for its popularity on the compact conventional crowd and audience present at the game itself than on the more diffuse mass and public spread throughout society (cf. Turner and Killian, 1972:chapters 3, 5, 7-10).

Functionalism. A functional analysis of baseball focuses on the game, at both micro and macro levels, as a social system (Parsons, 1951) that fulfills positive and negative, and latent and manifest, functions for society (cf. Merton, 1949:chapter 1; McIntosh, 1971:8-12). Baseball, therefore, is viewed from the perspective of society (cf. Coakley, 1978:23-26), particularly in terms of functional imperatives such as pattern maintenance and integration (Iso-Ahola, 1975:63). Functionalism emphasizes the role of baseball in exemplifying the values of the American "cultural system" (e.g., individualism, competition, teamwork), in assimilating immigrants and ethnic minorities into the mainstream of society, and in providing relaxation, "safe" tension release, affectivity, and expressive interests for citizens in a mass society (cf. Parsons, 1951:86–87, 512; Heinila, 1972: 112, 114).[22] Among baseball's "dysfunctions" might be that the game is often more work than play for the players and that it overstresses achievement values, thereby causing tension and even conflict with other values (cf. Lueschen, 1976b:105–6).

Another application of Parsonian functionalism was studies of the correlates of strategy, chance, and physical skill by Roberts and others. Using a cross-cultural analysis, the authors related games of strategy to social systems, games of chance to religious beliefs, and games of physical skill to environmental conditions (Roberts, Arth, and Bush, 1974:146). Given women's predilection to games of strategy and chance, and men's to games of physical skill, one can apply the Parsonian functional imperatives corresponding to social systems (integration), to religious beliefs (pattern maintenance), and to environmental conditions (adaptation) as a structural-functionlist explanation of differences in sex roles.

Another functionalist approach is to view the game as both work and play or leisure for ball players involving both instrumental and expressive behavior. As a famous umpire is reputed to have said: "You can't beat the hours!" This is less true for coaches, field managers, minor league players, and certainly for Japanese baseball players.[23] In any case, the place of leisure and of expressive behavior in baseball cannot be compared to industry in most respects but may resemble the university and religious institutions. That is, major league baseball's bottom "rung," the player, is far better paid and receives more honor and intrinsic reward from his work than does the bottom rung in business and politics.

In terms of organizations, generally, functionalism would emphasize baseball's different levels—technical (i.e., the players), managerial (field and general managers), and institutional (the club ownership, whether individual or corporate, and the league and commissioner structure)—as differentially fulfilling one or more of the four functional problems or imperatives of social systems—adaptation, goal attainment, pattern maintenance, and integration (cf. Parsons, 1951:chapter 3, 1959, 1966:7, 28–29), particularly the latter two (Lueschen, 1976b:104–5). This would be a benign view of management and of the person who bought the club or assumed its presidency. Not only are instrumental and economic considerations involved, therefore, but expressive and leisure ones as well (cf. Gilmartin, 1976), that is, the chance to relive one's childhood, to participate in a less serious activity, and/or, as Bob Hope, part owner of the Cleveland Indians in the 1940s and 1950s, once said, to be able to "give orders to men with muscles."

Finally, the late Talcott Parsons's work on "generalized or symbolic media of interchange" introduces four media that are symbolic rather than intrinsic (Parsons, 1975:95 and 1977:115), and "informational" rather than "energy," and that facilitate or control interchanges among baseball owners, players, advertisers, league presidents, and the like. For example, *money*, a medium of exchange related to the "adaptive" function of social systems, facilitates or controls exchanges of "practical rationality" within the baseball social system and between that system and other systems, e.g., negotiations over players' salaries and television contracts. Three other symbolic media are: *political power*, used in compliance or enforcement of baseball's rules and the owners' prerogatives; *influence*, involved in processes of persuasion between and among owners, players, managers, and umpires; and *value commitment*, facilitating or enforcing the obligations assumed by any of the above parties (Parsons, 1971:12–18; 1975:95–110).

Social Exchange Theory. Social exchange theory would stress the role of bargaining and negotiating in baseball, with emphasis upon resources, costs, rewards, and profits—broadly defined (cf. Homans, 1958, 1974; Cook and Emerson, 1978). With some Darwinian implications, baseball's competitive aspects would be emphasized. The focus would be on players competing for the same position, for limited resources and on relations between players and management, individually and collectively.

This theory would also apply to entrances and exits from baseball by owners, players, umpires, coaches, managers, etc. Cultural values, such as "macho," individualism, winning, teamwork, and fair play would be seen as macro variables arising out of the exchange processes that are emergent, indirect, and/or generalized exchange (cf. Sahlins, 1965:149–55; Lévi-Strauss, 1969). These, then act upon structural aspects of the macro level such as the ball club, the players' union, the league office, and the Baseball Writers' Association (cf. Blau, 1964, 1968; Emerson, 1976:355–59).

The success of minorities in entering baseball could be seen by exchange theorists in terms of (1) their exchange value, i.e., males with skills, (2) their increasing power in American society, and (3) changing values in the (macro) culture (cf. Blau, 1964). The smaller bonuses paid to blacks for signing, at least when they first entered organized baseball, and their less than proportionate share in commercial endorsements, might be explained in terms of a lesser exchange value. The absence of women in baseball may be explained in exchange terms, that is, the less their exchange value the less their power. Baseball in this way may reflect the slow change of cultural values relevant to women.

Finally, the principle of "distributive justice" (Homans, 1961: 72–78, 234; 1974: chapter 11) would mitigate against an affirmative action policy toward minorities and women in the game. The principle asserts that rewards are expected to be proportional to costs, and that profits are expected to be proportional to investments. Since baseball skills (costs) and outcomes are quantifiable (cf. Blalock, 1969: 418; Lueschen, 1969: 59), baseball is not likely to hire or reward minorities or women with inferior or even just average playing skills; this would also affect hiring at nonplaying positions. The principle of distributive justice can also help to explain why Kaline, Mays, and DiMaggio continued to draw high salaries (profit) toward the end of their careers when their skills (cost) were diminished; that is, they had been in the game and contributed to it and to their ball clubs at a high level of skill (cost) for a long time (investment, similar to seniority in industry). The drawing power of these players at the gate (cost), however, was still considerable even near the end of their careers.

As an outlook on baseball, social exchange theory tends to emphasize the more hard-headed, less openly ideological, aspects of the game. Perhaps it needs to be supplemented with ecological theory's emphasis on populations (players, teams, ball clubs, management) as units organized to deal with "scarce resources," that is, victories, championships, profits, recognition.

Conflict Theory. Conflict theory, of the earlier Gumplowicz-Ratzenhofer-Sumner-Simmel-Park-Vold varieties, and the Coser-Dahrendorf versions more recently (Park and Burgess, 1924:chapter 9; Vold, 1958; Dahrendorf, 1959, 1967, 1968; Coser, 1956, 1957, 1967), is similar to social exchange theory in its Darwinian flavor on both micro and macro levels. It could concern itself with the *political* aspect of baseball in that it stresses competition and conflict between players and between players and management, individually and collectively. Sports, including baseball, offer a "natural laboratory" for the detached study of conflict (E. Dunning, 1971 in Snyder and Spreitzer, 1974:473).

Conflict theory's "scarcity" assumption about the inevitability of scarce resources implies *incompatibilities* in baseball's competitive process. That is, only so many players can be stars or even kept on the team(s), only one team can win the World Series (or conference or national championship), only two can win the pennant, only four the division titles. Only one person can be the manager of a given team (though there have been "collective" experiments, e.g., the Chicago Cubs in the 1960s). In other areas, accommodations (i.e., adjustments of quantity or degree) are possible, for example, between players, between the player's or umpire's union and management, or in owner-player salary negotiations.

Conflict theory's position that the solidarity of baseball teams is enhanced by competition has some empirical support (cf. Meyers, 1969:376). Conflict theorists' confidence, however, that solidarity is also a cause or independent variable in its own right, that is, that it may aid in the competitive or conflict struggle, meets contradictory empirical findings (see above).

Conflict theorists would tend to see teams as *groups* organizing around *interests*. This applies not only to members of the same team sharing a common interest in the team's success, but also to players as a class, team owners as a class, umpires as a class or category, and perhaps managers or coaches as "quasi groups" (Dahrendorf, 1959:179–89). It also would apply to cliques and other subgroups on a team, not only organized around friendship, but also along racial, nationality (e.g., Latin Americans, for whom language is an important cohesive factor), and, perhaps in the near future, gender lines as well. Ethnic succession is, therefore, the rise, and perhaps the fall, of different interest groups.

Finally, even more than is true for exchange theory, conflict theory would deemphasize cultural values, norms, and ideas, seeing these as derivable, as misleading, and/or as weapons to be used instrumentally. Hence, the presumed norms in baseball, as well as the statements made by ball players, managers and owners (and by the commissioner) about the game would be seen as rationalizations. "Alibi Ike" is an established baseball character comparable to "Casey at the Bat" and accords with the low credibility of public statements by baseball players and officials, and sports writers, in anticipating or predicting the future or in explaining and justifying the past. Conflict theory, therefore, contrasts with symbolic interactionism and structural-functionalism in stressing interests (i.e., conflict, politics) of players and baseball organizations over interpersonal expectations and cultural values, respectively.

Marxist Theory. Marxists interpret baseball as part of the structure of corporate capitalism.24 As such, baseball reflects the alienation of the working classes, of employees in general, and others in the American labor force. Players are a comfortable proletariat imbued with "false consciousness," that is, they falsely see themselves as professionals despite intermittent activism, e.g., the reserve clause, playing and working conditions, and unionization. Minor league players, on the other hand, are not even a well-off proletariat. Baseball, like other sports, is seen to channel the potential for revolutionary activity by the masses into identification with safe and harmless teams and heroes; like other sports, it is part of the "superstructure" of society, covering or masking what is really going on in the rest of society (cf. R. Pankin, 1974:7; chapter 1.)

The game is seen to reflect the brutality of American society although it is less brutal than hockey, football, or basketball because of the fewer opportunities for body contact. Finally, baseball is seen to reinforce capitalist values by treating people as property or things, using trades and bonuses to improve efficiency and competitiveness, promoting specialization (that increases alienation), and standardizing and quantifyng the game (cf. Lahr, 1972:110–11).

The crucial point for Marxists is private ownership, making baseball part of the system of exploitation inherent in any capitalist society. One should not be fooled, therefore, by the culture of baseball (an arguement similar to that made by conflict theory, above) for, as part of baseball's ideology and superstructure, it is irrelevant to the real conditions of power and exploitation and even serves to support them. The profit motive supersedes all, including good will baseball arrangements with other nations (Onigman, 1978).

A Marxist critique of other theories would condemn their emphasis on variables such as values, on micro variables generally, and on variables that do not serve to question the mercenary and hopeless aspects of capitalism. A concentration on values, as emphasized in functionalism, gives a misleading view of what counts in baseball. Emphasis on the micro level, as in interactionism, obscures the macro level of baseball's private ownership. Stressing cost, reward, and profit in baseball, as exchange theory takes as given, albeit in a sophisticated manner, also reflects a market orientation characteristic of capitalism. For example, the "lesser exchange value" of women and blacks in advertising is explained by Marxists in terms of women and blacks being powerless and, thereby, exploitable. Finally, even conflict theory, which points to the role of power and conflict, group solidarity, and the falseness of ideas and values, sees conflict, power, and stratification as inevitable, as recurring and cyclical, and lies within the liberal ideology of freedom and market rationality (Dahrendorf, 1968: viii and chapter 8, 1967: footnote 16 and 38).

In contrast, Marxism and Marxist sport sociology as social theory and as ideological critique (cf. Hoberman, 1976) sees baseball as part of a dialectical historical process that passes from the current alienating society toward a future humanistic society (cf. Bennett, 1976:68-69). Like interactionism and Dahrendorf's version of conflict theory, Marxism stresses the emergent social movements that have been affecting baseball—of blacks, of women, of unionization of players and umpires, eventually of fans (cf. *Detroit Free Press*, 1977b; Boyle, 1979). These are seen to be part of a long and involved process of increasing conflict and heightened consciousness on the part of the exploited and the depressed. This process will eventually result in a condition of free "unalienated" producers (e.g., ball players) in control of economic necessity (i.e., of the resources and conditions of their baseball work) where forces and relations of production (i.e., the social structure of baseball organizations) will be integrated with the political, legal, and idea systems, that is, not only will racism and machismo disappear but also "Alibi Ike."

Conclusion. Each of the above five schools or theories deals with several aspects of baseball in its own way. That is, each theory has an outlook and tools that apply to some areas of the game and social life in general but not to other areas (for example, interactionism and functionalism in effect omit power while exchange theory omits the self). Moreover, even where they do overlap, the theories give different interpretations to the same phenomena (for example, the game's cultural values by functionism, exchange, conflict, and Marxist theories; social movements by interactionism and Marxism; expressive and leisure behavior in baseball by functionalism and Marxism; and power by exchange, conflict, and Marxist theories). Theory integration is not a fact, therefore, nor does it appear to be imminent in the study of baseball or of sociology in general.

Summary and Conclusion

Summary: Some Generalizations

This chapter brought a sociological approach to the examination of baseball. It first examined the game itself and contrasted it with other sports. The chapter then continued with an approach that was largely inductive and concluded with a deductive analysis (the five theories).

The inductive approach, in using important sociological concepts and ideas, was analytic in a loose or implicit sense. It began with a micro orientation that emphasized face-to-face interaction, then moved to structural variables that "intruded" on the micro—such as rules, statuses, and roles. Then, the macro level followed, dealing with the cultural, the historical, and the structural.

A deductive analysis was used that applied five existing sociological theories and schools to baseball. Here, examination of the game was analytic in an explicit sense.

Some generalizations that follow from the above approaches are:

1. Baseball, in contrast with footbal, basketball, and hockey, is a game for contemplation, punctuated with occasional peaks of intensity and anticipation. It is neither a timed game nor even much of a space or territory game (much of its spatial aspect being symbolic).

2. Baseball's explicit aspects tend to be micro, emphasizing interpersonal symbolic interaction, role-taking, and some intruding structural variable such as the baseball rules and the statuses or positions of players and officials. Among areas for further inquiry are the bases for the variations in the longevity of baseball field managers and other positions (e.g., third basemen), both currently and in the previous century. Other areas deserving further study are the relevance and limits of variables such as cohesiveness, cooperation, competition, and conflict to the actual winning and losing of games. Probably more important for the understanding of baseball is the limitations of micro analyses such as the above and the greater significance of macro analyses.

3. The macro level emphasized cultural, historical, and structural variables. Cultural variables stressed the role of individualism in

American baseball (comparison with baseball in a nonin-
dividualistic culture, such as Japan, might be instructive), though
this was moderated by the exigencies of team play. Moreover, con-
flicts between values of sportsmanship and winning, and between
formal and informal norms (e.g., for umpires), were emphasized.
Other significant norms in baseball were the role of and reasons
for superstition and the strength and future prospects of
"machismo" norms.

4. The second macro variable treated above, the historical,
brought in the other two, the cultural and structural, as well. For
example, it pointed to the early limitations set on sports development in colonial America by Puritan values, the limitations to
leisure set by early work conditions and by the class sytem, and
restrictions introduced by political and legal institutions. Another
dimension of the historical was the commercialization of baseball
in the nineteenth and twentieth centuries as the game developed
from "play," through "game," to "work," though it retains
aspects of all three. Of equal historical interest had been the
disinclination by baseball's leaders to attribute the game's origins
to non-American sources, thus leading to a long-held fiction that
the game was an American invention in 1839 rather than, as now
believed on the basis of better scholarship, an American refinement of earlier English games.

5. A third macro variable, or series of variables, examined the
structural level—organizational, the mass and public, the changing
role of the athlete, ethnicity, race, gender, and social stratification. Baseball's hierarchical corporate structure was emphasized,
particularly the power of team ownership, the relative importance
of baseball's highest officials, and the growing power of the
players' union, the last (in concert with an arbitrator's decisions)
causing severe modifications in the "reserve clause" in players'
contracts.

6. Related to the above organizational variables is the massifica-
tion brought about by radio and television, the question of the
credibility of baseball announcers, the role of "spectatoritis" and
the more *intrinsic* relation to baseball of the spectator than of the
players, and the increasing hedonism, egoism, and independence
of the modern player.

7. Study of ethnicity, race, and gender pointed to the *exclusion* of
blacks until after World War II and of women at least until the
1980s. Blacks have come to dominate the sport and have

represented a new and major source of talent recruitment at a time of the decline of the minor leagues; however, women are still almost completely excluded except at the amateur level. One interesting finding was the role and basis of "ethnic succession" in the game before the entrance of blacks. Of further interest are the changing roles of black players outside of game conditions, the remaining "social distance" between blacks and whites within the game (based on differential occupancy of near versus remote team positions), the possible emergence of Hispanic and American Indian consciousness, and the cyclical inclusion of women in certain sports and exclusion from others.

8. Baseball as a working-class sport and as a source of upward mobility was examined. The class level of both participants and spectators appears to have been curvilinear over time, that is, highest over a century ago, then dropping, and rising in recent years. Of interest to baseball's role as an aid to player upward mobility is the question of the player's initial class level, that is, the game may have aided many from immigrant, ethnic minority, and lower-class backgrounds to rise, although extensive participation in high school sports may have harmed the others' life chances.

9. Explicit application to baseball of current sociological theories and schools constituted a deductive sociological analysis of the game. Of the five theories mentioned, interactionism appeared to fit best the (micro) game situation although it also seemed relevant to emergent macro phenomena and to elementary collective behavior such as ethnic, gender, and unionization movements. Functionalism, on the macro and structural level, emphasized the positive and negative contributions that baseball as a system makes to society's values and to individual adjustment (e.g., assimilation, upward mobility, expressive functions).

10. In contrast, social exchange and conflict theories emphasized the more instrumental, harder, and "meaner" aspects of the game. In stressing resources, costs, profits, power, and conflict between and among players, managers, and owners, these two theories depart from the interactionist and functionalist emphasis on cooperation and symbols. Finally, a Marxist interpretation, similar to interactionism's process and emergence outlook and to conflict theory's emphasis on process, power, and conflict, offers, as does functionalism, a more complete theory of society and baseball. The game is viewed as a more beneficent version of relations in a capitalist society, one that is already participating in a

struggle (e.g., the unionization movement) against ownership in which players will come to realize their proletarian status despite their privileges.

11. A theoretical, deductive analysis of baseball may do more for theory than for baseball. It does highlight the limitations of using only one theory and there is a question about how much insight has been contributed. Interactionism's emphasis on emergent micro and macro processes added some insights to both ordinary and unusual baseball phenomena. The introduction of a functionalist focus brought an equilibrium and macro focus to baseball that contrasts with interactionism's process orientation; structural-functional theory is an almost complete theory with a conservative outlook that sees baseball's role in terms of its contributions to the status quo. Offering less typical views of the game are exchange and conflict theories, which stress the economic and political aspects of baseball, and Marxism's radical and moral class struggle interpretations of baseball's typical daily events as well as of its more dramatic movements and potential.

Conclusion: Sociology and the State of Baseball

Baseball cannot be studied sufficiently by sociology alone, or by any other single discipline, but a sociological approach is broad enough and insightful enough so that it offers a good beginning. Certainly, one learns by examining interaction and identity, status and role, organization and power, competition and conflict, cultural values and historical trends, both micro and macro aspects, inductively and deductively.

The game developed early within an urbanizing society, a society increasingly valuing organized leisure as well as business, competition as well as cooperation, and individualism as well as teamwork. The game may have reached its peak of popularity in the early decades of this century when the country was culturally rural and less educated. This meant that each town and village could have its own team without competition from college-based sports such as football and basketball which were not yet in a position to become successful professionally. By the 1960s, however, baseball's slower pace, said to be out of touch with a television-dominated urban and suburban college-trained society, and with a violent age (cf. Schwartz, 1973), had apparently become less popular than pro football and, perhaps, pro basketball as well.

The fact that interaction between baseball players during games is mediated by a ball and, in the case of batters, by bat and ball, may be a handicap in an age of sports that feature violent contact between players. Moreover, the slowness of baseball's leaders to respond effectively to television problems, territorial expansion, and player politicization and growing consciousness may have been a factor in the game's declining popularity.

Yet, baseball has begun to deal more intelligently with television and perhaps with expansion problems (cf. Spink, 1980). Players, aided by arbitration decisions, have forced reserve clause modifications. Further, in view of its increasing attendance and popularity (cf. Boswell, 1979b), notices of baseball's decline may be premature. Its slow pace may yet set it off to advantage as the popularity of its rivals wanes and people begin to appreciate baseball's different mood and symbolic aspects. Moreover, it still has part of the summer to itself. Of considerable importance may be its blending of different American values; e.g. speed and contemplation, power and precision, science and chance, idealism and pragmatism, democracy and opportunity.

Whether the game will continue to grow, to reflect the cultural and personal themes of the United States and other societies, and to retain and enhance its marginal hold on the majority of the population, remains a question. Sociologists, if they can restrain their love and loyalty to the game sufficiently so as to retain some objectivity and perspective, can devote more of their efforts to studying baseball so as to help answer this question. More generally, they and other social and behavioral scientists and humanists should do more research and analysis of baseball and other sports, thereby joining the baseball professionals and the countless amateurs who do much of this out of their love for the game.

Notes

I am grateful to Professor Jim Dowd, University of Georgia sociology department, and to Jim Benagh, *Detroit Free Press*, for many comments, additions, and corrections.

1. Perhaps, many national television announcers are not sufficiently aware of these baseball characteristics, judging from their rush to exaggerate the amount of action during slow or leisurely aspects of games.
2. Hence, the few times that games are "called" by darkness, weather conditions, transportation exigencies, or because of curfews indicate the distortions caused by time

limitations—such as the team that is behind wasting time and/or the team that is ahead trying to make out on purpose when at bat or to pitch only strikes, and to do so hurriedly, when afield.

3. Moreover, it is sometimes difficult to gain access to the macro-level since those who hold positions of power and control (e.g., team owners, high baseball officials), like upper and ruling classes generally, are reluctant to publicize, and to allow others to scrutinize, their positions and activities that imply power and privilege.

4. The American League, built out of a minor league, the Western League, in 1901 became the only successful challenger to the National League. Among the unsuccessful challengers were: the first Players' League (1871-75), the American Association (1882-91), the Union League or Association (1884), the second Players' League (1890), the Federal League (1913-15), the Mexican League (1945-46), and, on paper, the Continental League (about 1960). A temporary challenger in the mid-1970s was the World Baseball League (cf. Wallop, 1969:56-57, 62-73, 84-95; Koppett, 1969:7; Smith, 1970: 43, 60-62, 151-52, 190, Chapter 22; Detroit Free Press, 1976a; New York Times, 1976b). The latest variation, the Inter-American League, is a six club league that is unaffiliated with organized baseball; it began a five month, 130 game schedule in April 1979 with many former major league players in Miami, Florida, and five Latin American cities (cf. Janofsky, 1979; Colson, 1979).

5. The first paid admission occurred on 20 July 1859 at a game between Brooklyn and New York at which about 1,500 people paid fifty cents (WWJ radio station, 1978), although Lucas and Smith (1978:174) report a crowd of 2,000 that paid fifty cents to see a game in 1858. Numbers on uniforms were first worn, on their sleeves, by the Cleveland Indians in a game against the Chicago White Sox on 26 June 1916 (Falls, 1976a), and on their jerseys, by the New York Yankess in 1928, based on the order in which they batted—i.e., Durocher wore no. 1, Ruth no. 3, Gehrig no. 4 (Detroit Free Press, 1978). The White Sox, in turn, were the first team to have each player's name on the back of the uniform, an innovation introduced by Bill Veeck in 1960 (Sporting News, 1976b). The first major league night game was introduced in May 1935 in Cincinnati, with the home team defeating the Philadelphia Phillies (Hawkins, 1976:5-D). Sunday baseball first became legal in 1919, in New York, later in Massachusetts.

6. Professional boxing was declared to be subject to anti-trust laws in a 1955 Supreme Court decision and the Court held the same to be true for professional football in 1957 (cf. Robinson, 1969:228-29). The court, however, had declined to do the same to baseball in 1952 and 1972 decisions (cf. Koppett, 1976e:4, 12).

7. Earlier players' unions were: (l) the Players Brotherhood Fraternity, 1885-92 and 1900-1901, which set up the Players' League in 1890; (2) the Baseball Players Fraternity, 1912-18, which arose out of player support for Ty Cobb, suspended for fighting with a fan; and (3) the American Baseball Guild, set up by Robert Murphy in 1945, which lasted a little more than a year. The Major League Players' Association, under Marvin Miller, which was to become the first successful union, had been originally organized in 1968 with the owners'agreement to help administer the player's pension fund (cf. Smith, 1970:188-80, chapter 22; Twombly, 1976b; Lucas and Smith, 1978:185).

8. Low scoring in British football has been similarly corrected by modifying the "offside" rule (Elias and Dunning, 1972:76).

9. Moreover, an earlier analysis of professional baseball concludes that players in general receive no more than half of their economic value (Medoff, 1976a). Not surprisingly, Bob Woolf, a lawyer who represents athletes, does not believe their salaries to be too high (Woolf, 1978). A comparison of players' salaries as a proportion of the owner's gross income showed that while it increased from 15 percent in 1974-76 to 20 percent in 1977, 25

percent in 1978 and 27 percent in 1979, it had been as high as 32.4 percent in 1939 (Koppett, 1980a). A study of the 1978 season showed a positive relationship between the average salary paid to a team's players and that team's won-lost percentage (Pascas, 1978).

10. Nevertheless, the modern players may be better than earlier ones in that the former are bigger and more powerful (cf. Vincent, 1976; Elderkin, 1976c). This difference may explain the lower batting averages more than do night baseball, extensive travel and longer schedules, better gloves, larger outfields, more trying for home runs, or the tendency of the better little league players to try for the pitcher position; that is, the increased size and strength of modern players helps a pitcher's fast ball but does not improve a batter's timing, reflexes, etc.

11. A further sign of player independence, as well as of the internationalization of the game, is the number of Americans playing in Japan in recent years, where baseball is the most popular team sport (cf. Sugawara, 1972:47).

12. One possible sign of this decline is that there appear to be fewer colorful nicknames currently (Salin, 1979). There is little now to compare with Yogi Bera, Three-Fingered Mordecai Brown, the Georgia Peach (Cobb), Wahoo Crawford, Kiki Cuyler, Dizzy Dean, Joltin' Joe, the Yankee Clipper, or the Belting Beauty (DiMaggio), Larrupin' Lou or the Iron Horse (Gehrig), Goose Goslin (though there is Goose Gossage), the Rajah (Hornsby), King Carl or the Mealticket (Hubbel), the Big Train (Walter Johnson), Wee Willie Keeler, High Pockets Kelly, Heinie Manush, Rabbit Maranville, Big Six (Mathewson), Say Hey or Wonderful Willie (Mays), Ducky Wucky (Medwick), the Scooter (Rizzuto), Schoolboy Rowe, the Babe, the Bambino or, the Sultan of Swat (Ruth), the Grey Eagle (Speaker), "Big Ed" Walsh, Terrible Ted, the Splendid Splinter the Thumper, or the Kid (Williams). Among recent examples are Charlie Hustle (Pete Rose), Catfish Hunter, Mark "the Bird" Fidrych, and "Pops" Stargell. The most frequent nicknames appear to have been those referring to hair color, nationality, physical feature, and character, e.g., "Red," "Dutch," "Lefty," "Shorty," "Stubby," "Big Ed," "Available," "Boom Boom," "Pop," "Howling," and "Weeping" (cf. Salin, 1979).

13. There is reason to believe that the baseball "slide" was first devised in the nineteenth century to frighten, injure, and maim Negro players (Boyle, 1972:261; Rust, 1976, Voigt, 1976).

14. First Jackie Robinson, Doby, Easter, Jethroe, and Campanella; then Crowe, Gilliam, Thompson, Irvin, Mays, Bruton, Banks, Aaron, Elston Howard, Frank Robinson, Bill White, McCovey, Wills, and Pinson.

15. E.g., Bankhead, Paige, and Newcombe in the early years, later Joe Black, Sam Jones, Brooks Lawrence, Earl Wilson, Bob Gibson, Ferguson Jenkins, Vida Blue, J. R. Richard, and others.

16. A recent potential movement, weak as yet in baseball, is American Indian protests about racial stereotying encouraged by names and emblems of teams such as the Cleveland Indians and the Atlanta Braves, and the Washington Redskins in professional football (cf. Hoch, 1974:394-95).

17. The *British* names were: Alexander, Chance, Chase, Cobb, Eddie Collins, Crawford, Evers, Jackson, Johnson, Mathewson, Seymour, Speaker, and Young. The *Irish* names: Carey, Daugherty, Delahanty, Donlin, Donovan, Doyle, Kelly, McGinnity, Shannon, and Shawkey. The *German* names: Bescher, Groh, Heilmann, Reulbach, Roush, Ruth, Schulte, Steinfeldt, Wagner, and Zimmerman. The *French* names: Beaumont, Daubert, Fournier, Lajoie, Marquard, and Tesrau.

18. Some Jews used Irish names (Page, 1969:199). Johnny Kling, a leading catcher in the early years of this century, had changed his name from Kline (Smith, 1970:324; see also Hoch, 1974:395 n).

19. Using the above criteria of the apparent ethnic identity of leading batters, pitchers, and base stealers, the Latin American or Hispanic names would run from "Lefty" Gomez to Alou, Aparicio, Avila, Bithhorn, Campaneris, Carty, Cedeno, Cepeda, Clemente, Conseguera, Cuellar, Figueroa, Mike Garcia, Marichal, Minoso, Montañez, Omar Moreno, Oliva, Pascual, Jim Rivera, Segui, Taveras, Tiant, Tovar.

20. Women did create their own program, however, the Heraea games, in honor of Hera, the wife of Zeus, (Sage, 1974a:285).

21. Thus, umpires are another social category always sensitive but with recently increasing solidarity and consciousness (Boswell, 1979a; Lyon, 1980). In 1975, some umpires threatened to hold press conferences after games with evaluation and criticism of the performance of players, managers, and coaches in retaliation for published player ratings that denigrated the ability and efficiency of many umpires. In early 1977, the negotiator for the Umpires Association sought mediation of a dispute with the major leagues (*Detroit Free Press*, 1977a). Among umpires' demands were a thirty percent salary increase to match the percentage increase and a "gag rule" similar to that of the National Football League that prohibits public criticism of umpires by players, coaches, managers, or owners (*Detroit Free Press*, 1976f; Holtzman, 1977a). The umpires' strike in the first six weeks of the 1979 season won them most of their demands and further institutionalized their Association. There had been two earlier one-day strikes, in Pittsburgh and Minnesota in the first games of the 1970 National and American League playoffs and in regular season games of 25 August 1978 (cf. Hawkins, 1978b; Spink, 1978b).

22. All of these examples fall under Parsons's "pattern maintenance" functional imperative or problem (Parsons, 1966:7, 28-29).

23. Japanese players go to camp where they spend many hours each day doing calisthenics (Durslag, 1976b; *Detroit Free Press*, 1976d), in contrast with American players who are probably the worst conditioned of all team professional athletes (Puscas, 1976a; *Sporting News*, 1976d).

24. Cf. Jack Scott, Paul Hoch, and Dave Meggysey, referred to in Bennett, 1976:68; also Hoch, 1974 and Fitzpatrick, 1976.

Works Cited

Adams, R. C. "Mailbox: on Baseball When the Game was Very New" *New York Times* (13 April 1980): p. 55.

Anderson, Dave. "George Steinbrenner." *Sport* (October 1979): 27–33.

———. Column. *New York Times,* (1 June 1980): p. 55.

Angell, Roger. *The Summer Game.* New York: Viking, 1972.

———. Article. *New Yorker* (22 November 1976): 151–76.

Atkin, Ross. Article. *Christian Science Monitor* (27 September 1976): 20.

Axthelm, Pete. "The City Game." In M. Marie Hart, ed. *Sport in the Socio-Cultural Process.* Dubuque, Iowa: Brown, 1972, pp. 187–205.

Baseball Digest. "The Fans Speak Out." (October 1976): 6–15.

Benagh, Jim. Article. *Detroit Free Press* (23 May 1976a): 1-E.

———. Article *Detroit Free Press* (4 July 1976b): 3-D.

———. Article *Detroit Free Press* (22 July 1977): 1-D.

Bennett, William J. "In Defense of Sports." *Commentary* (February 1976): 68–70.

Berger, Peter, and Luckmann, Thomas. *The Social Construction of Reality.* Garden City, N.Y.: Doubleday, 1966.

Betts, John C. "The Technological Revolution and the Rise of Sport, 1850–1900." In M. Marie Hart, ed., *Sport in the Socio-Cultural Process.* Dubuque, Iowa: Brown, 1972, pp. 116–39.

Biederman, Les. Article. *Baseball Digest* (December 1979): 29–31.

Bisher, Furman. Column. *Sporting News,* (17 July 1976): 2, 44.

———. Column. *Sporting News* (3 September 1977): 2, 6.

Blalock, Hubert B., Jr. "Occupational Discrimination." In John W. Loy and Gerald S. Kenyon, eds. *Sport, Culture, and Society.* London: Macmillan, 1969, pp. 416–23.

Blau, Peter M. *Exchange and Power in Social Life.* New York: Wiley, 1964.

———. "Interaction: IV. Social Exchange." in David Sills, ed. *International Edition of the Social Sciences,* vol. 7. New York: Crowell-Collier and Macmillan, 1968, pp. 452–58.

Blumer, Herbert. "Social Psychology." In Emerson P. Schmidt, ed. *Man and Society.* New York: Prentice-Hall, 1937, chapter 4. "Society as Symbolic Interaction." In Arnold M. Rose, ed. *Human Behavior and Social Processes.* Boston: Houghton-Mifflin, 1962, pp. 179–92.

———. *Symbolic Interactionism.* Englewood Cliffs, N.J.: Prentice-Hall, 1969.

Bogart, Leo. "Television's Effect on Spectator Sports." In M. Marie Hart, ed. *Sport in the Socio-Cultural Process.* Dubuque, Iowa: Brown, 1972, pp. 386–96.

Boswell, Thomas. Article. *Baseball Digest* (April 1979a): 77–83.

———. Article. *Baseball Digest* (June 1979b): 38–44.

Bouton, Jim. *Ball Four.* New York: World, 1970.

Boyd, L. M. Column. *Detroit Free Press* (12 November 1979): 9-D.

Boyle, Robert H. "Negroes in Baseball." In Eric Dunning, ed. *Sport: Readings from a Sociological Perspective.* Toronto: University of Toronto Press, 1972, chapter 13.

———. "Scorecard." *Sports Illustrated* (21 May 1979): 18.

Broeg, Bob. Column. *Sporting News* (12 June 1976): 6.

———. Column. *Sporting News* (26 February 1977): 34.

Brower, Jonathan J. "Professional Sports Team Ownership: Fun, Profit and Ideology of the Power Elit" *International Review of Sport Sociology* 12 (1977): 79–98.

Buhrmann, Hans. G. "Scholarships and Athletics in High School." *International Review of Sport Sociology* 7 (1972): 119–31.

Burdge, Rabel J. "Levels of Occupational Prestige and Leisure Activity." In George H. Sage, ed. *Sport and American Society,* 2d. ed. Reading, Mass.: Addison-Wesley, 1974, pp. 234–49.

Burke, Kenneth. *A Grammar of Motives.* New York: Prentice-Hall, 1945.

———. *A Rhetoric of Motives.* New York: Prentice-Hall, 1950.

Burns, Bud. Article. *Baseball Digest* (April 1979): 60–63.

Caillois, Roger. *Man, Play, and Games.* Translated from French by Meyer Barash. London: Thames and Hudson, 1962.

Cattani, Richard J. Article. *Christian Science Monitor* (8 April 1976): 33.

Cavanaugh, Gerald J. Article. *New York Times* (3 October 1976): 2S.

Chass, Murray. Article. *New York Times* (25 July 1976): 8S.

———. Article. *New York Times* (6 January 1980a): 1S, 8S.

———. Article. *New York Times* (25 May 1980b): 1S-4S.

Clarke, Alfred C. "The Use of Leisure and Its Relation to Levels of Occupational Prestige." *American Social Review* 21 (1956): 301–7.

Coakley, Jay J. *Sport in Society: Issues and Controversies*. St. Louis: Mosby, 1978.

Cohen, Irwin. Article. *Baseball Bulletin* 3 (February 1977): 22.

Colborn, Jim. Article. *Baseball Bulletin* 3 (February 1977): 28.

Coleman, James S. *The Adolescent Society*. New York: Free Press, 1961.

Colson, Bill. "The Over-the-Hill League." *Sports Illustrated* (4 June 1979): 49–50.

Cook, Karen S., and Emerson, Richard M. "Power, Equity, and Commitment in Exchange Networks." *American Sociological Review* 43 (1978): 721–39.

Coser, Lewis A. *The Functions of Social Conflict*. Glencoe, Illinois: Free Press, 1967.

———. *Continuities in the Study of Social Conflict*. New York: Free Press, 1967.

———. "Social Conflict and Social Change." *British Journal of Sociology* 8 (1957): 197–207.

Cozens, Frederick, and Stumpf, Florence. "The Role of the School in the Sports Life of America." In George H. Sage, ed. *Sport and American Society*, 2d ed. Reading, Massachusetts: Addison-Wesley, 1974, pp. 104–31.

Craig, Jack. Column. *Sporting News* (28 February 1975a): 26.

———. Column. *Sporting News* (27 March 1976b): 33.

———. Column. *Sporting News* (24 April 1976c): 32.

———. Column. *Sporting News* (2 May 1976d): 20.

———. Column. *Sporting News* (24 July 1976e): 51.

———. Column. *Sporting News* (3 November 1979a): 38.

———. Column. *Sporting News* (15 December 1979b): 24.

Crepeau, Richard C. "Urban and Rural Images in Baseball." *Journal of Popular Culture* 9 (1975): 315–24.

Dahrendorf, Ralf. *Class and Class Conflict in Industrial Society*.Stanford: Stanford University Press, 1959.

———. *Conflict after Class*. London: Longmans, Green, 1967.

———. *Essays in the Theory of Society*. Stanford: Stanford University Press, 1968.

Detroit Free Press. Column (22 February 1976a): 2-E.

———. Article (4 May 1976b): 3-D.

———. Article (9 May 1976c): 4-E.

———. Article (10 July 1976d): 2-B.

———. Article (29 July 1976e): 3-D.

———. Article (9 December 1976f): 7-F.

———. Article (17 February 1977a): 10-D.

————. Article (22 December 1977b): 2-D.

————. Article (30 December 1977c): 2-D.

————. "For the Record" (1 February 1978a): 2–F.

————. Column (29 March 1978b): 2–D.

————. "Sports Hot Line" (16 April 1978c): 6–E.

————. Article (8 April 1979a): 1–E.

————. (caption under picture). (21 September 1979b): 1–D.

Director, Roger. Article. *Sport* (October 1979): 96.

Dorfman, Harvey A. Article. *New York Times* (6 June 1976): 2-E.

Dozer, Richard. Article. *Sporting News* (8 January 1977): 34, 38.

Dulles, Foster R. "In Detestation of Idleness." In George H. Sage, ed. *Sport and American Society*, 2d ed. Reading, Massachusetts: Addison-Wesley, 1974, pp. 64–71.

Duncan, Hugh D. *Communication and Social Order*. New York: Bedminster Press, 1962.

————. *Symbols in Society*. London: Oxford University Press, 1968.

Dunning, Eric. *Sport: Readings from a Sociological Perspective*. Toronto: University of Toronto Press, 1972.

Durslag, Melvin. Column. *Detroit Free Press* (16 March 1976a). 5-D.

————. Column. *Sporting News* (20 March 1976b): 46.

————. Column. *Sporting News* (15 May 1976c): 12.

————. Column. *Sporting News* (28 October 1978): 23.

Durso, Joseph. Article. *New York Times* (5 March 1978): 1-S.

Edwards, Harry. *"Preface to the Revolt of the Black Athlete."* In M. Marie Hart, ed. *Sport in the Socio-Cultural Process*. Dubuque, Iowa: Brown, 1972, pp. 304–7.

————. *Sociology of Sport*. Homewood, Illinois: Dorsey, 1973.

————. Article. *New York Times* (6 May 1979): 2-S.

Eitzen, D. Stanley, and Sage, George H. *Sociology of American Sport*. Dubuque, Iowa: Brown, 1978.

Eitzen, D. Stanley, and Yetman, Norman R. "Immune from Racism?" *Civil Rights Digest* 9 (1977): 2–13.

Elderkin, Phil. Article. *Christian Science Monitor* (17 May 1976a): 25.

————. Article. *Christian Science Monitor* (1 June 1976b): 26.

————. Article. *Christian Science Monitor* (14 June 1976c): 27.

————. Article. *Christian Science Monitor* (14 April 1978): 6.

————. Article. *Christian Science Monitor* (2 July 1980): 14. .

Eldridge, Larry. Article. *Christian Science Monitor* (11 March 1976): 10.

————. Article. *Christian Science Monitor* (8 August 1978a): 12–13.

————. Article. *Christian Science Monitor* (29 September 1978b): 16.

Elias, Norbert, and Dunning, Eric. "Dynamics of Sports Groups with Special Reference to Football." In Eric Dunning, ed. *Sport: Readings from a Sociological Perspective*. Toronto: University of Toronto Press, 1972, chapter 5.

Emerson, Richard M. "Social Exchange Theory." *Annual Review of Sociology* 2 (1976): 335–62.

Falls, Joe. Column. *Sporting News* (8 May 1976a): 24.

———. Column. *Sporting News* (5 June 1976b): 58.

Featherstone, Dennis C., and Studenmund, A. H. "A Statistical Model for Baseball Standings." *Research Quarterly* (1974): 80–85.

Fiedler, Fred E. "Assumed Similarity Measures as Predictors of Team Effectiveness." In John W. Loy, Jr., and Gerald S. Kenyon, eds. *Sport, Culture, and Society*. London: Macmillan, 1969, pp. 352–64.

Fitzpatrick, Tom. Article. *Detroit Free Press* (11 February 1976): 4-D.

Freeze, R. A. "An Analysis of Baseball Batting Order by Monte Carlo Simulation." *Operations Research* 22 (1974): 728–35.

Furst, R. Terry. "Social Change and the Commercialization of Professional Sports." *International Review of Sport Sociology* 6 (1971): 153–73.

Galloway, Randy. Article. *Baseball Digest* 38 (October 1979): 53–55.

Garagiola, Joe. Article. *New York Times* (20 February 1977): 2-S.

Gilmartin, Joe. Article. *Sporting News* (23 April 1976): 29.

Gmelch, George. "Baseball Magic." *Transaction* 8 (June 1971): 39–41, 54.

Grant, James. Article. *Sporting News* (1 January 1977): 29–30.

Green, Ted. Article. *Sporting News* (1 April 1978): 59.

Grimsley, Will. Article. *New York Times* (26 September 1976): 6-S.

Grossi, Tony. Article. *Cleveland Plain Dealer* (30 December 1979): 2-B.

Grusky, Oscar. "The Effects of Formal Structure on Managerial Recruitment." In John W. Loy, Jr., and Gerald S. Kenyon, eds. *Sport, Culture, and Society*. London: Macmillan, 1969, pp. 40–15.

Gwartney, James and Haworth, Charles. "Employer Costs and Discrimination: The Case of Baseball." *Journal of Political Economics* 82 (1974): 873–81.

Hagen, Paul. Article. *Baseball Digest* 38 (June 1979): 62–65.

Harris, Dorothy V. "The Sportswoman in Our Society." In George H. Sage, ed. *Sport and American Society*. Reading, Mass.: Addison-Wesley, 1974, pp. 310–14.

Harris, Louis. "Harris Survey." *Detroit Free Press* (19 November 1978): 7-D.

Hart M. Marie. "On Being Female in Sport." In M. Marie Hart, ed. *Sport in the Socio-Cultural Process*. Dubuque, Iowa: Brown, 1972a, pp. 291–302.

———. *Sport in the Socio-Cultural Process*. Dubuque, Iowa: Brown, 1972b.

———. *Sport in the Socio-Cultural Process*, 2d ed. Dubuque, Iowa: Brown, 1976.

Hauser, William J., and Lueptow, Lloyd B. "Participation in Athletics and Academic Achievement." *Sociological Quarterly* 19 (1978): 304–9.

Hawkins, Jim. Article. *Detroit Free Press* (25 May 1976): 1-D, 5-D.

———. Column. *Detroit Free Press* (25 June 1978a): 6-E.

———. Column. *Detroit Free Press* (26 August 1978b): 1-C, 3-C.

———. Column. *Detroit Free Press* (1 January 1980a): 1-D.

———. Column *Detroit Free Press* (27 January 1980b): 1-G.

Hecht, Henry. Article. *Baseball Digest* 35(December 1976): 26–28.

Hechter, William. "Law and Sports Violence." *Criminal Law Quarters* 19 (1977): 425–53.

Heinila, Kalevi. "Survey of the Value Orientations of Finnish Sports Leaders." *International Review of Sport Sociology* 7 (1972): 111–17.

Hoberman, John M. Article. *New York Times* (28 March 1976): 2–S.

Hoch, Paul. "The Battle Over Racism." In George H. Sage ed. *Sport in American Society*. 2d ed. Reading, Mass.: Addison-Wesley, 1974.

Holman, John. Article. *Sporting News* (29 October 1977): 16, 18.

Holtzman, Jerome. Column. *Sporting News* (24 January 1976a): 40, 43.

———. Column. *Sporting News* (3 July 1976b): 6, 49.

———. Column. *Sporting News* (8 January 1977a): 30.

———. Column. *Sporting News* (23 July 1977b): 17.

———. Column. *Sporting News* (20 August 1977c): 34.

———. Column. *Sporting News* (3 September 1977d): 13.

———. Article. *Official Baseball Guide*. St. Louis: Sporting News Co., 1978, pp. 309–40.

Holway, John. Article. *Sporting News* (29 October 1977): 16, 18.

Holzner, Burkhart. *Reality Construction in Society*. Rev. ed. Cambridge, Mass.: Schenkman, 1972.

Holzner, Burkhart, and Marx, John H. *Knowledge Application: The Knowledge System in Society*. Boston: Allyn and Bacon, 1979.

Homans, George C. "Social Behavior as Exchange." *American Journal of Sociology* 62 (1958): 597–606.

———. *Social Behavior: Its Elementary Forms*. New York: Harcourt, Brace & World, 1961.

———. *Social Behavior: Its Elementary Forms*. Rev. ed. New York: Harcourt Brace Jovanovich, 1974.

Hooke, Robert. "Statistics, Sports, and Some Other Things." In Judith M. Tanur, ed. *Statistics: A Guide to the Unknown*. San Francisco: Holden-Day, 1972.

Horrocks, J. E. *The Psychology of Adolescent Behavior and Development*, 3d ed. Boston: Houghton Mifflin, 1969.

Huizinga, Johan. *Homo Ludens: A Study of the Play-Element in Culture*. Boston: Beacon, 1950 [1938].

Isaacs, Stan. Column. *Sports Illustrated* (29 October 1979): 50.

Isle, Stan. Column. *Sporting News* (19 January 1980): 34.

Iso-Ahola, Seppo. "Leisure Patterns of American and Finnish Youth," *International Review of Sport Sociology* 10 (1975): 63–81.

Jacobson, Steve. Article. *Sporting News* (28 January 1978): 42, 52, 58.

Janofsky, Michael. Article. *Sporting News* (5 May 1979): 41.

Jares, Joe. Article. *Sports Illustrated* (15 October 1979): 8.

Kagan, J., and Moss, H. L. "The Stability of Passive and Dependent Behavior from Childhood through Adulthood." *Child Development* 31 (1960): 577–91.

Kahn, Roger. Article. *Life* (20 March 1970): p. 101.

Kennedy, Ray, and Williamson, Nancy. Article. *Sports Illustrated* (28 April 1980): 34–45.

Kenyon, Gerald S., ed. *Aspects of Contemporary Sport Sociology* (proceedings of C.I.C. Symposium on the Sociology of Sport, University of Wisconsin, 18–20 November 1968). Madison: The Athletic Institute, 1969.

Kirshenbaum, Jerry. "Scorecard." *Sports Illustrated* (26 March 1979a): 11–12.

———. "Scorecard." *Sports Illustrated* (5 November 1979b): 25–26.

Klapp, Orrin. *Symbolic Leaders.* Chicago: Aldine, 1964.

———. *Collective Search for Identity.* New York: Holt, Rinehart and Winston, 1969.

———. *Heroes, Villains, and Fools.* 2d ed. Englewood Cliffs, New Jersey: Prentice-Hall, 1972.

Klein, Michael, and Christiansen, Gerd. "Group Composition, Group Structure, and Group Effectiveness of Basketball Teams." In John W. Loy, Jr. and Gerald S. Kenyon, eds. *Sport, Culture, Society.* London: Macmillan, 1969, pp. 397–408.

Koppett, Leonard, "Baseball: After 100 Years Quo Vadis the Game?" *New York Times* (16 February 1969): 1-S, 7-S.

———. Column. *Sporting News* (31 January 1976a): 4.

———. Column. *Sporting News* (3 April 1976b): 4.

———. Column. *Sporting News* (29 May 1976c): 4.

———. Column. *Sporting News* (26 June 1976d): 4, 12.

———. Column. *Sporting News* (10 July 1976e): 4.

———. Column, *Sporting News* (15 October 1977): 4, 10.

———. Column. *Sporting News* (27 October 1979a): 23.

———. Column. *Sporting News* (3 November 1979b): 53.

———. Column. *Sporting News* (29 March 1980a): 17.

———. Column. *Sporting News* (11 May 1980b): 38.

Koster, Rich. Article. *Baseball Digest* 38 (September 1979): 66–68.

Kritzer, Cy. Article. Columbus (Ohio) *Citizen-Journal* (18 April 1969): 28.

Lahr, John. "The Theater of Sports." In M. Marie Hart, ed. *Sport in the Socio-Cultural Process.* Dubuque, Iowa: Brown, 1972, pp. 105–15.

Lapoint, Joe. Article. *Detroit Free Press* (27 July 1980a): p. H13.

———. Article. *Detroit Free Press* (28 July 1980b): pp. 1F, 6F.

———. Article. *Detroit Free Press* (30 July 1980c): pp. 1F, 5F.

Lenk, Hans. "Top Performance despite Internal Conflict." In John W. Loy, Jr., and Gerald S. Kenyon, eds. *Sport Culture, and Society.* London: Macmillan, 1969, pp. 393–97.

Leonard, Wilbert M. "An Extension of the Black, Latin, White Report." *International Review of Sport Sociology* 12 (1977): 85–95.

Lévi-Strauss, Claude. *Elementary Structures of Kinship,* Rev. Boston: Beacon, 1969.

Lincoln, Melissa Ludtke. Article. *New York Times* (23 April 1979): 2-S.

Lipsyte, Robert. *Sports World*. New York: Quadrangle/New York Times Book Co., 1976. Referred to and quoted in Art Spander.

———. Column. *Sporting News* (8 May 1976): 25 (see Spander, 1976b).

London, Herbert I. Article. *New York Times* (23 April 1978): 2-S.

Loy, John W., Jr., "The Study of Sport and Social Mobility." In Gerald S. Kenyon, ed. *Aspects of Contemporary Sport Sociology*. Madison, Wisc.: Athletic Institute, 1969, pp. 101–19.

———. "Social Origins and Occupational Mobility Patterns of a Selected Sample of American Athletes." *International Review of Sport Sociology* 7 (1972): 5–25.

Loy, John W. Jr., and Kenyon, Gerald S., eds. *Sport, Culture, and Society: A Reader on the Sociology of Sport*. London: Macmillan, 1969.

Loy, John W., Jr., and McElvogue, Joseph F. "Racial Segregation in American Sport." *International Review of Sport Sociology* 5 (1970): 5–23.

Lucas, John A., and Smith, Ronald A. *Saga of American Sport*. Philadelphia: Lea & Febiger, 1978.

Lueschen, Gunther. "Small Group Research and the Group in Sport." In Gerald S. Kenyon, ed. *Aspects of contemporary Sport Sociology*. Madison, Wisc.: Athletic Institute, 1969, pp. 57–66.

———. "Social Stratification and Mobility among Young German Sportsmen." In Eric Dunning, ed. *Sport: Readings from a Sociological Perspective*. Toronto: University of Toronto Press, 1972, chapter 12.

———. "The Interdependence of Sport and Culture." In M. Marie Hart, ed. *Sport in the Socio-Cultural Process*, 2d ed. Dubuque, Iowa: Brown, 1976.

Lukes, Bonnie L. "Viewpoint." *Sports Illustrated* (5 November 1979): 24–25.

Lyon, Bill. Article. *Baseball Digest* 39 (February 1980): 45–53.

Maccoby, Eleanor E., ed. *The Development of Sex Differences*. Stanford: Stanford University Press, 1966.

Maccoby, Eleanor E., and Jacklin, C. M. *The Psychology of Sex Differences*. Stanford: Stanford University Press, 1974.

McGrath, Joseph E. "The Influence of Positive Interpersonal Relations on Adjustment and Effectiveness of Rifle Teams." In John W. Loy, Jr., and Gerald S. Kenyon, eds. *Sport, Culture, and Society*. London: Macmillan, 1969, pp. 378–93.

McIntosh, P. C. "An Historical Review of Sport and Social Control." *International Review of Sport Sociology* 6 (1971): 5–16.

McLuhan, Marshall. "Games: The Extensions of Man." In M. Marie Hart, ed. *Sport in the Socio-Cultural Process*, 2d ed., Dubuque, Iowa: Brown, 1976.

Madden, Bill. Column. *Sporting News* (12 June 1976): 46.

———. Column. *Sporting News* (18 March 1978): 58.

———. Column. *Sporting News* (5 January 1980): 38.

Marcin, Joe. Article. *Sporting News* (10 September 1977): 25, 36.

Martens, Rainer, and Peterson, James A. "Group Cohesiveness as a Determinant of Success and Member Satisfaction in Team Performance." *International Review of Sport Sociology* 6 (1971): 49–61.

Mead, George Herbert. *Mind, Self and Society*. Chicago: University of Chicago Press, 1934.

Medoff, Marshall H. "On Monopolistic Exploitation in Professional Baseball." *Quarterly Review of Economics* 47 (Summer 1976a): 113–21.

———. "Racial Segregation in Baseball: The Economic Hypthesis versus the Sociology Hypothesis." *Journal of Black Studies* 6 (1976b): 393–99.

Merry, Don. Column. *New York Times* (9 July 1978): 2-S.

Merton, Robert K. *Social Theory and Social Structure*. Glencoe, Ill.: Free Press, 1949.

———. *Social Theory and Social Structure*, 3d enl. ed. ed. New York: Free Press, 1968.

Metheny, Eleanor. "Symbolic Forms of Movement: The Feminine Image in Sports." In M. Marie Hart, ed. *Sport in the Socio-Cultural Process*, 2d ed. Dubuque, Iowa: Brown, 1976, pp. 75–83.

Metropolitan Life Insurance Company. "Longevity of Major League Baseball Players." *Statistical Bulletin* 56 (April 1975a): 3–4.

———. "Characteristics of Major League Baseball Players." *Statistical Bulletin* 56 (August 1975b): 6–8.

Miller, Dick. Article. *Sporting News* (27 August 1977): 18, 38.

Moore, Terence. Article. *Baseball Digest* 39 (January 1980): 33–34.

Mosteller, Frederick. "The World Series Competition," *Journal of the American Statistical Association* 47 (September 1952): 355–80.

Murphy, Edward F. Article. *New York Times* (25 April 1976): 2-S.

Meyers, Albert. "Team Competition, Success, and the Adjustment of Group Members." In John W. Loy, Jr., and Gerald S. Kenyon, eds. *Sport, Culture, and Society*. London: Macmillan, 1969, pp. 365–77.

New York Times. Column. (28 March 1976a): 9-S.

———. Article. (4 April 1976b): 9-S.

———. Column. (6 May 1979): 2-S.

New Yorker. "The Bicentennial Beat." In "The Talk of the Town" (5 July 1976): 19–21.

Newell, K. M. "Decision Processes of Baseball Batters." *Human Factors* 16 (1974) 520–27.

Newhouse, Dave. Article. *Baseball Digest* 39 (February 1980): 86–91.

Nigro, Ken. Article. *The Sporting News* (22 July 1978): 17.

Nixon, Howard L. "Reinforcement Effects of Sports Team Success Cohesiveness-Related Factors." *International Review of Sport Sociology* 12 (1977): 17–36.

Novikov, A. D., and Maximenko, A. M. "The Influence of Selected Socio-economic Factors on the Level of Sports Achievements in the Various Countries." *International Review of Sport Sociology* 7 (1972): 27–44

Official Baseball Guide. St. Louis: The Sporting News, 1980.

Official Baseball Rules. Official Playing Rules Committee, St. Louis: The Sporting News, 1974.

Onigman, Marc. Article. *New York Times* (19 March 1978): 2-S.

Opotowsky, Stan. "Symposium Summary with Reflections upon the Sociology of Sport as a Research Field." In Gerald S. Kenyon, ed. *Aspects of Contemporary Sport*

Sociology. Madison, Wisc.: Athletic Institute, 1969, pp. 189–202.

Pankin, Robert M. "The Mask of Sports." Paper presented at the Popular Culture Association meetings, Milwaukee, 3 May 1974.

Park, Robert E., and Burgess, Ernest W. *Introduction to the Science of Sociology*, 2d ed. Chicago: University of Chicago Press, 1924.

Parsons, Talcott. *The Social System*. Glencoe, Ill.: Free Press, 1951.

———. "General Theory in Sociology." In Robert K. Merton, Leonard Broom, and Leonard S. Cottrell, Jr., eds. *Sociology Today*. New York: Basic Books, 1959, pp. 3–38.

———. *Societies*. Englewood Cliffs, New Jersey: Prentice-Hall, 1966.

———. *The System of Modern Societies*. Englewood Cliffs, New Jersey: Prentice-Hall, 1971.

———. "Social Structure and the Symbolic Media of Exchange." In Peter M. Blau, ed. *Approaches to the Study of Social Structure*. New York: Free Press, 1975, chapter 8.

———. *Social Systems and the Evolution of Action Theory*. New York: Free Press, 1977.

Paxson, Frederic L. "The Rise of Sport." In George H. Sage, ed. *Sport and American Society* 2d ed. Reading, Mass.: Addison-Wesley, 1974.

Pepe, Phil. Article. *Sporting News* (5 June 1976): 9.

Petrie, Brian M. "Achievement Orientations in Adolescent Attitudes toward Play." *International Review of Sport Sociology* 6 (1971): 89–101.

———. "Examination of a Stereotype: Athletes as Conservatives." *International Review of Sport Sociology* 12 (1977): 51–61.

Pezzano, Chuck. Column. *Sporting News* (21 February 1976): 29.

Phillips, John C., and Schafer, Walter E. "Consequences of Participation in Interscholastic Sports: A Review and Prospectus." In George H. Sage, ed. *Sport and American Society,* 2d ed. Reading, Mass.: Addison-Wesley, 1974.

Pope, Edwin. Article. *Baseball Digest* 38 (July 1979): 22–28j.

Pucas, George. Column. *Detroit Free Press* (4 March 1976a): 1-F.

———. Column. *Detroit Free Press* (12 May 1976b): 1-D.

———. Column. *Detroit Free Press* (13 February 1980): 1-D.

Reese, (Harold) "Pee Wee." Article. *New York Times* (17 July 1977): 2-S.

Rehberg, Richard A., and Schafer, Walter E. "Participation in Interscholastic Athletics and College Expectations." In George H. Sage, ed. *Sport and American Society*. Reading, Mass.: Addison-Wesley, 1974, pp. 454–66.

Richman, Milton. Article. *Baseball Digest* 39 (September 1980), pp. 78–80.

Riesman, David, and Denney, Reuel. "Football in America: A Study in Cultural Diffusion." In John W. Loy, and Gerald S. Kenyon, eds. *Sport Culture, and Society*. London: Macmillan, 1969, pp. 306–19.

Roberts, John M; Arth, Malcolm J.; and Bush, Robert R. "Games in Culture." In George H. Sage, ed. *Sport and American Society*. Reading, Mass.: Addison-Wesley, 1974, pp. 138–48.

Robinson, W. Clyde. "Professional Sports and Antitrust Law." In John W. Loy, Jr., and Gerald S. Kenyon, eds. *Sport, Culture, and Society*. London: Macmillan, 1969, pp.

Rosenblatt, A. "Negroes in Baseball. The Failure of Success." *Trans-Action* (September 1967): 51–53.

Rust, Art, Jr. "Black Man and Baseball: Disillusionments of Youth." *New York Times* (9 May 1976): 2-S.

Sage, George H., ed. *"Sport and American Society: Selected Readings,"* 2d ed. Reading, Mass.: Addison-Wesley, 1974a.

————. "Sport in American Society." In George H. Sage, ed. *Sport and American Society*, 2d ed. Reading, Mass.: Addison-Wesley, 1974b (Sage, 1974a, above).

Sahlins, Marshall D. "On the Sociology of Primitive Exchange." In Michael Banton, ed. *The Relevance of Models for Social Anthropology*. London: Tavistock, 1965, pp. 139–236.

Salin, Tony. Article. *Baseball Digest* 38 (August 1979): 34–36.

Schafer, Walter E., and Armer, J. Michael. "On Scholarship and Interscholastic Athletics." In Eric Dunning, ed. *Sport: Readings from a Sociological Perspective*. Toronto: University of Toronto Press, 1972, chapter 11.

Scherer, Ron. Article. *Christian Science Monitor* (11 August 1976): 11.

Schwartz, Barry, and Barsky, Stephen. "The Home Advantage." *Social Forces* 55 (1977): 641–61.

Schwartz, J. Michael. "Causes and Effects of Spectator Sports." *International Review of Sport Sociology* 8 (1973): 25–43.

Scott, Walter. Column. *Parade, Detroit Free Press* (23 April 1978): 2.

Scully, G. W. *Economic Discrimination in Professional Sports: Symposium on Athletics*. Durham, N.C.: Duke University School of Law, 1973.

Shaw, Irwin. "Before the 'Pros.'" In *Professional Baseball: The First 100 Years*. New York: Portez-Ross, 1969.

Sherif, Carolyn. "Females in the Competitive Process." In George H. Sage, ed. *Sport and American Society*, 2d ed. Reading, Mass.: Addison-Wesley, 1974, pp. 314–40.

Sifford, Darrell. Article. *Detroit Free Press* (21 May 1976): 7-D.

Slocum, Frank. Article. *Sporting News* (14 April 1979): 39, 42.

Smith, "Red." Column. *New York Times* (22 April 1979): 3-S.

Smith, Robert. *Baseball*. Rev. ed. New York: Simon and Schuster, 1970.

————. Letter, *New York Times* (23 April 1977): 2-S.

Snyder, Eldon E., and Spreitzer, Elmer. "Sociology of Sport: An Overview." *Sociological Quarterly* 15 (1974): 467–87.

Sorrentino, Gilbert. Article. *New York Times* (9 April 1978): 2-S.

Spander, Art. Column. *Sporting News* (3 April 1976a): 26.

————. Column. *Sporting News* (8 May 1976b): 25.

————. Column. *Sporting News* (12 June 1976c): 18.

————. Column. *Sporting News* (26 June 1976d): 60.

————. Column. *Sporting News* (22 January 1977a): 47.

————. Column. *Sporting News* (27 August 1977b): 15.

Spink, C. C. Johnson. Column. *Sporting News* (1 May 1976): 12.

————. Column. *Sporting News* (13 August 1977a): 15.

————. Column. *Sporting News* (27 August 1977b): 15.

————. Column. *Sporting News* (11 March 1978a): 16.

————. Column. *Sporting News* (16 September 1978b): 14.

————. Column. *Sporting News* (12 January 1980): 12.

Sport. "Overtime: Sport Talk" (October 1979): 11.

Sporting News. Editorial (3 January 1976a): 12.

————. Editorial (24 January 1976b): 14.

————. Editorial (13 March 1976c): 12.

————. Editorial (26 June 1976d): 18.

————. Editorial (17 July 1976e): 14.

————. Editorial (22 January 1977a): 47.

————. Editorial (27 August 1977b): 15.

Stone, Gregory P. "Appearance and the Self." In Arnold M. Rose, ed. *Human Behavior and Social Processes.* Boston: Houghton Mifflin, 1962, chapter 5.

————. "Some Meanings of American Sport." In Gerald S. Kenyon, ed. *Aspects of Contemporary Sport Sociology.* Madison, Wis.: Athletic Institute, 1969.

————. "American Sports: Play and Display." In Eric Dunning, ed. *Sport: Readings from a Sociological Perspective.* Toronto: University of Toronto Press, 1972, chapter 4.

Sugawara, Ray. "The Study of Top Sportsmen in Japan." *International Review of Sport Sociology,* (1972): 45–68.

Sutton-Smith, Brian, and Roberts, John M. "The Cross-cultural and Psychological Study of Games." *International Review of Sport Sociology* 6 (1971): 79–87.

Sutton-Smith, Brian; Roberts, John M.; and Kozelka, Robert M. "Game Involvement in Adults." In John W. Loy, Jr., and Gerald S. Kenyon, eds. *Sport, Culture, and Society.* London: Macmillan, 1969, pp. 244–58.

Sutton-Smith, Brian; Rosenberg, B. G.; and Morgan, E. F., Jr. "Development of Sex Differences in Play Choices during Preadolescence." In George H. Sage, ed. *Sport and American Society,* 2d ed. Reading, Mass.: Addison-Wesley, 1974, pp. 302–10.

Sylvester, Curt. Article. *Detroit Free Press* (28 May 1976a): 3-D.

————. Article. *Detroit Free Press* (13 July 1976b): 1-D, 2-D.

Tuley, Tom. Article. *Baseball Digest* 38 (September 1979): 90–92.

Turner, Jonathan. *The Structure of Sociological Theory.* Rev. ed. Homewood, Ill.: Dorsey Press, 1978.

Turner, Ralph H., and Killian, Lewis M. *Collective Behavior.* 2d ed. Englewood Cliffs, N.J.: Prentice-Hall, 1972.

Twombly, Wells. Column. *Sporting News* (17 January 1976a): 46.

————. Column. *Sporting News* (13 April 1976b): 30, 38.

————. Column. *Sporting News* (29 May 1967c): 17.

Vass, George. Article. *Baseball Digest* 39 (May 1980), p. 68.

Vescey, George. Article. *Detroit Free Press.* (9 August 1978): 5-D.

Vincent, Charlie. Article. *Detroit Free Press* (9 May 1976): 5-D.

Voigt, David O. Article. *New York Times* (9 May 1976): 2-S.

Vold, George B. *Theoretical Criminology*. New York: Oxford University Press, 1958.

Wallop, Douglass. *Baseball: An Informal History*. New York: Norton, 1969.

Walter, Claire. Article. *Christian Science Monitor* (24 June 1976): 11.

Warren, Bruce. Article. *Baseball Digest* 36 (January 1977): 48–54.

Warshay, Leon H. *The Current State of Sociological Theory*. New York: David McKay, 1975.

Weigel, Tim. Article. *Detroit Free Press* (18 April 1976a): 4-E.

————. Article. *Detroit Free Press* (8 June 1976b): 5-D.

Weinberg, S., Kirson, and Arond, Henry. "The Occupational Culture of the Boxer." In Eric Dunning, ed. *Sport: Readings from a Sociological Perspective*. Toronto: University of Toronto Press, 1972, chapter 14.

Weiss, Paul. *Sport: A Philosophical Inquiry*. Carbondale and Edwardsville: Southern Illinois University Press, 1969.

Whiteside, Larry. Article. *Sporting News* (1 January 1977): 13.

Woolf, Bob. Article. *Christian Science Monitor* (18 July 1978): 22.

WWJ (Radio station, Detroit). Statement made in a 20 July 1978 broadcast at about 10:27 A.M.

Young, Dick. Column. *Sporting News* (26 June 1976): 69.

————. Column. *Sporting News* (1 January 1977a): 13.

————. Column. *Sporting News* (30 July 1977b): 15.

Zeitlin, Irving M. *Rethinking Sociology: A Critique of Contemporary Theory*. Englewood Cliffs, N.J.: Prentice-Hall, 1973.

Zurcher, Louis A., and Meadow, Arnold. "On Bullfights and Baseball." In Eric Dunning, ed. *Sport: Readings from a Sociological Perspective*. Toronto: University of Toronto Press, 1972, chapter 10.

Afterword

We began this book by proposing that an organizational power theory should lead us to an analysis of sports in Western industrial society, suggesting several avenues of approach that combine: power in complex organizations, the power of the media to publicly define sports situations, the combined power of organizational and media control, and the necessity to combine power and situational definition with the phenomenon of "masking." Sports are a primary example of the masking phenomenon but the notion could be generalized further.

This book has only begun to explore the complexity of sports reality in Western Industrial Society. Power, where it is exercised in defining situations that are then accepted as real, combined with the phenomenon of masking, leads to the social differentiation that the authors of this book have pointed out in several different ways. The social world of sports is a differentiated world within itself that helps produce and reinforce the differentiation that is structured into the larger society.

Laughlin and McManus gave us some strong leads about how this process occurs through evolution. The intersection of the operational environment with the cognized environment allows us to simultaneously, but dialectically, cope with a world that is at the same time presented to and created by us. The sports world presents us with organization and difference and accepted definitions of both our organization and the organized differences among us. We cognize this environment, then recreate it and change it through processes of play and gaming.

The processes of play and gaming provide a model for us to think that we are different from each other. As Johnsen has so eloquently demonstrated, the organization of team sports for children socializes males to use females as a negative reference group, while at the same time socializing females to use males as a positive reference group. This has enormous consequences when we recognize that the organizational world of work is a world dominated by males who understand the symbiotic competitive-cooperative process quite "naturally." The complex set of male definitions of the situation, part of which are drawn from early socialization in team sports (with its corresponding negative view of women), can explain why women are first excluded from the work place and when they are admitted are then undervalued both personally and monetarily. Women, finally, can only be accepted when they, as individuals, can be defined as "one of the boys." In this case the organization masks the male domination of females by presenting a set of so-called objective and impersonal rules that everyone must follow. Yet, as most people recognize when working in organizations, the trick is not to follow the rules but know when to bend or break them.

LeFlore, by combining information theory with systems theory, has illuminated another aspect of the differentiation process. He adds Weber's assumption of intentionality or rationality. Information is made available through the media about the organization of various team sports. From the point of view of potential black athletes this includes material on where blacks are generally visable and accepted, and where they are not visible and apparently unaccepted. As this is more or less accepted within the black athlete subculture it is used as the basis of sport choice as well as playing position within the sport.

Once again it appears that we have a set of norms or rules that are impersonal and nondiscriminatory because they are generated by organizations (the sports clubs and the media), not people. Yet, it is people who have ideas about other people and discriminate against them. But insofar as these patterns of discrimination are seen as "natural," and made a part of day to day organizational behavior, it is difficult to break through the barriers for it seems as if the group discriminated against (women in the first case, and blacks in this case), accept the definitions of the situation produced by the dominant majority. Not accepting common definitions of their situation can make things appear even more difficult for individual members of minority groups. What appears to be individual choice making is based on a predefined rationality and logic that is originated as ideological support for bureaucratically structured complex organizations.

Acceptance of an organizational mask denoted by a predefined social situation is nowhere more apparent than among older people. Harootyan's evidence shows that for the majority of them there is no reason to reduce the level of their physical activity, let alone stop participating altogether. Yet, the subcultural information pool among older people seems to provide the single rational that if you are old you must retire from life. Retirement from life is signaled by retirement from the complex organizations for which most of us work. The import of organizational strength is shown in the other direction by Harootyan's data on Senior Olympics. Still in a rudimentary form, we might predict that once that organization is further developed (and it will be due to the increasing numbers of older people in our population) the complete retirement of older people from physical activity will be lessened. This is just another way of saying that one of the major reasons older people do not participate in sports, particularly team sports, is that there are few complex organizations which support that activity. What businesses make a point of developing and selling special equipment for use in older people's physical activity? When some enterprising entrepreneur discovers that older people want to be, and can be, more active and that they have money to spend on physical activity, clubs will be formed and equipment produced.

One of the effects of severe differentiation has been developed in depth by Eitzen and Yetman. Their data indicate fairly conclusively that blacks are kept out of positions of outcome control within sports organizations. This directly parallels conditions in the general society. Blacks are not found in positions of outcome control in corporations or government. The one sporting exception to this is basketball that simply could not keep the black superstars from dominating all positions. Yet, for years whites were overrepresented at the outcome control positions of center and guard. But what chance is there for twelve percent of a population to overwhelm any other but a small aspect of life such as basketball. The paradox is apparent. Professional team sports make it appear that blacks can be successful and basketball can be held out as an example. The situation in basketball, however, is completely unique. This uniqueness provides a mask. Blacks are being told today that they may even have (and some really do have) responsible positions in corporations and government while the black middle class has been permitted to move out of the ghetto. Yet the twelve percent of the population who are blacks can never be in the dominant positions where they make decisions that effect the very quality of their lives. The white majority will continue to rule and define acceptable pluralism.

Those decisions that effect the quality of everybody's lives may often be made in the atmosphere of private clubs. As its major focus one type of private club has a golf course (that may be another type of mask). Golf may not be the most important activity that occurs at them. Davidson pointed out how we separate ourselves into social classes and reinforce our social associations in terms of whom we play with. We do this by sex, race, religion, and social class. Yet, as any beginning student in sociology will point out, the major determinant of social class position in Western industrial society is occupation. In the modern world a person's occupation most generally depends on his or her connection (or lack of connection) to some complex organization. How often you get to play is determined by your occupation, and whom you play with is dependent on your social class. It is a complete circle.

The explanations of organizational masking and differentiation can be many and varied. Warshay, through his examination of baseball, and its micro and macro aspects, has given us suggestions on how to look at sports as a social organization form from a variety of sociological positions. It is well recognized in modern sociology that these positions are derived from sociopolitical ideological perspectives. These can be broken down on a continuum of support or rejection of the differentiation structure. Warshay's contribution is that positions on any point on the continuum may be used to see how sports help to develop and maintain the organizational structure of society that produces differentiation.

Conclusion

This book, written by several people, has come to focus on the processes of social organization. Each chapter in some way focuses on how people behave as they come to organize their social lives. The surprising outcome for the reader may be that this has occurred even though several different theoretical perspectives were employed.

Two chapters, those by Johnsen and Harootyan, use life cycle and socialization theoretical notions to get at the processes of social organization. LeFlore, on the other hand, introduces a systems theory organizational informational pooling analysis to account for decisions in a particular part of a subculture. Two other chapters—by Eitzen and Yetman, and Davidson—use classical sociological approaches to race relations and social stratification to study the macro-aspects of social organization. Warshay, however, uses a metatheoretical taxonomy to examine ways of approaching the organization of a particular sport, baseball.

The two opening theoretical chapters of this book approach the problem of social organization in two different but complementary ways. Laughlin and McManus offer a biopsychological explanation of the way the social world is modeled and the contributions of play and games toward that modeling. On the other hand, I have suggested that the sports world is organized much as the business world and this particular model is what we learn and develop through biopsychological processes. When these approaches are integrated they should be able to deal with all of the aspects of social organization discussed throughout this book.

The conjunction and focus on social organization from several different points of view is what brings this book together; it is the unifying theme. All of the authors of this book hope that they have provided many ideas for further research and theoretical speculation. Our task will have been complete if we cause some controversy and end up raising more questions than we have answered.

Notes on Contributors

ROBERT M. PANKIN, the editor, has been practicing sociology (teaching and research) for eleven years since receiving the Ph.D. at Purdue University. He recently returned from Asia, having taught at the Chinese University of Hong Kong and completed a study tour of Japan and three Southeast Asian countries. At present, he teaches at and the University of Wisconsin-Eau Claire.

JAMES D. DAVIDSON of Purdue University is well known for his work in the sociology of religion.

D. STANLEY EITZEN is a sociologist who is presently at Colorado State University. He is the author of many books and articles.

ROBERT HAROOTYAN is a sociologist and associate director for research at the Western Gerontological Society.

KATHRYN P. JOHNSEN has taught for several years in the department of sociology at Purdue University. She is well known in the area of the sociology of the family.

CHARLES D. LAUGHLIN has been teaching anthropology for eleven years and is now located at Carleton University in Ottawa, Canada. He is co-author of *Biogenetic Structuralism* and two other books.

JAMES LeFLORE teaches anthropology at the State University of New York in Oswego. His research in the Caribbean is well known.

JOHN McMANUS is a psychologist who has been a program director for the city of Philadelphia and at the present time is a private consultant in that city.

LEON WARSHAY teaches sociological theory at Wayne State University and has published a book on theoretical taxonomy.

NORMAN R. YETMAN is a senior member of the department of sociology at Kansas University. He has collaborated with Dr. Eitzen on much of the work that has been most significant in the area of race and sport.

Index